The History of Television

Dedication

To all the innovators, engineers, writers, actors, and viewers who have shaped the ever-evolving landscape of television—your contributions have illuminated our screens and enriched our lives.

This book is a testament to your collective ingenuity and the enduring power of the medium. It is dedicated to the countless individuals, often unsung, whose tireless work and creative visions have brought the magic of television to homes around the world, across generations. From the earliest tinkerers in their workshops to the modern-day streaming giants and the creative minds crafting today's content, this work celebrates the human spirit behind the technology and the stories told. This is a tribute to the power of visual storytelling and the enduring human need for connection, fostered and facilitated by the marvel of television. It is with deep respect and appreciation that this book is presented to all those who have made, and continue to make, television the compelling force it is today. We recognize the societal impact, both positive and negative, acknowledging the complexity of this revolutionary medium's trajectory, while celebrating its triumphs and illuminating its challenges.

Preface

Television. The very word conjures images – flickering black and white, vibrant color, the glow of the screen illuminating countless faces across decades. It's a medium deeply woven into the fabric of modern life, a constant companion offering entertainment, information, and a window into worlds both real and imagined.

This book aims to provide a comprehensive exploration of television's rich and multifaceted history, from its humble beginnings as a technological marvel to its current status as a dynamic, ever-evolving force in global communication. We'll journey through the ingenious inventions, fierce rivalries, and groundbreaking innovations that have shaped the medium, exploring the technological leaps and bounds alongside the cultural and societal impacts. But this is not merely a chronicle of technological advancements. It's a narrative of human creativity, entrepreneurial spirit, and the enduring desire for connection. We will delve into the stories behind the inventors, the programmers, the actors, and the viewers, showcasing the human element central to television's success. This journey will take us from the spinning disks of mechanical television to the sophisticated algorithms powering today's streaming services, examining not only the "what" but also the "why" and "how" of television's evolution. The goal is to provide a clear, accessible, and engaging account that appeals to both technology enthusiasts and those simply fascinated by the profound influence of this extraordinary medium on our lives. The history of television is, in essence, a reflection of our own history, showcasing innovation, creativity, and societal shifts in a constantly changing world.

Introduction

The history of television is a captivating tale of technological innovation, creative vision, and profound societal impact. From its nascent stages as a series of flickering images projected onto a screen, to its present-day form as a multi-faceted global entertainment and information powerhouse, television has relentlessly redefined how we consume media, interact with each other, and understand the world around us. This book undertakes a detailed examination of this remarkable evolution, tracing its journey from the early experiments of pioneers like John Logie Baird and Philo Farnsworth, through the golden age of network television and the advent of cable, to the digital revolution and the rise of streaming services. We will explore the technological breakthroughs that enabled the transition from mechanical to electronic television, from black and white to color, and from analog to digital broadcasting. More than just a technical history, this narrative will also explore the cultural and societal contexts that shaped television's development and reception. We will examine its impact on politics, popular culture, family dynamics, and global communication. We will explore the rise of interactive television, the integration of social media, the emergence of smart TVs, and the increasingly important role of artificial intelligence in shaping the viewing experience. Ultimately, this book aims to provide a comprehensive understanding of television's multifaceted history, highlighting not only its technological achievements but also its profound and enduring cultural legacy. This comprehensive overview will serve as both an informative resource and an engaging narrative, illuminating the captivating story behind one of the most influential media inventions of the 20th and 21st centuries. The future of television, as we will see, remains as dynamic and unpredictable as its past, promising further innovation and evolution.

Telegraph and Radio Pioneering Technologies

The seemingly simple act of watching television today belies a complex history of technological innovation, scientific breakthroughs, and societal shifts. Before the flickering images of electronic television captivated audiences, the groundwork was laid by two groundbreaking technologies: the telegraph and the radio.

Understanding their contributions is essential to appreciating the full evolution of the television medium. The telegraph, born from the ingenuity of inventors like Samuel Morse and Charles Wheatstone in the mid-19th century, dramatically altered the speed and reach of communication. Morse's code, a system of dots and dashes representing letters and numbers, enabled the transmission of messages over long distances via electrical signals along wires. This was revolutionary; news that once took days or weeks to travel now zipped across continents in mere minutes. While not directly involved in image transmission, the telegraph established fundamental principles of long-distance signal transmission and the use of electrical impulses to convey information – principles that would prove invaluable in the later development of television. The success of the telegraph demonstrated the feasibility and the demand for instantaneous, far-reaching communication, paving the way for even more ambitious endeavors.

The advent of radio in the late 19th and early 20th centuries represented a further significant leap. While the telegraph relied on physical wires, radio utilized electromagnetic waves to transmit signals wirelessly. Pioneering figures like Guglielmo Marconi and Nikola Tesla made pivotal contributions, refining and commercializing wireless technologies. Marconi, through meticulous experimentation and practical application, successfully transmitted signals across the Atlantic, marking a turning point in global communication. Tesla's theoretical work, though less commercially successful in his lifetime, laid the foundation for many wireless technologies, including those that would ultimately find their way into the television. The wireless aspect of radio was especially crucial: it broke free from the limitations of wired systems, promising a broadcast medium capable of reaching a vast and dispersed audience. Radio also introduced the concept of broadcasting, where a single signal could be received by many simultaneously, a concept that would be integral to television broadcasting. Moreover, radio's development of sophisticated amplification and signal processing techniques provided essential building blocks for the later amplification and manipulation of video signals.

The societal impact of the telegraph and radio was immense. The telegraph's speed transformed news dissemination and business operations, creating new markets and fostering rapid economic growth. The immediate availability of information broke down geographical barriers and fostered a sense of interconnectedness across vast distances. Newspapers saw a radical transformation, able to publish stories from far-flung locations with unprecedented speed. The stock market, reliant on rapid information flow, experienced a revolution, leading to more efficient trading and faster response to market changes. The military also benefited from the telegraph's speed, significantly improving strategic coordination and communication during wartime. The societal changes brought about by the telegraph were transformative, impacting the very fabric of commerce, politics, and daily life.

Radio's impact was equally profound, expanding communication beyond the written word and entering the realm of audible information. It provided a new avenue for entertainment, news dissemination, and political discourse. Radio programs became part of the daily fabric of millions of lives, providing companionship, information, and entertainment in a way that transcended traditional media. The immediate broadcast of news events allowed for shared experiences and collective responses, forging a sense of community among listeners. Radio broadcasts during wartime played a critical role in informing the public, building morale, and disseminating propaganda. The cultural impact was monumental, shaping social attitudes, trends, and musical tastes. The widespread adoption of radio receivers in homes signified a technological revolution, transforming the way people received information and interacted with the world. The groundwork laid by both the telegraph and radio—the mastery of long-distance signal transmission, the amplification and refinement of signals, the concept of broadcasting, and the impact on societal communication

—created a fertile ground for the eventual emergence of television. The challenges of transmitting images, however, would require a separate but related series of inventive solutions.

The transition from transmitting sound to images proved far more complex. While the underlying principles of signal transmission were similar, the technical hurdles in capturing, encoding, and transmitting images were monumental. Early experiments with image transmission faced substantial difficulties. The sheer volume of data required to represent a visual image far exceeded that of sound, demanding more sophisticated encoding and transmission techniques. The bandwidth limitations of early transmission technologies further constrained the quality and resolution of the images. Moreover, the challenge of synchronizing image transmission with the receiver's display mechanism presented substantial engineering challenges.

The early years of television development witnessed a period of intense experimentation and fierce competition among inventors. Different approaches emerged, most notably mechanical and electronic systems. Mechanical television, spearheaded by inventors like John Logie Baird in the UK and Charles Francis Jenkins in the USA, utilized spinning disks with perforated patterns (like the Nipkow disk) to scan and recreate images. These systems, though crude by modern standards, demonstrated the possibility of transmitting moving images. Baird's 1926 demonstration of a transmitted image, though of low resolution and flickering quality, marked a milestone in television history, capturing the public imagination and sparking immense interest in the new technology.

Jenkins, a contemporary of Baird, also made significant contributions, developing mechanical television systems that competed with Baird's technology. These early mechanical systems, while demonstrating the basic principles, suffered from significant limitations. Image quality was poor, resolution was low, and the systems were susceptible to various mechanical problems, resulting in unstable and often unreliable transmissions.

The limitations of mechanical television spurred the development of electronic television, a significantly more robust and efficient approach. This technology, pioneered by Philo Farnsworth in the

USA and Vladimir Zworykin in the USSR, utilized electron beams to scan and recreate images, eliminating the mechanical limitations of Baird's and Jenkins' systems. Farnsworth, a remarkably inventive young man, conceived the essential principle of electronic image scanning at the age of 14. His innovative approach, involving the use of a cathode ray tube to generate and display the image, marked a profound shift in television technology. Zworykin, working independently, developed a similar system, leading to a protracted patent dispute between Farnsworth and RCA (Radio Corporation of America), which employed Zworykin. The legal battle ultimately affirmed Farnsworth's priority in the development of essential electronic television technology, although the widespread commercial success of electronic television was primarily achieved through RCA's significant resources and marketing power. Electronic television offered superior image quality, higher resolution, and greater stability compared to its mechanical counterpart, rapidly surpassing mechanical systems in performance and popularity. The transition to electronic television was a technological watershed moment, setting the stage for the rapid expansion of television broadcasting and the transformation of entertainment and information dissemination.

The early broadcasts of television programs, while rudimentary, signaled the dawn of a new era in communication. The first broadcasts, often featuring simple demonstrations or test patterns, gradually evolved to incorporate live performances and simple news reports. The limited range of early broadcasts and the relatively small number of receivers initially constrained the reach of the medium. However, the growing public interest and the gradual improvements in technology propelled the expansion of broadcasting infrastructure. The technical challenges of early television broadcasts were substantial. Signal quality varied significantly due to factors like atmospheric conditions and interference from other radio signals. Maintaining stable and consistent transmission over long distances remained a considerable engineering hurdle. The resolution of early television images was drastically low compared to today's standards, often resulting in blurry and indistinct pictures. Despite these limitations, the very existence of television broadcasts, however imperfect, ignited the public's imagination and fueled the desire for a better and more accessible technology. The early years of television were a testament to human ingenuity and the relentless drive to overcome technological challenges in pursuit of a compelling new communication medium. The path to the sophisticated television sets that dominate modern life was paved with significant challenges, creative solutions, and passionate inventors who pushed the boundaries of what was thought possible.

Mechanical Television Bairds Nipkow Disk and Early Systems

The quest to transmit moving images, a seemingly simple concept today, presented an immense technological hurdle in the early 20th century. While the telegraph and radio had laid the foundation for long-distance signal transmission, the sheer volume of data required to represent a visual image dwarfed that of sound. This necessitated innovative approaches to encoding, transmitting, and receiving visual information, leading to the development of mechanical television. John Logie Baird, a Scottish inventor, stands as a pivotal figure in this early stage of television's history. His relentless experimentation and determination to overcome the inherent challenges of image transmission resulted in the creation of a functional, albeit rudimentary, mechanical television system.

Baird's ingenuity centered on the Nipkow disk, a rotating disk with a spiral of small apertures. This seemingly simple device was the cornerstone of his mechanical television system. The disk, when rotated at a specific speed, acted as a scanning mechanism. A light source illuminated the scene to be transmitted, and the light passing through the apertures on the spinning disk was focused onto a photoelectric cell. This cell, a light-sensitive device, converted the varying light intensity into corresponding electrical signals. These signals, representing the varying brightness levels across the image, were then transmitted over a wire to a receiving end.

At the receiver, a second Nipkow disk, synchronized with the transmitting disk, rotated in tandem. The received electrical signals modulated the intensity of a light source, which then shone through the apertures of the receiving disk. This modulated light, projected onto a screen, recreated the original image, albeit in a drastically simplified form. The number of apertures on the disk directly determined the resolution of the image; more apertures meant a more detailed image, but also required a faster rotation speed and increased bandwidth for transmission.

Baird's early systems produced images of incredibly low resolution and suffered from significant flickering. The images were often blurry and indistinct, with limited detail. Moreover, the synchronization between the transmitting and receiving disks was critical. Even minor discrepancies in the rotation speed could result in a distorted or completely unintelligible image. Furthermore, the mechanical nature of the system introduced inherent instability; the moving parts were prone to wear and tear, requiring constant maintenance and adjustment. Despite these limitations, Baird's demonstrations in the mid-1920s captivated the public and marked a significant milestone in television's development. His 1926 transmission of a recognizable image, though of poor quality, was a testament to his pioneering efforts and sparked widespread interest in the burgeoning field of television.

The success of Baird's demonstrations, however imperfect, ignited a wave of competition among inventors. Charles Francis Jenkins, an American inventor, emerged as a notable rival to Baird. Jenkins, having experimented with image transmission for years, developed his own mechanical television system, employing a similar scanning disk mechanism but with different design features. He also used a different approach to image reception, emphasizing the use of improved light sources and screens to enhance image visibility. His system, while also suffering from the limitations inherent in mechanical scanning technology, offered slight improvements in image quality and stability compared to some of Baird's earlier models.

The rivalry between Baird and Jenkins, while intense, spurred innovation. Both inventors continuously refined their systems, striving for better image quality, increased resolution, and more reliable transmissions. They also focused on improving the synchronization mechanisms and enhancing the durability of the rotating disks. The competition between these pioneers was crucial in driving progress and fostering public interest in the technology, demonstrating the power of competitive innovation.

While both Baird and Jenkins made significant contributions to early mechanical television, their systems shared fundamental limitations. The resolution of the images remained stubbornly low, restricting the detail that could be conveyed. The flickering inherent in the rotating disk mechanism was also unavoidable, resulting in a viewing experience far removed from the smooth images we enjoy today. The relatively slow scanning speed dictated the refresh rate of the images, further contributing to the perceived flickering.

Transmission range was limited by the signal strength and the susceptibility of the signals to interference. Furthermore, the systems were highly sensitive to changes in lighting conditions, further impairing image quality. Mechanical issues, such as wear on the rotating disks and the need for precise synchronization, proved to be a constant challenge.

The inherent complexity of synchronizing the transmitting and receiving disks across long distances was a significant technical hurdle. The precise speed and timing of the rotation were crucial, and any slight deviation could lead to image distortion or complete failure of the transmission. Even minor variations in the electric power supply could disrupt synchronization, resulting in unreliable image transmission. The need for careful calibration and frequent adjustments meant that these early systems demanded expert handling. The practical challenges associated with maintaining synchronized mechanical systems across distances proved a significant obstacle to widespread adoption. Furthermore, the manufacturing precision required for the Nipkow disks and associated components was a considerable cost factor, making the systems expensive to produce.

Despite these significant limitations, mechanical television systems played a crucial role in the history of television. They demonstrated, unequivocally, the feasibility of transmitting moving images, capturing the public's imagination and paving the way for the subsequent development of electronic television. They served as a crucial proving ground, demonstrating the underlying principles of image scanning, transmission, and reception, providing invaluable lessons for future inventors. The insights gained from the experimentation and limitations of mechanical television were instrumental in shaping the subsequent development of electronic systems, which ultimately superseded mechanical technology and ushered in the era of high-quality, readily accessible television broadcasting. Mechanical television's legacy lies not in its longevity but in its role as a critical stepping stone on the path to the sophisticated television systems we take for granted today. The inherent limitations of mechanical systems underscored the need for a more efficient and robust approach, setting the stage for the revolutionary breakthroughs that came with electronic television.

The Rise of Electronic Television A Technological Revolution

The limitations of mechanical television, as starkly evident in the flickering images and low resolution produced by Baird and Jenkins' systems, ultimately paved the way for a revolutionary leap forward: electronic television. While mechanical systems relied on the cumbersome and inherently unstable mechanics of rotating disks, electronic television utilized entirely different principles, leveraging the power of electron beams to scan and reproduce images with significantly greater precision and fidelity. This shift represented not merely an incremental improvement but a fundamental paradigm change in television technology.

Two prominent figures emerged as key players in this technological revolution: Philo Farnsworth and Vladimir Zworykin. Their contrasting paths, independent inventions, and subsequent legal battles vividly illustrate the intense competition and creative ingenuity of the era. Philo Farnsworth, a young American inventor, conceived the fundamental principles of electronic television while still a teenager. His vision, remarkably prescient, involved using an electron beam to scan an image and convert it into electrical signals for transmission. This concept, far more elegant and efficient than the mechanical scanning methods, formed the bedrock of electronic television.

Farnsworth's innovation rested on his understanding of the principles of image dissection and electronic scanning. Unlike the mechanical systems that physically scanned the image using a rotating disk with apertures, Farnsworth's system employed a cathode ray tube (CRT) to generate an electron beam. This beam, meticulously controlled, swept across the image, sequentially reading its brightness values. These values were then converted into electrical signals, representing the image's visual information. At the receiving end, another CRT recreated the image by modulating the intensity of its electron beam according to the received signals.

This seemingly simple concept, however, required a remarkable level of precision and engineering prowess. The challenge lay in generating and controlling the electron beam with sufficient accuracy and speed to scan the image quickly enough to create the illusion of continuous motion, avoiding the flickering that plagued mechanical systems. Farnsworth's brilliance lay in his ability to overcome this fundamental hurdle, developing innovative circuitry and vacuum tube technology to achieve the necessary level of control and precision. The development of the image dissector tube, a crucial component of his invention, represented a significant technological achievement. This tube efficiently converted the optical image into electrical signals, forming the heart of his transmitting system.

Meanwhile, across the Atlantic, Vladimir Zworykin, a Russian-born engineer working for RCA (Radio Corporation of America), independently developed a similar electronic television system. Zworykin's approach, while ultimately converging on the same fundamental principles as Farnsworth's, involved different technological choices and design implementations. His system utilized a different type of CRT, the iconoscope, as the camera tube, which had its own unique advantages and disadvantages compared to Farnsworth's image dissector. The iconoscope, while more complex to manufacture, proved more sensitive to light and thus capable of producing better images in lower-light conditions.

The simultaneous development of electronic television by Farnsworth and Zworykin led to an inevitable clash, a protracted and acrimonious patent battle that reverberated through the television industry for years. Both inventors fiercely defended their claims, sparking a legal war that involved protracted litigation and expert testimony. The complexities of the patent claims and the intricate nature of the underlying technologies fueled the intensity of the dispute. Ultimately, while the details of the legal battles remained contested, Farnsworth's pioneering role in conceiving the fundamental principles of electronic television is widely acknowledged, even though Zworykin's technological contributions were significant and commercially influential.

The advantages of electronic television over its mechanical predecessor were undeniable. Electronic systems offered vastly superior image quality, far exceeding the resolution and clarity of mechanical systems. The elimination of the rotating disks, with their inherent mechanical limitations and susceptibility to wear, resulted in significantly improved stability and reliability. The smoother, less flickering images created a substantially enhanced viewing experience. This superior image quality, coupled with the higher resolution, marked a profound improvement over the crude, blurry images of mechanical television.

Beyond the improvements in image quality, electronic television systems also offered greater flexibility and scalability. The electronic scanning process could be readily adapted to various formats and resolutions, allowing for greater versatility in image transmission. Furthermore, electronic systems proved more readily adaptable to color television technology, a further advance that would dramatically enhance the viewer experience.

The transition from mechanical to electronic television marked a pivotal moment in the history of broadcasting. The superior image quality, improved stability, and enhanced scalability of electronic systems quickly led to their widespread adoption, effectively rendering mechanical television obsolete. While mechanical television served as a crucial stepping stone, demonstrating the feasibility of image transmission, it was electronic television that truly unlocked the potential of the medium, paving the way for the mass consumption of television and its profound impact on society.

The ensuing decades saw the rapid advancement of electronic television technology, culminating in the widespread adoption of color television and ultimately the digital revolution that transformed the medium once more. The legacy of Farnsworth and Zworykin, despite their contentious relationship, remains inextricably linked to this technological transformation, shaping the television landscape we inhabit today. Their innovations not only improved the viewing experience but also laid the foundation for the incredible technological advancements that would follow, transforming television from a novelty into a ubiquitous form of media and entertainment. The ongoing evolution of television technology, from high-definition to ultra-high definition and beyond, owes its foundation to the groundbreaking work of these pioneering inventors, a testament to their enduring contributions to the history of communication.

Early Broadcasts and Technological Challenges

The successful development of electronic television, however, was only the first step in a long and complex journey. The early broadcasts were far from the polished productions we are accustomed to today. These initial transmissions were characterized by a number of significant technical limitations, which profoundly impacted both the quality of the viewing experience and the extent of the medium's reach. The image quality, for example, was often surprisingly poor, even by the standards of the time. Resolution was extremely low, resulting in blurry, indistinct pictures. Contrast and brightness levels were often erratic, creating images that were sometimes difficult to decipher. Furthermore, the broadcasts were frequently plagued by interference, resulting in a snowy or static-filled image that disrupted the viewing experience. These technical issues were not merely aesthetic inconveniences; they fundamentally limited the appeal and effectiveness of the early broadcasts.

One of the most significant challenges was the limited range of the early television broadcasts. The early transmission systems lacked the power and sophistication needed to send signals over long distances. This meant that the broadcasts were largely confined to small geographical areas, often within the immediate vicinity of the transmitting station. This severely limited the potential audience for these early broadcasts, hindering the development of a mass television audience. Viewers were often dependent on the proximity of the receiver to the transmitter and on the signal strength, which was frequently inconsistent. Even small geographical features, such as hills or tall buildings, could significantly disrupt or attenuate the signal, resulting in poor reception or no reception at all. The problem of signal attenuation and interference posed a serious technological hurdle that had to be overcome before television could achieve its full potential.

The inconsistent signal strength was another major problem facing early television broadcasts. The early transmission systems were far from stable, and signal strength often fluctuated wildly, leading to a variable viewing experience. One moment the image might be relatively clear, only to be swallowed up by static or interference the next. This unpredictability made television viewing a frustrating and often unrewarding experience. The lack of standardized transmission protocols further compounded this problem, adding to the complexity of ensuring consistent signal quality across different receiving stations. This lack of standardization also meant that receivers designed for one transmission system were not necessarily compatible with others, further limiting the potential reach of the medium.

Early television programming itself was also limited. The earliest broadcasts were extremely rudimentary, often consisting of little more than simple test patterns, rudimentary animations, or short news bulletins. The technical limitations of the time constrained the complexity and scope of the programs. Live broadcasts were often fraught with problems, with cameras prone to malfunction and sudden drops in signal strength frequently interrupting the program flow. Furthermore, the limited bandwidth available for transmission restricted the visual resolution and the possibilities for sophisticated camerawork. The range of programming options was understandably limited, reflecting the nascent stage of the medium's development.

Despite these technical challenges, the societal impact of those first broadcasts was profound, even if the impact was initially felt in a limited geographical area. The very novelty of watching moving images in one's own home held a powerful allure. The early broadcasts, rudimentary as they were, ignited the public's imagination and fostered a sense of anticipation about the future potential of the medium. For many, television represented a window into a new world, offering a glimpse of events happening elsewhere and opportunities to consume entertainment in a format that differed from radio. The limited programming available often featured short newsreels, experimental dramas, or simple demonstrations of the technology's capabilities. Despite their limitations, these early broadcasts captured the public imagination and sparked considerable interest in the nascent medium.

The reaction to the first television broadcasts was a mixture of excitement and skepticism. Many were captivated by the wonder of watching moving pictures, even if the quality of the images was far from perfect. Others remained skeptical, questioning the practical value and potential of this new technology. Some commentators raised concerns about the potential for social and cultural disruption. Others were impressed by the technology's potential educational and entertainment value. The diverse reactions reflected the nascent and uncertain nature of the medium at this stage of development. The early broadcasts, despite their imperfections, stimulated heated debate about television's potential and role in society.

The challenges faced by early broadcasters extended beyond mere technological limitations. The establishment of broadcasting infrastructure was itself a significant undertaking. Setting up transmitting stations and establishing networks to connect them posed considerable logistical and financial obstacles. The lack of consistent standards for transmission across various systems further added to the challenges, resulting in incompatibility between different receivers and transmitters. Moreover, the training and employment of qualified technical personnel was crucial for the operation and maintenance of broadcasting equipment. These early broadcasters faced considerable challenges in establishing and operating transmission facilities and training personnel in the operation and maintenance of often-complex equipment.

As the technology matured, however, so did the programming. Initially, broadcasts often consisted of simple demonstrations of the medium's capabilities. As the quality of the image improved, and as broadcasters gained more experience, more complex and sophisticated programming became feasible. The development of new camera techniques, editing methods, and broadcasting infrastructure gradually improved the viewing experience. This evolution of programming, fueled by technological advances, marked a transition from crude demonstrations to the creation of professionally produced programs. This evolutionary trajectory saw a gradual shift in the types of programs being broadcast, ranging from experimental dramas and newsreels to more ambitious productions that capitalized on the growing technical capabilities of the medium.

The transition from experimental to commercially viable broadcasts marked another critical milestone in the early history of television.

This meant a change from demonstrations of technology to the establishment of regular programming schedules aimed at attracting larger audiences and generating revenue. This marked the formal inception of television as a mass-market communications and entertainment medium. The transition to commercially viable television programs required not only advances in technology but also the creation of a business model that would support regular programming and the operation of broadcasting stations.

In conclusion, the early days of television broadcasts were a period of both remarkable innovation and significant technical challenges. The initial transmissions, far from perfect, nonetheless captured the public's imagination and laid the groundwork for the future development of the medium. The technical hurdles, including low resolution, limited range, and inconsistent signal strength, highlighted the limitations of early television technology.

Nevertheless, the sheer novelty of the medium, coupled with the promise of future improvements, propelled television towards its ultimate dominance as a mass communications medium. The societal response to these early broadcasts, a mixture of excitement and skepticism, reflected the uncertainty and transformative potential of this new technology. The subsequent years would witness the relentless pursuit of technological improvement, laying the groundwork for the golden age of television and the digital revolution that would transform the medium beyond recognition.

The Social Impact of Early Television The Beginning of a New Medium

The arrival of television, despite its initial technical imperfections, irrevocably altered the social fabric. Its impact transcended the mere provision of entertainment; it fundamentally reshaped how people communicated, consumed information, and interacted with the world around them. The ability to bring moving images into the home, a previously unimaginable feat, fostered a sense of collective experience unlike anything seen before. While radio had united audiences through shared auditory experiences, television offered a visual dimension, creating a deeper, more immersive connection.

Early television broadcasts, though limited in scope and quality, captured the public imagination in ways that are difficult to fully appreciate today. Imagine the awe of witnessing, for the first time, a live sporting event unfold in your living room, the immediacy of seeing news unfold as it happened, or the vicarious thrill of experiencing faraway places through the lens of a television camera. For many, these moments represented a profound shift in their relationship with the world. The small, flickering screen became a portal to distant realities, both mundane and extraordinary.

Public reaction to these broadcasts was far from uniform. While many were captivated by the novelty, even the low-quality images holding a certain charm, others greeted the new medium with skepticism or outright apprehension. Concerns were raised about the potential negative impacts on society, reflecting anxieties about the power of visual media to shape perceptions and influence behavior. Some feared the allure of television might draw people away from more active pursuits, leading to passivity and social isolation. The potential for propaganda and the manipulation of public opinion were also voiced concerns.

These anxieties were not unfounded. The power of television to shape public opinion and disseminate information rapidly, both accurate and inaccurate, was immediately apparent. Early news broadcasts, even with their limitations, demonstrated the potential of television to influence public discourse and shape political perceptions. Similarly, early advertising campaigns, though simpler than their modern counterparts, showcased the medium's persuasive power and its effectiveness in shaping consumer behavior.

The very act of watching television became a shared social experience. Families gathered around the set, bonding over shared viewing experiences. While this created a sense of community within the home, it also raised questions about the role of television in family life. Concerns emerged about the time spent watching television, potentially diverting time away from more traditional forms of family interaction. The potential for television to isolate individuals and families from their communities was also discussed.

The limited programming available in the early days of television further influenced its social impact. The initial broadcasts often consisted of newsreels, simple dramas, and educational programs. However, the technical limitations of the time meant that these programs were often crude and simplistic, reflecting the technological infancy of the medium. The limited variety in programming also meant that the audience's viewing options were extremely restricted, often leading to a sense of uniformity in tastes and experiences.

The development of commercial television profoundly impacted the social landscape. The transition from experimental broadcasts to commercially driven programming created a new arena for advertising and the dissemination of consumer culture. This meant the integration of advertising into programming itself, effectively merging entertainment with the promotion of goods and services. The implications for consumer behavior and societal values were profound, leading to questions about the role of commercial interests in shaping television content and public perceptions.

The impact extended beyond entertainment and advertising. Educational programs, despite their limited resources, demonstrated the potential of television to reach large audiences with information and educational materials. These early programs, though often rudimentary, paved the way for more sophisticated educational television programming that would later play a significant role in shaping learning experiences, especially for those in remote areas or those with limited access to traditional educational resources.

As television technology continued to evolve, the social impact intensified. The development of color television, for example, enhanced the viewing experience, making the images more realistic and engaging. This, in turn, broadened its appeal and further cemented its role in popular culture. The shift to color represented more than a technical improvement; it was a cultural shift, underscoring television's increasingly pervasive influence on daily life.

The arrival of television was not just a technological leap; it was a social revolution. It reshaped the cultural landscape, redefined how people spent their leisure time, and transformed the way families interacted. It offered a new form of community, both within the household and across wider society, while simultaneously raising concerns about the homogenization of culture and the potential for social isolation. These early broadcasts, however imperfect, laid the groundwork for the profound influence television would come to exert in subsequent decades, paving the way for the golden age of television and beyond.

The rapid adoption of television across the globe brought with it a range of societal consequences. The spread of television broadcasts across national borders fostered a sense of global interconnectedness, allowing individuals in different countries to share similar experiences and engage with similar narratives. This increased cultural exchange, however, also sparked debates about cultural homogenization and the potential loss of local traditions. The anxieties associated with the dominance of Western cultural exports were also expressed.

The evolution of television technology continued unabated, laying the foundation for future innovations. The invention of the remote control, seemingly minor today, marked a significant step in transforming television from a communal experience to a more personalized form of entertainment. The introduction of cable television further expanded programming options, increasing competition and creating a more diverse range of content available to viewers. These developments, seemingly small in retrospect, had profound implications for how people engaged with television and the impact it had on their lives.

In conclusion, the early days of television, with all its technical shortcomings, marked a watershed moment in human history. Its influence on society was immediate and profound, transforming entertainment, communication, and the way individuals and communities interacted. While initially greeted with a mixture of excitement and apprehension, television's inexorable rise demonstrated its power to shape the cultural, political, and social landscape. The foundations laid during those early years of broadcasting would continue to resonate through the following decades and beyond, shaping the trajectory of the medium and its ongoing impact on human life. The anxieties and excitement surrounding early television serve as a reminder of the transformative power of new technologies and the importance of understanding their societal consequences.

The Technological Advancements of Postwar Era

The end of World War II marked a turning point not only in global politics but also in the technological landscape. The war years had spurred immense innovation in various fields, and this momentum carried over into the post-war era, significantly impacting the development and accessibility of television. The immediate post-war period witnessed a surge in consumer demand for durable goods, fueled by pent-up demand, a burgeoning middle class, and the relative economic prosperity of the time. Television, still a relatively new technology, found itself perfectly positioned to capitalize on this wave of consumer optimism.

One of the most significant factors contributing to the post-war boom in television was the mass production techniques refined during the war. The manufacturing processes developed to produce military equipment were readily adapted to the production of television sets, leading to significant economies of scale. This resulted in a dramatic decrease in the cost of manufacturing, making television sets increasingly affordable for the average American household. The price point, once prohibitive for all but the wealthiest, began to fall within the reach of a significantly larger segment of the population. This affordability was pivotal in driving the rapid expansion of television ownership. Factories that had once churned out weaponry were retooled to produce the cathode ray tubes, chassis, and cabinets that formed the heart of the television set. The assembly line techniques, honed to a high degree of efficiency during the war, were instrumental in accelerating the production process and driving down manufacturing costs. This allowed for the mass production of affordable sets that could flood the market.

Simultaneously, significant advancements in television technology improved the quality of the viewing experience. Early television sets were plagued by problems such as poor resolution, limited contrast, and frequent interference. However, the post-war period saw rapid improvements in these areas. Engineers and scientists continued to refine the cathode ray tube technology, leading to sharper images, richer colors (eventually leading to color television), and a more stable signal. The development of improved circuitry and more sensitive receiving components further enhanced picture quality and reception range. These technological improvements, along with the economies of scale achieved through mass production, worked in tandem to deliver a better product at a more attractive price, fueling the demand further.

The expansion of broadcasting infrastructure was equally crucial. The government recognized the potential of television as a medium for both entertainment and information dissemination, and it supported the expansion of broadcasting networks across the country. This involved the construction of new television stations, the allocation of broadcast frequencies, and the development of the technical infrastructure required to transmit television signals over long distances. The rapid expansion of the number of television stations, coupled with the development of powerful transmitters, greatly increased the geographic reach of television broadcasts. This meant that more and more people could receive a clear signal, widening the market for television sets considerably. The establishment of the networks (NBC, CBS, and ABC) as dominant forces played a critical role in the standardization of broadcast frequencies and programming schedules, fostering a national television viewing experience and driving further demand.

The improved reliability of television sets was another significant factor. Early models were notoriously prone to breakdowns and required frequent maintenance. However, advancements in component technology, coupled with improvements in manufacturing processes, led to more reliable and durable sets. This reduced the frequency of repairs and increased the overall lifespan of television sets, boosting consumer confidence and further accelerating adoption rates. The increased lifespan meant a stronger return on investment for consumers, which further boosted sales.

The integration of more robust and longer-lasting components translated into a less frustrating ownership experience. This added to the growing confidence in the technology itself and influenced purchasing decisions.

Beyond the technological and manufacturing improvements, the social and cultural context of the post-war era played a vital role in shaping the television boom. The widespread availability of inexpensive housing in the suburbs, the rise of the middle class, and a growing culture of consumerism all contributed to a climate where owning a television became increasingly aspirational.

Television offered a new form of family entertainment, bringing families together in the evening to watch shared programs. This new sense of family togetherness was very appealing after the hardship and separation brought about by war. The television set became a symbol of suburban prosperity and the ideal American family. Advertising heavily played on this association to increase sales.

The impact on the workforce was substantial. The booming television industry created thousands of jobs in manufacturing, broadcasting, and related fields. This created employment opportunities for returning veterans and helped fuel post-war economic growth. Television became a significant job-creating sector, driving employment across various aspects of the production, distribution, and broadcasting chain. This not only contributed to economic prosperity but also played a role in stabilizing the post-war society.

The transition to color television in the late 1950s and early 1960s marked another significant milestone. While initially expensive, the eventual widespread adoption of color television drastically improved the visual appeal of the medium. This upgrade added further allure, pushing consumers to upgrade their existing black and white sets, further boosting the industry. The enhanced visual experience, though initially a premium feature, ultimately became the standard, further driving the market and cementing television's position in mainstream culture.

The expansion of programming beyond simple newsreels and limited-budget shows also played a key role. The emergence of variety shows, sitcoms, dramas, and sporting events created a diverse range of content that appealed to a broad audience. This diversification of programming helped to solidify television's position as the dominant form of entertainment and solidified the medium's role in mainstream culture. This diverse content contributed not only to the increase in viewership but also to the growth of related industries like advertising and entertainment production.

The post-war boom was not without its challenges. The rapid expansion of the television industry led to concerns about the quality of programming, the potential for broadcasting harmful or misleading information, and the societal impacts of television's growing influence on viewers. These concerns, though present, did not diminish the immense growth and impact of television technology during this period. The very real anxieties about the influence of television on society were largely overshadowed by the undeniable appeal and widespread adoption of the medium. The initial anxieties and concerns did not slow the momentum or prevent the rapid and significant changes to social dynamics that television brought about.

In essence, the post-war boom in television was a confluence of technological advancements, economic prosperity, and evolving social trends. The combination of mass production techniques, improvements in television technology, the expansion of broadcasting infrastructure, and the cultural embrace of consumerism created the perfect storm for the rapid proliferation of television sets into American homes and, subsequently, across the globe. This period set the stage for the "golden age" of television and laid the foundations for the ongoing evolution of the medium.

The post-war era was not merely a period of technological advancement; it was a cultural shift, inextricably linking the rise of television to the shaping of postwar society. The lasting impact of this boom continues to be felt even today, as television remains a central feature of our lives, albeit in constantly evolving forms.

The Rise of Network Television

The post-war boom wasn't simply about the availability of affordable television sets; it was about the creation of a shared national experience. This shared experience was largely orchestrated by the rise of the major television networks: NBC, CBS, and ABC. These networks, initially radio broadcasting giants, quickly recognized the potential of the visual medium and aggressively moved to establish their dominance in the burgeoning television landscape. Their strategies were multifaceted, impacting not only the technological development of television but also its social and cultural influence.

One of the most significant contributions of the networks was the standardization of broadcasting practices. Before the networks' consolidation of power, television programming was fragmented and inconsistent. Local stations operated independently, broadcasting a mixture of live performances, newsreels, and experimental programming. There was little in the way of a coordinated national schedule or consistent programming formats. The networks, however, brought order to this chaos. By establishing national programming schedules and developing standardized formats for various program types – news broadcasts, sitcoms, dramas, and variety shows – they created a sense of national cohesion in television viewing. This consistency proved incredibly effective in attracting large audiences and establishing a common cultural touchstone across the country.

The development of standardized program formats was equally crucial. The networks understood the importance of creating easily replicated and repeatable content. This led to the emergence of distinct television genres that are still recognizable today. The sitcom, with its episodic structure and focus on family dynamics or workplace comedy, became a staple of network programming.

Similarly, the half-hour drama format, often featuring serialized storylines and continuing characters, gained popularity. Variety shows, with their blend of music, comedy, and celebrity appearances, provided a diverse form of entertainment. These standardized formats provided a template for program production, allowing networks to produce a large volume of content efficiently and cost-effectively. The standardization of these formats also greatly increased the ease and efficiency of advertising integration, a key component of the networks' revenue model.

The networks' influence extended beyond the mere standardization of programming. They also played a key role in shaping the content itself. Through their control over programming schedules and production resources, they dictated the types of shows that were produced and the values they promoted. While some programming was locally sourced or independently produced, a significant portion was produced in-house or through network-affiliated production companies. This control gave the networks considerable power to influence public opinion and shape cultural norms. For instance, the portrayal of family life in sitcoms, the representation of different social groups in dramas, and the presentation of news and current events all reflected and, in many cases, reinforced the prevailing social values and perspectives of the time.

The networks' reach also led to a homogenization of the television experience across different regions of the country. While regional differences still existed, the dominance of network programming created a shared national culture, albeit one that was sometimes criticized for its lack of diversity. However, this standardization provided a platform for the creation of national celebrities, a phenomenon previously unheard of on the same scale. Actors, musicians, and comedians, who may have only been known regionally, achieved nationwide fame through their appearances on network television. This also facilitated the spread of national trends and the growth of a mass consumer culture.

The influence of the networks was not without its challenges. Their control over programming was often criticized for stifling creativity and diversity. Independent producers and local stations often felt marginalized by the dominance of the networks. Critics argued that the standardization of programming led to a bland uniformity and a lack of regional or local representation. The power concentrated within the networks raised questions about media monopolies and their potential impact on society. The content itself often reflected the prevailing social norms and biases, leading to accusations of limited representation of minorities and marginalized groups. Nevertheless, despite these criticisms, the networks' contribution to the rise of network television and the creation of a national television culture is undeniable.

The introduction of color television in the late 1950s further enhanced the networks' influence. The transition to color brought about a significant upgrade in the quality of the viewing experience.

The initially higher cost of color television sets didn't deter consumers, and the networks seized the opportunity to showcase the enhanced capabilities of the new technology. Color programming brought a new vibrancy and realism to television, further increasing its appeal and viewership. This upgrade significantly impacted the networks' bottom lines as well as influencing consumer demand and leading to a rapid transition to the new color standard across the nation.

The economic impact of the networks was also substantial. They were not only major employers themselves, but they also fueled the growth of related industries, such as advertising, production companies, and talent agencies. Advertising revenues became a crucial component of the network business model, and the networks developed sophisticated strategies to maximize their advertising income. This relationship between networks and advertisers further shaped the content of television programming, as shows were often designed to appeal to specific demographic groups that advertisers targeted. The revenue generated enabled further investment in technological advancements, talent acquisition, and content creation.

The networks' impact on political discourse and information dissemination was equally significant. Network news broadcasts became a primary source of information for millions of Americans.

The nightly news, with its standardized format and clear presentation of information, established a trusted, if sometimes biased, source of news. This influence, while arguably beneficial in some ways, also raised concerns about the networks' potential to shape public opinion and manipulate the news agenda. This gave the networks considerable influence, not just in shaping entertainment, but in influencing public opinion and political viewpoints as well.

The golden age of television, often associated with the 1950s and 1960s, was largely defined by the dominance of the major networks. Their influence extended to every aspect of television, from programming formats and content to the technical standards and broadcasting infrastructure. Their role in creating a shared national experience, promoting consumerism, and shaping public opinion was substantial and long-lasting. While the landscape of television has changed dramatically since then, the foundation laid by these networks continues to shape the industry even today. The structure of network television, though evolving, still bears the imprint of the systems, formats, and cultural norms established during this period of intense growth and influence. The legacy of the networks in creating a shared national television culture is undeniable, and their influence resonates through the many iterations of the medium we consume today. The post-war television boom was, in many ways, the making of the modern television landscape, a story still unfolding as technology continues to redefine how we watch and interact with this ubiquitous medium.

The Golden Age of Television Iconic Shows and Cultural Impact

The post-war economic boom fueled a surge in television ownership, transforming the medium from a novelty into a ubiquitous fixture in American homes. This widespread adoption coincided with a flourishing of creative talent and innovative programming, marking what is widely considered the "Golden Age" of television. This era, roughly spanning from the mid-1950s to the late 1960s, witnessed the emergence of iconic shows that not only entertained but also profoundly impacted American culture, shaping social attitudes, fashion trends, and even the very language we use.

One of the key characteristics of this Golden Age was the rise of distinct television genres. The sitcom, already established, blossomed into a dominant force, offering a window into the lives of everyday families. Shows like *I Love Lucy*, with its groundbreaking use of film techniques and Lucille Ball's comedic genius, redefined what was possible in television comedy. The show's influence extended beyond mere entertainment; its portrayal of a working wife and mother challenged traditional gender roles, subtly influencing shifting societal attitudes towards women in the workplace. Similarly, *The Dick Van Dyke Show*, with its sharp writing and ensemble cast, became a model for workplace sitcoms, its influence still visible in contemporary shows. The show cleverly explored the creative process and the comedic dynamics of a television writing room, subtly commenting on the television industry itself.

Simultaneously, the anthology series, with its varied themes and single-episode narratives, provided a platform for diverse storytelling. Series like *Alfred Hitchcock Presents* and *The Twilight Zone* showcased the versatility of the medium, exploring a range of genres, from suspense and horror to science fiction and fantasy. They pushed the boundaries of television storytelling, experimenting with different narrative styles and tackling complex themes that were often absent from other primetime programs.

These shows demonstrated that television could be a vehicle for sophisticated and thought-provoking narratives. Their impact lay not only in their individual stories but also in their influence on the broader evolution of television storytelling, paving the way for future dramatic series.

The Western genre flourished during this period, offering viewers a glimpse into the romanticized frontier of the American West. Shows like *Gunsmoke* , with its realistic portrayal of life in Dodge City, and *Bonanza* , with its focus on a sprawling Ponderosa ranch, captivated audiences with their larger-than-life characters and exciting storylines. These shows, while often romanticizing the past and sometimes perpetuating harmful stereotypes, provided a sense of national identity, reflecting and shaping American perceptions of its own history and its sense of destiny. Their enduring popularity is a testament to their enduring power to capture the American imagination.

Dramatic series also gained prominence, exploring complex themes and showcasing nuanced characters. Shows like *The Twilight Zone* , though technically an anthology, frequently used dramatic elements, while shows like *Peyton Place* and *The Fugitive* introduced serialized storylines and complex characters, paving the way for the intricate narratives of modern television dramas. These shows, often dealing with social issues and personal conflicts, demonstrated television's ability to tackle serious and emotional subject matter in a compelling manner. Their impact on subsequent drama programming was substantial, establishing the foundation for many later series that embraced serialized narratives and complex character development.

Beyond the genre-specific shows, the variety show dominated the landscape, providing a kaleidoscope of entertainment. Shows like *The Ed Sullivan Show* showcased a wide range of musical acts, comedians, and other performers, introducing many to iconic talents and shaping popular musical culture. *The Tonight Show* under Jack Paar and then Johnny Carson became an institution, establishing the late-night talk show format that persists to this day. These shows, through their diverse guest list and host personalities, not only provided entertainment but also reflected the evolving cultural tastes of the nation and served as a powerful platform for both emerging and established artists. The influence of these variety shows extended to the development of many later television formats, from talk shows to musical competitions, continuing to shape television even into the present.

The cultural impact of these shows extended beyond their entertainment value. The fashion choices of characters, the slang they used, and the social attitudes they represented often became pervasive influences in American society. The hairstyles of *I Love Lucy*'s Lucy Ricardo, for instance, became instantly popular, influencing fashion trends. The casual wit and phrasing of characters on shows like *The Dick Van Dyke Show* contributed to American vernacular. The plots and themes of many shows reflected the societal anxieties and aspirations of the time, making them culturally significant touchstones for their era. Shows dealt with issues like racial prejudice, gender roles, and social class, sometimes subtly, sometimes more directly, influencing social conversations and attitudes.

Moreover, the "Golden Age" wasn't just about the shows themselves; it was about the personalities who brought them to life. Lucille Ball, Desi Arnaz, Jack Benny, Milton Berle, and Sid Caesar became household names, their fame extending far beyond the television screen. These performers transcended their roles, becoming iconic figures that shaped the public's perception of entertainers and influencing how the industry itself would grow and develop. Their talent, charisma, and comedic timing contributed to a golden era in comedy that continues to inspire artists today.

The Golden Age of television was also a time of technical innovation. The transition to color broadcasting in the late 1950s dramatically enhanced the visual appeal of television, further increasing its appeal. This technological advancement, while initially expensive, spurred technological innovation and led to higher-quality production values, further enhancing the immersion and aesthetic pleasure of viewing. The change not only improved the television watching experience but also fueled further innovation and development of the television industry.

The influence of the networks on the Golden Age is undeniable. Their control over scheduling and production significantly shaped the types of programs that were produced and the values they promoted. However, the creativity and innovation of the era also resulted from the talent and vision of independent producers and writers who pushed boundaries and explored new thematic territory. While networks held considerable power, the quality of the programs also relied on the talents and visions of the independent producers and artists involved. This combined effort ultimately shaped this formative era of the medium, leaving an indelible mark on American culture. The legacy of the Golden Age continues to influence television today, inspiring new shows and shaping our understanding of the medium's creative potential. The enduring appeal of many of these shows testifies to their impact on American culture, proving that the magic of that era still resonates with viewers today.

The Transition to Color Television A New Era of Visuals

The transition to color television marked a watershed moment in the medium's history, dramatically altering the viewing experience and profoundly impacting the industry's creative landscape. While the monochrome era had established television as a dominant force in American homes, the introduction of color added a new dimension of realism and vibrancy, further cementing its position as the primary source of entertainment and information. This shift, however, was far from seamless. It involved years of technical development, significant financial investment, and a gradual shift in consumer attitudes.

The initial experiments with color television date back to the 1920s and 30s, even preceding the widespread adoption of black-and-white technology. Early systems, however, were plagued by technical limitations, including incompatibility between different systems, poor picture quality, and the impracticality of producing and broadcasting color signals. These challenges hindered the development and widespread adoption of color television for several decades. Several competing systems emerged, each employing different methods to generate and display color images. This lack of standardization was a major obstacle to the widespread adoption of color television, as it made it difficult for broadcasters and manufacturers to create compatible equipment. The lack of a unified standard meant that viewers often needed to purchase multiple sets to receive broadcasts from various networks. This fragmentation of the market made it economically difficult for the industry to mass-produce affordable color televisions.

The development of compatible color television standards was a critical breakthrough in the 1950s. The National Television System Committee (NTSC) in the United States developed a system that addressed the issues of incompatibility and picture quality. The NTSC system, which utilized a compatible color encoding scheme, allowed color signals to be received by both color and monochrome televisions, thus mitigating the risk of alienating the existing monochrome television audience. This compatibility was a key factor in the eventual triumph of the NTSC standard, making it possible for broadcasters to gradually introduce color programming without requiring all viewers to upgrade their equipment immediately. This crucial compatibility factor removed a significant barrier to the adoption of color television.

Even with a standardized system in place, the transition to color was not an overnight success. The cost of color televisions was initially prohibitive for many consumers, limiting their widespread adoption in the early years. The higher cost of production and broadcast equipment also hampered the immediate transition to widespread color broadcasting. Many television stations were initially hesitant to invest in expensive new equipment, while consumers were slow to adopt color technology due to high initial costs. Consequently, color broadcasting started slowly, with only a few programs adopting color initially.

The gradual introduction of color programming further shaped audience reception. Viewers initially accustomed to black and white imagery needed time to adjust to the enhanced visual experience offered by color television. The vividness of color not only improved the aesthetic quality of the programs, but it also allowed for a richer and more expressive visual storytelling. Gradually, the superior visual quality of color programming became increasingly apparent, enhancing the storytelling power of television significantly.

Network television played a pivotal role in driving the adoption of color television. The major networks, including NBC, CBS, and ABC, gradually began to increase the amount of color programming in their schedules. High-profile shows were chosen to debut in color, enticing viewers to upgrade their television sets. The strategic decision to showcase high-profile programs in color was a persuasive strategy that greatly accelerated the transition to color television. The impact was significant: the networks' investments in color programming directly influenced consumer purchasing decisions, creating a powerful positive feedback loop that rapidly increased color television adoption.

The impact of color television on programming extended beyond a mere aesthetic improvement. The enhanced visuals opened up new creative possibilities for producers and directors. Color could be used to create specific moods, enhance the dramatic impact of scenes, and elevate the storytelling capabilities of the medium. The enhanced visual possibilities also transformed the way directors approached scenes and storytelling. Color created a more dynamic environment and allowed filmmakers to use the visual aspect of their storytelling to a much greater degree than black and white allowed. The enhanced visual palette also offered opportunities to create new visual aesthetics tailored specifically for the color medium.

Color television further redefined the standards of television production. As color broadcasting became more common, the quality and aesthetic values of television programs generally increased. The higher production values encouraged filmmakers and artists to consider the impact and value of color. This emphasis on visual aesthetics elevated the overall viewing experience, thereby enhancing the prestige of television programs.

The social significance of color television extends beyond the realm of entertainment. The vibrant colors and enhanced realism brought a sense of immediacy and intimacy to television viewing, contributing to a more profound and emotional engagement. In turn, this new immersion also fostered stronger emotional connections between the viewers and the content they consumed. The transformation from black-and-white to color fundamentally altered the way audiences perceived and interacted with the medium. Color added a deeper layer of emotional resonance, impacting viewers on a more visceral level.

In conclusion, the transition to color television was a complex process involving technological breakthroughs, economic factors, and a gradual shift in consumer preferences. Its impact, however, was undeniable. Color television significantly enhanced the visual appeal and entertainment value of television, transforming its role as a primary source of entertainment and information for millions. It not only improved the technical capabilities of the medium but also significantly impacted the cultural landscape and the way audiences interacted with and perceived television. The introduction of color was far more than a technological advancement; it was a cultural transformation.

The Growing Popularity of Television and its Impact on Society

The post-war economic boom in the United States provided fertile ground for the burgeoning television industry. Returning soldiers, coupled with a burgeoning middle class, fueled a consumerist frenzy, and television became a highly sought-after symbol of this prosperity. The affordability of sets, initially a luxury item, gradually decreased throughout the 1950s, making television ownership attainable for a significantly larger segment of the population. This accessibility dramatically altered the social landscape, transforming how Americans spent their leisure time and fundamentally reshaping family dynamics and social interactions.

Prior to the widespread adoption of television, evening entertainment was often centered around family-oriented activities such as board games, reading, or attending local events. Radio, while a powerful medium, offered a more passive and solitary form of entertainment. Television, however, brought families together in a shared experience, often gathered around the same set, watching the same programs. This shared viewing experience created a common ground for conversation and family bonding, albeit with its own set of unique dynamics. The very structure of the evening changed, with families adjusting their dinner schedules to accommodate primetime programming. The television set became a focal point of the living room, a silent observer of family life, both reflecting and influencing the domestic sphere.

The impact on family dynamics was multifaceted. While television provided a shared experience, it also introduced new challenges. The passive nature of television viewing could lead to a decline in family interaction, replacing more active forms of engagement. Concerns arose about the potential for television to reduce face-to-face communication within families, leading to a shift in relational dynamics. The shared viewing experience, however, also opened up opportunities for conversation and common ground, fostering a sense of shared experience and common cultural understanding within the family unit.

Children were particularly affected by the rise of television.

Educational programs offered a new avenue for learning, while cartoons and other children's shows provided entertainment tailored to their age group. However, concerns emerged regarding the potential negative impacts of excessive television viewing, such as exposure to violence, unhealthy role models, and the potential for addiction. The burgeoning debate surrounding the effects of television on children's development became a significant area of public and academic discourse, shaping policy and parental guidance surrounding screen time.

Beyond the family unit, television's impact extended to broader society. The creation of a shared viewing experience led to the formation of a common cultural landscape. Popular television shows, like "I Love Lucy," "The Honeymooners," and "The Milton Berle Show," became national cultural phenomena, providing a common vocabulary and shared references that transcended geographical boundaries. These programs were not only entertaining; they reflected and shaped prevailing cultural norms, attitudes, and values.

The influence of advertising also played a pivotal role in shaping the social and cultural impact of television. Commercial breaks, initially brief interruptions, gradually expanded, becoming an integral part of the viewing experience. Television advertisements, unlike their radio counterparts, offered a more visually compelling way to reach a mass audience, leading to a dramatic increase in consumerism. The pervasive nature of advertising on television transformed consumer culture, influencing purchasing decisions and shaping desires for material goods. The impact of television advertising was not limited to product sales; it also contributed to the creation of brand identities and the establishment of social trends.

The rise of television also altered the political landscape. Politicians increasingly recognized the power of television to reach voters directly, transforming political campaigns and the nature of political discourse. The use of television in political advertising and campaign coverage influenced voter behavior, leading to debates about the ethical implications of using the medium to influence public opinion. The ability of television to disseminate information rapidly and widely also contributed to heightened political awareness and engagement, though this access also led to concerns about the potential for manipulation and the spread of misinformation.

The increasing popularity of television also impacted other media industries. Radio, once the dominant form of mass communication, faced stiff competition from television. Radio adapted by focusing on niche audiences and developing specialized programming, but the competition forced significant changes in the structure and content of radio broadcasting. The film industry also felt the impact, as movie attendance declined, prompting Hollywood to adapt and innovate, including experimenting with technologies like widescreen and color cinematography to compete for audience attention.

The social impact of television wasn't solely positive. The pervasive nature of the medium raised concerns about its potential negative consequences, including potential increases in violence and aggression, the promotion of unrealistic beauty standards, and the passive consumption of information. These concerns led to increased scrutiny of television programming and calls for regulations and ethical standards.

In summary, the post-war boom and the rise of television profoundly transformed American society. It reshaped family dynamics, leisure activities, consumer culture, political discourse, and the broader media landscape. While television brought many benefits, including increased access to information and entertainment, it also presented a range of societal challenges that continue to be debated and analyzed to this day. The transition from a primarily radio-based society to one dominated by television was not simply a technological advancement but a significant cultural and social upheaval, laying the groundwork for future media transformations. The seeds of later debates about media influence, violence, and cultural homogeneity were all sown during this period of rapid television adoption. The next chapter will explore how television evolved to meet the demands and challenges of a rapidly changing world, moving beyond the dominance of the three major networks and into the era of cable, satellite, and ultimately, the digital revolution.

The Emergence of Cable Television Expanding Channels and Content

The limitations of over-the-air broadcasting, inherent in its reliance on limited frequency bands, became increasingly apparent as television's popularity soared. The three major networks—ABC, CBS, and NBC—dominated the airwaves, offering a relatively narrow range of programming that often catered to a broad, general audience. This limited selection, while successful in achieving mass appeal, left many viewers yearning for more diverse and specialized content. This desire, coupled with technological advancements, paved the way for the emergence of cable television, a revolutionary development that would irrevocably reshape the television landscape.

The earliest forms of cable television were far from the sophisticated networks we know today. They began as community antenna television (CATV) systems, primarily in areas with poor over-the-air reception. Mountains, tall buildings, and distance from broadcast towers often resulted in weak or non-existent signals, leaving residents with limited or no access to television programming. To overcome this, communities began installing large antennas on hilltops or other elevated locations to receive broadcast signals, then distributing them via coaxial cables to subscribers'homes. These early systems offered a limited number of channels—typically just the local stations amplified with improved reception—but they represented a critical first step towards expanding television access and laying the foundation for the cable television industry's future growth.

The 1960s witnessed the significant expansion of CATV systems, driven by several factors. Technological advancements made it possible to transmit more channels over a single coaxial cable, increasing capacity and enhancing the appeal of cable television.

Furthermore, the development of improved amplifiers and other equipment improved signal quality and reliability. Beyond technical considerations, the growing demand for diverse programming fuelled the expansion of cable networks. Viewers, no longer satisfied with the limited selection offered by over-the-air broadcasting, were eager to access a wider variety of content.

This period saw the emergence of the first dedicated cable channels, though the programming was initially limited. Early cable networks often focused on rebroadcasting existing programming from other sources or offering niche content that wasn't commercially viable for broadcast television. Educational channels, public access channels dedicated to community programming, and channels focused on specific interests, such as sports or religious programming, started to appear. The content on these early channels was often low-budget and comparatively rudimentary in terms of production quality, yet they represented a crucial step in broadening the range of programming available to viewers.

The watershed moment in the development of cable television came with the launch of HBO (Home Box Office) in 1972. HBO marked a paradigm shift by introducing the concept of premium cable channels, offering subscribers a selection of movies and other programming for a monthly fee. This represented a significant departure from the ad-supported model of broadcast television. HBO's success demonstrated the considerable commercial potential of premium cable, demonstrating viewers' willingness to pay for high-quality, diverse programming beyond what was offered by free-to-air channels. This financial model proved pivotal, enabling the expansion and development of higher-budget cable programming and the creation of more specialized channels.

HBO's success spurred a surge in the creation of premium and specialty cable channels. The following years witnessed the launch of Showtime, Cinemax, and other premium channels that followed HBO's model, offering movies, original programming, and other content for a subscription fee. Simultaneously, specialized networks began to emerge, catering to specific demographics and interests. ESPN (Entertainment and Sports Programming Network), launched in 1979, revolutionized sports broadcasting, becoming one of the most successful and influential cable networks. The success of ESPN proved the demand for dedicated sports channels, setting a precedent for the proliferation of specialized networks that would soon follow, focusing on interests such as news, music, and children's programming.

The growth of cable television was not without its challenges. The initial expansion of cable systems faced significant regulatory hurdles. Local authorities often had to be convinced of the benefits of cable television and the need for franchises allowing cable companies to operate within their jurisdictions. Negotiations with broadcasters over carriage agreements—the process by which cable networks secured the right to carry broadcast channels on their systems—were often complex and contentious. Competition among cable operators also led to market consolidation and the formation of larger cable companies. Despite these challenges, the growth of the cable industry continued unabated, fueled by technological innovation and the increasing demand for diverse programming.

The expansion of channel selection brought about significant changes in the television viewing experience. The shift from a limited selection of broadcast channels to a wide array of specialized cable networks enabled viewers to tailor their viewing experience to their individual tastes and preferences. This personalization profoundly influenced how individuals consumed television content, moving away from the more homogenous, mass-audience approach of the broadcast era. The diversity of content also reflected the increasingly fragmented nature of the American audience, with cable channels catering to increasingly niche interests and demographics.

The emergence of cable television also altered the balance of power in the television industry. The dominance of the three major broadcast networks began to erode as cable networks increasingly challenged their position. Cable networks offered the advantage of greater creative freedom and less restrictive regulatory oversight, enabling them to develop programming that often pushed boundaries and experimented with new formats and styles. This competitive landscape, in turn, pushed broadcast television to adapt and innovate, leading to greater diversity and higher production values in broadcast programming as well.

The rise of cable television, therefore, represented a transformative moment in television history. It wasn't simply an incremental improvement in technology or distribution; it was a fundamental shift in how television content was produced, distributed, and consumed. The expansion of channel choices and the diversification of programming offered viewers greater control over their viewing experience, and ultimately changed television from a largely passive experience into a more interactive and personalized one. This diversification also paved the way for the future of television, setting the stage for the eventual digital revolution and the rise of streaming services. The cable television era, however, marked a crucial turning point, forever altering the relationship between viewers, programmers, and the technology itself. The limitations of broadcast television's limited bandwidth and reliance on geographical constraints had been bypassed, creating a more fluid and adaptable landscape for the decades to come. This expansion allowed for the emergence of niche programming, catering to a diverse range of interests and demographics, creating a television landscape far more diverse and engaging than ever before. The seeds of future changes – satellite television, and eventually streaming – were all sown during this period of cable's ascendency.

Satellite Television Reaching a Wider Audience

The burgeoning success of cable television, with its expanding channel selection and specialized programming, didn't signal the end of innovation in television distribution. In fact, it laid the groundwork for an even more ambitious leap forward: satellite television. While cable relied on a network of terrestrial cables, satellite television harnessed the power of orbiting satellites to beam signals directly to homes, transcending geographical limitations and dramatically increasing the potential for channel diversity.

The concept of using satellites for television broadcasting wasn't immediately apparent. Early experiments with satellite communication, primarily for telephone and data transmission, paved the way. The technology needed to transmit and receive high-quality television signals from geostationary orbit—a point above the equator where a satellite appears stationary relative to the Earth—was challenging to develop. The power requirements for the transmission of television signals were significantly higher than those for simpler communication systems and required larger, more powerful satellites. Additionally, receiving signals from these distant satellites required sophisticated and relatively expensive receiving equipment, limiting initial market penetration.

The development of more powerful and efficient transponders—devices on satellites that receive, amplify, and retransmit signals—proved critical. These advancements made it feasible to transmit multiple television channels simultaneously from a single satellite, significantly improving cost-effectiveness and channel capacity. Furthermore, advancements in antenna technology on the receiving end allowed for smaller, more affordable satellite dishes, thereby broadening the appeal and accessibility of the technology to the average consumer.

Early satellite television systems often faced technical challenges. Signal strength could be affected by weather conditions, particularly heavy rainfall or snow, causing disruptions in transmission. The relatively high cost of initial setup, including the satellite dish, receiver, and installation, presented a barrier to entry for many potential subscribers. Furthermore, issues related to signal interference from other satellites or terrestrial sources required careful frequency planning and coordination between different satellite operators.

Despite these initial hurdles, the potential benefits of satellite television were undeniable. Unlike cable, which relied on a physical network of cables that required significant infrastructure investment, satellite television offered a way to reach even the most remote areas without the need for extensive terrestrial infrastructure. This was particularly significant for underserved populations in rural areas, mountainous regions, and other geographically challenging locations, where the expansion of cable networks was often impractical or prohibitively expensive. This geographical advantage directly translated to reaching a wider and more diverse audience, expanding the television viewing experience beyond the constraints of geographical limitations.

The launch of several pioneering satellite television services in the 1970s and 1980s marked a turning point. Services like HBO, initially offered via cable, expanded their reach through satellite distribution, extending their programming to a vastly larger audience. Early satellite providers often partnered with cable companies to distribute their programming, effectively using satellite as a crucial transmission link in a hybrid system. This approach allowed satellite operators to leverage the existing cable infrastructure while expanding their reach beyond the limitations of cable's geographical constraints.

The introduction of Direct Broadcast Satellite (DBS) technology in the late 1980s and early 1990s signified a significant shift. DBS systems eliminated the need for cable infrastructure altogether, transmitting signals directly to individual satellite dishes. This direct-to-home technology proved particularly transformative. The improved signal quality and the ability to receive a vastly larger number of channels directly from the satellite made DBS extremely appealing to consumers. The increased channel capacity significantly expanded programming options, offering viewers a diverse array of choices far surpassing what was available through cable or terrestrial broadcasting.

The competition between cable and satellite providers intensified during this period. Both technologies offered a wider variety of channels compared to over-the-air broadcasting, but their strengths and weaknesses differentiated their market appeal. Cable offered consistent signal quality, free from weather interference, but was limited by the geographical reach of its network. Satellite television overcame geographical limitations but was susceptible to signal disruption from weather and required a significant upfront investment in equipment. This competitive pressure drove both industries to innovate. Cable companies invested in improving their networks and expanding their channel lineups, while satellite operators continued to enhance their technology, making satellite dishes smaller and more efficient, and continuously improving signal quality and reliability.

The rise of satellite television also significantly impacted the media landscape. It allowed for the emergence of new channels catering to niche interests and global audiences, creating a more fragmented yet diverse television environment. Independent programmers and content producers gained access to a broader market, bypassing the gatekeepers of terrestrial and cable networks. International programming became increasingly accessible, breaking down geographical barriers and exposing viewers to a wider range of cultures and perspectives.

The impact on advertising revenue was also profound. The increased channel selection offered advertisers a wider range of options to reach their target audiences, while the expanded reach of satellite television provided them with access to a larger market.

This created new opportunities for niche advertising, targeting specific demographics and interests with tailored marketing campaigns.

Satellite television's legacy extends beyond its technical contributions. Its role in shaping global communication and cultural exchange is undeniable. The ability to receive international news, movies, and television shows across national borders not only enhanced the diversity of programming but also fostered cross-cultural understanding and dialogue. Furthermore, the technology's role in providing television access to remote and underserved communities remains a significant accomplishment.

However, satellite television wasn't without its drawbacks. The reliance on specialized equipment and ongoing subscription fees, along with its vulnerability to weather conditions, remained barriers for some consumers. The increasing congestion of the geostationary orbit, with more and more satellites vying for space and frequency, also posed a challenge. Furthermore, the high cost of launching and maintaining satellites meant that this industry remained dominated by larger, well-funded corporations. This consolidated market structure inevitably introduced its own set of economic and regulatory challenges.

The rise of satellite television stands as a significant chapter in the history of television broadcasting. It demonstrated the transformative power of technological innovation in extending access to information and entertainment, shaping cultural landscapes, and reshaping the competitive dynamics of the television industry. The ability to reach a wider audience and deliver an unprecedented number of channels not only redefined what was possible in television but also laid the foundation for the next wave of technological advancements that would further revolutionize how we consume television – the digital revolution and the rise of streaming services. The satellite era represented a crucial bridge between the analog and digital worlds, and its influence is still felt in the global television landscape today.

The Competition between Cable and Satellite A Battle for Viewers

The battle for viewer loyalty between cable and satellite television unfolded as a dynamic interplay of technological innovation, strategic marketing, and shifting consumer preferences. While both offered a significant upgrade from terrestrial broadcasting, their distinct strengths and weaknesses shaped their respective market positions and fueled a period of intense competition.

Cable television, with its established infrastructure and relatively consistent signal quality, enjoyed an early advantage. The expansion of cable networks into more suburban and even rural areas, coupled with aggressive marketing campaigns highlighting the increased channel selection and specialized programming, attracted a substantial subscriber base. Cable operators invested heavily in building and upgrading their networks, continually adding new channels to their lineups, and offering bundled packages that included telephone and internet services to enhance their value proposition. This bundling strategy proved highly effective in locking in subscribers, making it more difficult for satellite providers to compete on sheer convenience. The readily available local channels, a key draw for many viewers accustomed to over-the-air broadcasts, were a further advantage cable consistently possessed over satellite in the early years. Moreover, the relative simplicity of cable installation, requiring only a connection to the existing infrastructure, made it a more straightforward and appealing option compared to the more involved installation required for satellite dishes.

Satellite television, however, held a crucial trump card: its geographical reach. Unlike cable, which relied on the gradual and expensive expansion of its physical network, satellite technology allowed for the immediate delivery of programming to virtually any location with a clear view of the sky. This was particularly significant in rural areas, mountainous regions, and sparsely populated territories where cable infrastructure was economically impractical to implement. Satellite providers capitalized on this advantage by aggressively targeting these underserved markets, offering an alternative to the limited channel options available through terrestrial broadcasting. The promise of a wider variety of channels, including premium movie channels and specialized programming, proved incredibly attractive to viewers previously limited by their geographical location.

The technological advancements in satellite technology further strengthened its competitive position. The development of smaller, more efficient satellite dishes dramatically reduced the installation cost and aesthetic impact, making the technology more accessible and appealing to a broader range of consumers. Improvements in transponder technology increased channel capacity, enabling the transmission of a greater number of channels from a single satellite, which in turn led to further price reductions and even more channel choices for the consumers. While initial set-up costs for satellite systems remained higher compared to cable, the broader range of channels and the geographical access often outweighed this consideration for many viewers.

The strategies employed by both cable and satellite providers to capture and retain subscribers became increasingly sophisticated. Cable companies began offering interactive features like on-demand programming and video-on-demand services, enhancing the viewer experience and enhancing their appeal to younger audiences.

Satellite operators countered by offering high-definition (HD) channels earlier and more extensively than cable providers, initially setting themselves apart by a superior picture quality. Both industries fiercely competed for programming rights, vying to secure popular television shows, movies, and sporting events, understanding the critical role that programming played in customer loyalty. The race to capture the most sought-after content led to escalating licensing fees, impacting the overall pricing structure of both cable and satellite television services.

The evolution of consumer preferences played a significant role in shaping the dynamics of the competition. As consumers became more discerning, demanding both broader program choices and higher picture quality, both cable and satellite providers struggled to keep pace. The rise of digital technology opened up avenues for specialized, niche channels catering to narrow interests, a trend that further diversified the television landscape. This fragmentation of viewership made it more difficult for both cable and satellite providers to capture large, homogenous audiences. Furthermore, the emergence of digital video recorders (DVRs) and later, digital streaming platforms, offered consumers more control over their viewing habits, allowing them to skip commercials and watch shows at their convenience. This shift in consumer behavior further intensified the competitive pressure on both cable and satellite providers to adapt and innovate.

The competition also played out in the realm of pricing strategies.

Cable companies often leveraged bundled services to offer seemingly attractive packages, but faced criticism for opaque pricing structures and hidden fees. Satellite providers, while offering a wider selection of channels, frequently came under scrutiny for their relatively high upfront equipment costs.

Consumers often found themselves navigating a complex landscape of packages, options and add-ons, struggling to discern the best value for their needs. This complexity often led to customer dissatisfaction and even churn, as consumers searched for more transparent and customized viewing solutions.

The legal and regulatory landscape also played a role in shaping the competitive dynamics. Government regulations regarding broadcasting licensing, antitrust laws, and consumer protection played a significant part in determining the scope of competition and preventing monopolies. The interplay between these regulatory bodies and the evolving technological landscape further complicated the competitive landscape for both cable and satellite companies.

In conclusion, the competition between cable and satellite television was a complex and multi-faceted struggle, shaped by technological innovation, shifting consumer preferences, and strategic business decisions. Both industries constantly had to adapt and innovate to remain competitive. Although satellite television initially had a competitive edge due to its geographical reach, cable's established infrastructure and bundling strategies proved highly effective. The evolving television environment eventually led to further disruptions in the form of streaming platforms, fundamentally altering the entire industry and presenting both cable and satellite companies with the challenge of adapting to a new era of television consumption. The narrative of this competition serves as a compelling case study of the constant interplay between technology, business models, and consumer behavior in the dynamic world of media and communications.

The Changing Television Landscape Increased Choice and Competition

The proliferation of cable and satellite television fundamentally reshaped the television landscape, ushering in an era of unprecedented channel choice and intensified competition. Before their widespread adoption, viewers were largely limited to a handful of terrestrial broadcast channels, their programming dictated by the networks themselves. Cable and satellite dramatically expanded this selection, offering hundreds of channels catering to a diverse range of interests and demographics. This increase in choice had a profound impact on both the content produced and the way television was consumed.

One of the most immediate consequences of increased channel choice was the rise of niche programming. With more channels vying for viewers' attention, networks began to specialize, targeting specific demographics or interests. This led to the emergence of channels dedicated to news, sports, music, movies, documentaries, and countless other genres, each carving out its own niche within the broader television ecosystem. Previously marginalized communities and interests found their voices amplified through dedicated channels, showcasing diverse perspectives and cultural experiences previously unseen on mainstream television. The rise of cable also created opportunities for independent producers and smaller production companies to gain exposure, diversifying the creative landscape and challenging the dominance of the major networks.

This explosion of channel diversity, however, also presented challenges. The sheer volume of available channels could be overwhelming for viewers, leading to "channel surfing" and a perceived lack of focus. The challenge for networks became not just producing quality content, but also effectively marketing their channels and attracting audiences in a highly competitive environment. The fragmentation of viewership meant that networks could no longer rely on large, homogenous audiences. They had to become more targeted and sophisticated in their programming strategies, tailoring their content to specific demographics and interests to maximize their reach and advertising potential.

The increased competition among networks also had a significant impact on the quality of television programming. With more channels vying for attention, networks had to invest in high-quality production values, compelling storylines, and recognizable talent to attract and retain viewers. This led to a noticeable improvement in the overall quality of many programs, especially in genres like drama, comedy, and reality television. However, the pressure to compete also led to a proliferation of reality television shows and other less expensive programming formats, which often came at the expense of more ambitious and creatively challenging projects.

The advertising landscape also underwent a significant transformation. With the proliferation of channels, advertisers had to develop more targeted advertising strategies to reach their desired audiences. This led to the development of sophisticated audience measurement systems and increasingly niche advertising opportunities. The influx of advertising revenue into the expanded television ecosystem fueled further growth and investment in programming, creating a positive feedback loop that accelerated the overall expansion of the television industry. However, this growth also brought with it concerns about advertising saturation and the impact of excessive commercial breaks on the viewer experience.

The increased competition also led to innovation in programming formats and delivery methods. The advent of interactive television, pay-per-view services, and video-on-demand expanded the ways in which viewers could engage with television content. Consumers were no longer passive recipients of pre-scheduled broadcasts; they gained greater control over their viewing experience. This trend culminated in the later rise of streaming services, which further disrupted the television landscape by offering on-demand access to an even wider range of content.

The impact on the economics of the television industry was substantial. The rise of cable and satellite television created new revenue streams for broadcasters and content providers. Cable operators generated revenue through subscription fees, while networks earned money through advertising and affiliate fees paid by cable operators for carrying their channels. This diversification of revenue sources strengthened the television industry's financial base and fueled continued growth and innovation. However, the escalating costs of securing programming rights, coupled with the increasing competition for viewers and advertising dollars, created a complex and often volatile economic environment for both broadcasters and cable operators. The challenge of balancing the cost of acquiring high-quality programming with the need to maintain competitive subscription prices became a critical factor in the success or failure of television networks.

Furthermore, the rise of cable and satellite impacted the role of local broadcasters. While local stations remained important for local news and certain syndicated programs, their dominance in overall viewership diminished as viewers turned to the wider array of channels offered by cable and satellite services. This shift led local broadcasters to adapt their programming and business strategies, often seeking partnerships and affiliations with larger networks or investing in niche programming to maintain their relevance and appeal to audiences. The once-unquestioned dominance of the three major networks was undeniably challenged, creating a more fragmented and competitive media landscape.

The technological advancements driving the expansion of cable and satellite television also impacted the regulatory environment.
Government agencies had to grapple with the implications of increased channel choice, the need for fair competition among networks, and the potential for monopolies to emerge. The regulatory landscape evolved in response, attempting to balance the need for innovation and competition with the desire to protect consumers and ensure diversity in programming. This ongoing tension between regulatory oversight and technological innovation remains a defining characteristic of the television industry to this day.

In the end, the increased choice and competition brought about by cable and satellite television irrevocably transformed the television landscape. It not only expanded the range of programming available to consumers but also reshaped the economics, technology, and regulatory environment of the television industry. The legacy of this period continues to influence the current era of streaming and on-demand content, demonstrating the enduring impact of these technological breakthroughs on our media consumption habits. The evolution from a handful of terrestrial channels to the vast and diverse selection available today stands as a testament to the dynamic and ever-changing nature of television and its ongoing adaptation to technological progress and evolving viewer preferences. The competition that ensued, while often fierce, ultimately benefited the viewer, leading to a richer, more diverse, and ultimately more engaging television experience.

The Beginning of Fragmentation of Television Viewership

The proliferation of channels brought about by cable and satellite television didn't simply increase the *quantity* of programming; it fundamentally altered the *quality* of the television viewing experience. The once-unified audience, largely captive to the three major networks, fractured into a mosaic of niche interests. This fragmentation had profound and lasting consequences, reshaping programming strategies, advertising models, and even the very nature of what constituted "television."

The rise of specialized channels—ESPN for sports fanatics, MTV for music lovers, CNN for news junkies—signaled a significant shift. No longer were viewers forced to consume a generalized mix of programming. They could now curate their viewing experience, selecting channels that precisely mirrored their preferences. This hyper-segmentation of the audience had a direct impact on the types of programs produced. Networks could tailor their offerings to specific demographics, leading to the emergence of shows catering to increasingly specific tastes and interests. The result was a broader range of content, but also a more fragmented and less shared cultural experience. The water-cooler moments of shared viewing, once common around network sitcoms and primetime dramas, became less frequent, replaced by individualized viewing experiences.

This fragmentation also impacted the economics of television. The advertising model, which had thrived on large, homogenous audiences, had to adapt. Advertisers now needed more targeted approaches to reach their desired demographics. This spurred the development of sophisticated audience measurement tools, enabling advertisers to pinpoint specific viewers and tailor their messages accordingly. The rise of cable also introduced a new revenue stream—subscription fees—which became a significant source of income for cable companies, lessening their dependence on advertising alone. This diversification of revenue streams, however, also introduced new complexities, forcing networks to balance the demands of advertisers with the needs of subscribers. The pressure to attract and retain subscribers led to a focus on providing high-quality content that catered to specialized interests, but also increased the importance of marketing and promotion in a highly competitive landscape.

The impact on programming itself was dramatic. The abundance of channels created intense competition for viewers' attention.

Networks were forced to invest in high-quality production, compelling storylines, and recognizable talent to stand out from the crowd. This led to an improvement in the overall quality of many programs, particularly in genres like drama and comedy. However, the pressure to produce compelling content at a reasonable cost also fueled the rise of reality television, a genre that proved to be relatively inexpensive to produce while still capable of attracting large audiences. While reality TV provided an affordable alternative, critics argued that it often came at the expense of more ambitious and creatively challenging projects, potentially leading to a decline in the overall artistic merit of some television programming. The debate surrounding the quality and cultural impact of reality television remains a point of contention among television critics and scholars even today.

The increase in channel choice also presented logistical challenges for viewers. The sheer volume of programming available could be overwhelming, leading to what came to be known as "channel surfing"—a seemingly endless search for something engaging to watch. The remote control, initially hailed as a tool for greater control over viewing, became a symbol of the fragmentation itself.

Viewers found themselves constantly flicking through channels, often settling for something less than satisfying, rather than making a deliberate choice. This constant switching and the abundance of options paradoxically created a sense of dissatisfaction and a perceived lack of engagement with individual programs. This contributed to a feeling of being overwhelmed and ultimately potentially disconnected from the television experience altogether.

This fragmentation also had implications for the role of local broadcasters. With the availability of hundreds of channels offering diverse content, the importance of local news and local programming lessened for many viewers. Local stations, once the primary source of news and entertainment, had to adapt to maintain relevance. Many developed partnerships with larger networks, while others focused on niche programming to serve a specific community need. The decrease in viewership led to reduced advertising revenue, placing pressure on local news operations and impacting the quality and depth of local news coverage. The challenge facing local stations became maintaining local relevance in a world increasingly dominated by national and international news sources readily available on cable and satellite.

The regulatory landscape struggled to keep pace with the rapid changes brought about by cable and satellite television.

Government agencies faced new challenges in balancing competition with the need to ensure diversity in programming and protect consumers. The increase in channels raised concerns about potential monopolies and the need for fair access to cable systems.

This resulted in ongoing debates and policy changes aimed at fostering competition, promoting diversity, and ensuring a fair and equitable television marketplace.

The arrival of cable and satellite television marked a decisive turning point in television history. It wasn't just an expansion of channels; it was a fundamental shift in the relationship between viewers and the medium. The fragmentation of viewership, while presenting challenges, also fostered innovation and diversity. It created new opportunities for niche programming, diverse perspectives, and independent production companies. The period laid the foundation for the subsequent digital revolution, setting the stage for the streaming services and on-demand viewing habits that dominate the television landscape today. The impact of this era of fragmentation continues to resonate, shaping the way television content is created, distributed, and consumed in the modern era, highlighting the enduring consequences of this technological and cultural shift. The legacy of this period serves as a crucial chapter in the ongoing story of television's evolution, highlighting both its successes and challenges in adapting to the ever-changing technological and cultural landscapes.

The Transition to Digital Broadcasting Technological Changes

The dawn of the 21st century witnessed a seismic shift in television broadcasting: the transition from analog to digital. This wasn't merely a technological upgrade; it represented a fundamental change in how television signals were generated, transmitted, and received, profoundly impacting picture quality, channel capacity, and broadcast efficiency. The analog system, with its inherent limitations, had reached its technological ceiling. The analog signal, a continuously varying waveform representing the image and sound, was susceptible to noise and interference, leading to picture degradation and audio distortion, especially over long distances or in areas with significant electromagnetic interference. The limited bandwidth of analog signals also restricted the number of channels that could be broadcast simultaneously, resulting in a constant struggle for airtime and a limited range of program choices for viewers.

The digital revolution offered a solution to these inherent limitations. Digital signals, representing images and sound as discrete data packets, were inherently more robust against noise and interference. This inherent resilience ensured a significantly improved picture and sound quality, regardless of transmission distance or environmental conditions. Furthermore, the sophisticated compression techniques used in digital broadcasting allowed for multiple channels to be transmitted within the same bandwidth previously occupied by a single analog channel. This dramatic increase in channel capacity led to a proliferation of channels, offering viewers an unprecedented level of choice and diversity in programming.

The transition to digital wasn't instantaneous. It was a gradual process, phased in over several years in most countries. Early digital television broadcasts were often experimental, limited in scope, and faced challenges in reaching a wider audience due to the lack of widespread digital receivers. The cost of upgrading infrastructure, both at the broadcasting end and in individual homes, presented a significant barrier to widespread adoption. Consumers were initially reluctant to invest in new digital television sets or set-top boxes, particularly in the absence of a compelling reason to switch from their existing analog systems. Government policies and incentives played a crucial role in accelerating this transition. Many governments established deadlines for the switchover, gradually phasing out analog broadcasts and encouraging consumers to adopt digital technology through subsidies and public awareness campaigns.

One of the pivotal technological developments underlying this transformation was the development of digital compression algorithms. These algorithms, such as MPEG-2 and later MPEG-4, drastically reduced the amount of data required to represent a video signal without significant loss in quality. This compression was essential for efficient transmission of digital signals, as it allowed multiple channels to be squeezed into the same bandwidth previously occupied by a single analog channel. Without effective compression, the massive amount of data required for digital television broadcasting would have rendered the whole concept economically unviable and technologically impractical. The development of these algorithms marked a major technological milestone, allowing for the practical implementation of digital television broadcasting on a large scale.

The transition also involved substantial changes in broadcasting infrastructure. Television stations had to invest in new digital transmission equipment, including digital encoders, transmitters, and antennas. This involved considerable capital expenditure, requiring broadcasters to adapt to new technologies and update their infrastructure. The deployment of new transmission towers and improved signal distribution networks was also necessary to ensure widespread coverage of digital signals. This infrastructural upgrade was a key factor influencing the timeline of the digital transition. In many countries, the upgrade process was gradual, with digital signals initially supplementing analog broadcasts until analog transmission eventually ceased altogether. This phased rollout helped to mitigate disruption and ensure a smooth transition for viewers.

Beyond the technological aspects, the move to digital broadcasting had significant legal and regulatory implications. Governments had to devise strategies to allocate the newly available spectrum, addressing issues of fairness and competition among broadcasters.

The increased channel capacity raised questions regarding the licensing of new channels and the potential for monopolization. Furthermore, the transition created a need for revised broadcasting regulations, reflecting the changed technical landscape and the increased opportunities for interactive and multimedia content delivery. The regulatory framework had to adapt to the new realities of digital television, ensuring fair competition, promoting diversity in programming, and preventing abuses of the increased channel capacity.

The implementation of digital broadcasting also spurred innovations in television set design and functionalities. Digital television sets offered a range of new features and functionalities unavailable in their analog counterparts. High-definition (HD) television, with its vastly improved picture resolution, became a major selling point, attracting consumers to upgrade their equipment. Digital television sets also provided improved sound quality, enhanced color reproduction, and the ability to receive multiple channels simultaneously. These technological advancements transformed the television viewing experience, enhancing the visual and auditory appeal of television programming. The introduction of interactive services, allowing viewers to engage with programs and services in novel ways, became another significant benefit of digital broadcasting.

However, the transition wasn't without its drawbacks. The digital divide, the gap between those with access to digital technology and those without, presented a significant challenge. Many low-income households struggled to afford new digital television sets or set-top boxes, potentially excluding them from the benefits of digital broadcasting. This social equity issue forced governments to implement programs to address the digital divide, ensuring equitable access to digital television for all citizens. Strategies included subsidies for low-income households, public access centers offering digital television viewing, and educational campaigns to bridge the technological gap between different social groups.

The switchover also created temporary disruptions for some

viewers, particularly those who lacked the necessary equipment or were unfamiliar with the new technology. The transition period often saw confusion, technical difficulties, and a steep learning curve for some consumers. The need for widespread public education and technical support during the transition was crucial to ensure a smooth switchover and prevent viewers from being left behind. The implementation of comprehensive public education programs played a pivotal role in the overall success of the transition to digital television.

In conclusion, the transition from analog to digital broadcasting was a landmark moment in television history. While it presented challenges, particularly concerning the digital divide and the need for infrastructural upgrades, the benefits of digital broadcasting –including superior picture and sound quality, increased channel capacity, and enhanced interactive features – were undeniable. The shift marked not only a technological upgrade but a significant step forward in the evolution of television as a medium, paving the way for the further technological advancements and innovations that would continue to shape the television landscape in the decades to come. The legacy of this digital transition continues to resonate today, shaping the way television content is produced, distributed, and consumed in the modern era of streaming services, high- definition formats, and the increasing integration of digital television with the internet.

The Rise of the Internet and its Impact on Television

The digital revolution in broadcasting, as detailed previously, laid the groundwork for a profound and ongoing transformation of the television industry, a transformation inextricably linked to the rise of the internet. While the transition to digital television significantly enhanced picture quality and channel capacity, the internet introduced a new paradigm, one that fundamentally altered how television content was created, delivered, and consumed. No longer confined to the limitations of broadcast schedules and terrestrial signals, television embraced the boundless potential of the internet, resulting in a revolution that continues to reshape the media landscape.

One of the most immediate impacts of the internet was its ability to offer viewers a far greater degree of control over their viewing experience. The traditional broadcast model, with its rigid schedules and limited channel selection, gave way to a world of on-demand viewing. Websites and applications began offering access to television shows, movies, and other video content, allowing viewers to watch what they wanted, when they wanted, eliminating the need to adhere to broadcast schedules. This shift empowered viewers, placing them at the center of the viewing experience and dramatically altering their relationship with television programming. The rise of video-on-demand (VOD) services was a critical step in this transformation. Early VOD services were often limited to offering a relatively small selection of content, often at a cost per view or per rental. However, as broadband internet penetration increased, so did the scale and scope of VOD services.

The emergence of streaming services represents a watershed moment in this evolution. Netflix, initially a DVD rental service, pioneered the streaming model, offering a subscription-based service with a vast library of movies and television shows. The success of Netflix proved the viability of a subscription-based streaming model, attracting a large subscriber base and demonstrating the considerable consumer demand for on-demand, internet-delivered television content. This success spurred a wave of competition, with other companies launching their own streaming services, each offering a unique selection of content, pricing models, and features. Amazon Prime Video, Hulu, HBO Max (now Max), Disney+, Apple TV+, and countless others joined the fray, creating a fiercely competitive market characterized by a relentless pursuit of original programming and exclusive content deals.

This competition has fueled a golden age of television production. With streaming services vying for subscribers, there's been a surge in the creation of high-quality, original television programming. The traditional constraints of network television, such as concerns about broad appeal and limited budgets, have been lessened, allowing for greater creative freedom and experimentation.

Streaming platforms have been instrumental in supporting ambitious and niche programming, providing a platform for diverse voices and narratives that might not have found a home on traditional broadcast television. This expansion of creative possibilities has led to a flowering of creativity, resulting in television shows that are both critically acclaimed and widely popular. The success of these streaming services has also influenced the production strategies of traditional television networks, which have increasingly incorporated streaming platforms into their business models, creating content for both broadcast and digital distribution.

The internet's impact on television extends beyond content delivery; it fundamentally reshaped viewer behavior. The rise of "binge-watching," the practice of watching multiple episodes of a television series in a single sitting, is directly attributable to the on-demand nature of streaming services. This phenomenon reflects a shift in how audiences consume television content, moving from a scheduled viewing pattern to a more individualized and personalized experience. The internet also fostered the growth of online communities centered around television shows, providing spaces for viewers to discuss episodes, share opinions, and connect with other fans. These online communities enrich the viewing experience, extending the engagement beyond the screen and creating a sense of shared cultural experience. Social media platforms have become integral to this communal aspect of television viewing, with viewers often using platforms like Twitter and Facebook to share their reactions and thoughts in real-time, creating a dynamic and interactive viewing experience.

Moreover, the internet facilitated the emergence of new forms of programming. The rise of web series, short-form videos specifically designed for online consumption, exemplifies this. Web series often challenge traditional television formats, embracing experimental storytelling styles and unconventional structures. The low cost of production and the ease of online distribution allowed for independent creators and smaller production companies to gain a wider audience, bypassing the gatekeepers of traditional television. The proliferation of YouTube channels devoted to television-related content, featuring reviews, commentary, and fan-made videos, further reflects the interactive and community-driven nature of television viewing in the internet age. These channels not only offer alternative perspectives and analyses of existing television shows but also foster a culture of participatory engagement. Viewers are no longer passive recipients of content; they are active participants in a dynamic and interactive media ecosystem.

The internet's integration with television sets themselves has further blurred the lines between traditional television and online video. Smart TVs, equipped with internet connectivity and access to streaming apps, have become the primary point of access for many viewers. The convenience of having all their streaming services available on one device has contributed to the decline of traditional cable television subscriptions, as consumers increasingly opt for the flexibility and affordability of streaming services. The integration of internet capabilities into television sets also enables interactive functionalities, such as personalized recommendations and social media integration, enhancing the viewing experience and further deepening the relationship between viewers and television content. This convergence of television and internet technologies points to a future where the distinction between the two may become increasingly blurred.

However, the internet's influence on television is not without its challenges. The proliferation of streaming services has led to a phenomenon known as "content fragmentation," where viewers are faced with a dizzying array of choices, making it difficult to discover new content or keep track of their favorite shows. The cost of subscribing to multiple streaming services can also be a barrier for many consumers, creating a new form of "subscription fatigue." Furthermore, the dominance of a few major streaming platforms raises concerns about the diversity of content and the potential for market consolidation. The need for regulations to address these challenges, while protecting the dynamism and innovation of the streaming market, is a crucial aspect of navigating the future of television.

The ongoing evolution of television technology, driven in large part by internet advancements, presents both opportunities and challenges. High-definition (HD) and ultra-high-definition (UHD) or 4K and 8K resolutions, fueled by advances in internet bandwidth and compression techniques, have significantly enhanced the visual quality of television programming, creating a more immersive viewing experience. The integration of artificial intelligence (AI) is poised to further revolutionize television production and consumption, with AI-powered tools capable of automating tasks such as editing, special effects, and content recommendation. AI can also be used to personalize the viewing experience, offering tailored recommendations based on individual preferences and viewing habits. The potential applications of AI in the television industry are immense, promising a future where television content is not only visually stunning but also highly personalized and engaging.

In conclusion, the rise of the internet has fundamentally transformed the television industry. From the introduction of on-demand viewing and streaming services to the emergence of new forms of programming and the integration of television sets with the internet, the impact has been profound. While the digital revolution in broadcasting laid the foundation for this transformation, the internet has taken it to a new level, creating a media landscape characterized by greater viewer control, a wealth of content choices, and an ongoing convergence of television and online video. The challenges presented by this transformation, such as content fragmentation and the cost of streaming subscriptions, necessitate ongoing discussion and the development of strategies to ensure a sustainable and equitable future for the television industry. The next chapter will delve into the future prospects of television, examining the potential of emerging technologies and the challenges that lie ahead in this rapidly evolving media landscape.

The Emergence of Streaming Services A New Way to Watch TV

The emergence of streaming services marks a pivotal moment in television history, a radical shift from the established broadcast model that fundamentally altered how content was produced, distributed, and consumed. Netflix, initially a DVD-by-mail service, played a pioneering role. Its transition to streaming in the early 2000s, offering a vast library of movies and TV shows for a monthly subscription fee, was a calculated gamble that paid off handsomely. This subscription model, unlike the pay-per-view or rental models prevalent at the time, offered unparalleled value and convenience.

Viewers gained access to a seemingly endless catalog of content, eliminating the limitations of broadcast schedules and the inconvenience of physical media. The success of Netflix's approach demonstrated a significant untapped market demand for on- demand, internet-delivered entertainment. This success was not just a technological achievement; it was a masterful demonstration of understanding evolving consumer preferences. Viewers craved control, convenience, and a wider range of choices than traditional broadcast television could offer.

Netflix's early success spurred intense competition. Other companies, recognizing the lucrative potential of the streaming market, quickly followed suit. Amazon, already a dominant force in e-commerce, leveraged its existing infrastructure and customer base to launch Amazon Prime Video, bundling streaming access with its Prime membership program. This shrewd strategy quickly attracted a substantial user base, capitalizing on the existing loyalty of Prime subscribers. Hulu, a joint venture initially involving several major broadcast networks, offered a different approach, focusing on current-season episodes of popular network shows alongside a library of older content. This strategy catered to viewers seeking immediate access to their favorite shows while also providing a substantial back catalog. HBO, long known for its premium cable programming, launched HBO Max (later rebranded as Max), leveraging its reputation for high-quality original content to attract a discerning audience. Disney, a latecomer to the streaming wars, quickly established itself as a major player with Disney+, capitalizing on its vast library of beloved films and television shows spanning decades and appealing to families and children. Apple TV + adopted a different strategy, focusing on producing high-quality original programming, attracting prominent talent and investing heavily in content creation to compete with established players.

The proliferation of streaming services ignited a fierce battle for subscribers, fueling an unprecedented boom in television production. Unlike the traditional broadcast model, where network executives often prioritized broad appeal and limited budgets, streaming platforms provided a degree of creative freedom rarely seen before. The pressure to attract and retain subscribers drove streaming services to commission ambitious projects, often with significant budgets and creative risks. This competition fostered a golden age of television, resulting in a surge of critically acclaimed and widely popular shows that explored diverse genres, themes, and perspectives. Streaming platforms provided a refuge for niche programming that might not have found a home on traditional networks, offering opportunities for diverse voices and untold stories to reach wider audiences. The emphasis on original content became a defining characteristic of the streaming wars, with platforms investing heavily in securing exclusive rights to popular franchises and commissioning high-profile productions. This intense competition spurred innovation in storytelling, production techniques, and even distribution models.

The impact of streaming services extended far beyond the realm of production. The very nature of these platforms reshaped viewing habits. The advent of binge-watching—the practice of consuming multiple episodes of a series in rapid succession—became a defining characteristic of streaming culture. This phenomenon, fueled by the on-demand nature of streaming services and the lack of commercial interruptions, fundamentally altered how audiences engage with television. The traditional viewing experience, punctuated by commercials and adhering to a rigid schedule, yielded to a more individualized, personalized, and immersive experience. Viewers gained control over their viewing schedules, able to watch what they wanted, when they wanted, and at their own pace. This shift contributed significantly to the decline of traditional television viewership, as audiences increasingly turned to the convenience and flexibility offered by streaming services.

The rise of streaming also dramatically altered the social landscape of television. Online communities and social media platforms became integral to the viewing experience. Viewers actively engaged in discussions, shared opinions, and reacted to episodes in real-time, creating a dynamic and interactive ecosystem surrounding their favorite shows. Platforms like Twitter and Facebook became virtual water coolers, where viewers shared their thoughts and connected with fellow fans. This social dimension enriched the viewing experience, extending the engagement beyond the screen itself and fostering a sense of shared cultural experience.

This phenomenon also influenced the way television shows were promoted and marketed, with producers and networks actively engaging with online communities and leveraging social media to generate buzz and build anticipation. The integration of social media into the viewing experience fundamentally transformed the relationship between audiences and the content they consumed.

However, the rise of streaming also presented challenges. The abundance of choices, sometimes referred to as "content fragmentation," created its own set of problems. Viewers faced a dizzying array of options, making it difficult to navigate the vast landscape of available content and discover new shows or movies.

The phenomenon of "subscription fatigue," where viewers found themselves subscribing to multiple services to access their preferred content, resulted in considerable expense. The dominance of a few major platforms raised concerns about market consolidation and the potential for a decrease in content diversity. These concerns underscored the need for ongoing discussions and potential regulatory measures to ensure a sustainable and equitable streaming landscape. The dynamic and rapidly evolving nature of the industry required both adaptation and careful consideration of the potential consequences of unchecked growth.

The technical aspects of streaming were also instrumental in its success. Advances in broadband internet access, video compression technologies, and network infrastructure made it possible to stream high-quality video content to a wide range of devices. The development of streaming protocols and technologies enabled efficient and reliable delivery of video over the internet, overcoming the limitations of earlier attempts at online video distribution. The improvements in bandwidth and data transfer rates facilitated higher-resolution streaming, culminating in the widespread adoption of high-definition (HD) and, more recently, ultra-high-definition (UHD) or 4K and 8K resolutions. These technological advances enhanced the viewing experience significantly, creating a more immersive and visually stunning experience for audiences. The ability to seamlessly stream high-quality video to diverse devices, from smartphones and tablets to smart TVs and game consoles, further contributed to the widespread adoption of streaming services.

The convergence of television and the internet continues to reshape the media landscape. Smart TVs, with built-in internet connectivity and access to a wide range of streaming apps, became the central hubs of home entertainment. The convenience of having all streaming services readily accessible on a single device contributed significantly to the decline of traditional cable television subscriptions, as consumers opted for the flexibility and affordability of streaming platforms. The integration of artificial intelligence (AI) holds the potential to further revolutionize television, both in terms of production and consumption. AI- powered tools are being employed to automate tasks such as editing, special effects, and content recommendation, potentially transforming the production pipeline. AI-powered personalization engines can tailor content recommendations to individual viewers, enhancing engagement and improving the overall viewing experience. The ongoing technological innovations promise to deliver ever-more immersive, personalized, and engaging experiences for audiences in the future.

In conclusion, the emergence of streaming services represents a watershed moment in television history. The business models, content strategies, and technological advancements underpinning the rise of platforms like Netflix, Amazon Prime Video, Hulu, and Disney+ fundamentally transformed how television is produced, consumed, and experienced. While the initial success of these services was predicated on convenience and offering a wide selection of pre-existing content, the subsequent competition spurred a surge in original programming, creating a "golden age" of television. The ongoing challenges presented by content fragmentation, subscription fatigue, and the dominance of a few major players require continuous evaluation and potential regulatory measures to ensure a sustainable and inclusive streaming landscape. The convergence of television, internet technology, and artificial intelligence promises to further reshape the media landscape in ways we are only beginning to understand.

The Changing Nature of Content Consumption OnDemand and Personalized Viewing

The shift from scheduled television programming to on-demand viewing represents a profound alteration in the relationship between audiences and the content they consume. For decades, television viewers were largely passive recipients of broadcast schedules dictated by networks. Programming was broadcast at specific times, and viewers had little choice but to conform to these schedules or miss their favorite shows. The advent of VCRs and later DVRs offered a degree of control, allowing viewers to record programs for later viewing, but this technology still remained largely reactive, adapting to the existing broadcast schedule rather than fundamentally altering it. The true paradigm shift arrived with the rise of streaming services and the internet's ubiquitous reach.

On-demand viewing, enabled by high-speed internet access and advanced streaming technologies, empowers viewers to consume content at their own convenience. No longer bound by broadcast schedules, viewers can access a vast library of movies and TV shows at any time, day or night. This unprecedented flexibility fundamentally reshaped viewing habits, allowing audiences to tailor their viewing experiences to their own schedules and preferences. The implications of this shift extend far beyond simple convenience; it transformed the very nature of television consumption from a scheduled, passive activity to an individualized, active process.

This newfound control over viewing experiences extends beyond timing; on-demand platforms also offer viewers unprecedented choice. Broadcast television, with its limited channel offerings and fixed programming, offered a relatively narrow range of content.

Streaming services, by contrast, provide access to vast catalogs encompassing diverse genres, languages, and cultural perspectives.

Viewers are no longer limited by the preferences of network executives or the constraints of broadcast regulations; they can choose from a nearly limitless selection of content, reflecting their own unique tastes and interests. This abundance of choice, however, also presents its own set of challenges, as viewers grapple with the overwhelming number of options available and the potential for "decision fatigue." The sheer scale of content libraries can be paralyzing, making it difficult for viewers to discover new shows or movies that might resonate with them.

The personalization of the viewing experience further differentiates on-demand platforms from traditional broadcast television. AI-powered recommendation algorithms analyze viewers' past viewing habits, preferences, and ratings to suggest content that might appeal to them. This sophisticated level of personalization creates highly curated viewing experiences tailored to individual viewers, ensuring a constant supply of engaging content. While personalized recommendations can enhance the viewing experience, concerns remain about the potential for "filter bubbles" – personalized content selections that limit exposure to diverse perspectives and reinforce existing biases. The algorithmic curation of content raises ethical considerations surrounding transparency, data privacy, and the potential for manipulation. The extent to which algorithms shape our viewing choices and influence our understanding of the world remains a subject of ongoing discussion and research.

The impact of on-demand viewing extends to the social dynamics surrounding television. In the era of broadcast television, shared viewing experiences were often defined by communal gatherings around a television set, providing opportunities for discussion and shared cultural experiences. While on-demand viewing can be a solitary activity, it has also fostered new forms of social interaction through online communities and social media platforms. Viewers now engage in real-time discussions about their favorite shows, share opinions, and create a dynamic ecosystem surrounding television content. Platforms like Twitter, Reddit, and Facebook have become virtual water coolers, enabling fans to connect with others who share their interests. This social interaction enriches the viewing experience, extending its reach beyond the screen and creating a sense of shared cultural experience, even in the context of individualized viewing habits.

However, this shift towards on-demand and personalized viewing has also introduced new challenges for the television industry. The traditional advertising model, deeply integrated into broadcast television, has been significantly disrupted by the rise of streaming.

While some streaming services still incorporate advertising, many others operate on a subscription model, eliminating traditional commercial breaks. This shift has forced the industry to adapt, leading to the exploration of new advertising models and revenue streams. The implications for the production and distribution of television content are substantial. With advertising revenue reduced or eliminated for some platforms, the industry is increasingly reliant on subscription fees and other revenue sources. This has led to intensified competition among streaming services and an ongoing struggle to attract and retain subscribers. The economics of streaming have also impacted the production of television programming, creating a complex interplay between creative freedom, budgetary constraints, and the need to deliver engaging content that attracts a wide audience.

Furthermore, the proliferation of streaming services has led to what some have termed "content fragmentation," a scenario where content is scattered across numerous platforms, making it challenging for viewers to access everything they want to see. This necessitates subscriptions to multiple services, leading to "subscription fatigue," a phenomenon where viewers become overwhelmed by the costs and complexities of managing multiple accounts. The industry faces an ongoing challenge in finding ways to balance consumer choice with the practicalities of managing diverse content libraries and sustainable business models. This includes exploration of content aggregation, bundled services, and innovative pricing strategies.

The future of television viewing is likely to involve an even greater degree of personalization and interactivity. Advances in artificial intelligence are poised to transform both the production and consumption of television content. AI-powered tools are already being used to automate tasks such as editing, special effects, and content creation, improving efficiency and potentially lowering production costs. Moreover, AI-powered recommendation systems are becoming increasingly sophisticated, offering ever-more tailored content suggestions. Virtual and augmented reality technologies have the potential to further revolutionize the viewing experience, creating more immersive and interactive forms of entertainment.

The incorporation of personalized interactive elements into

television programs could transform passive viewing into an active and participatory experience.

The evolution of television continues at a rapid pace, shaped by technological advancements, changing consumer preferences, and the creative ingenuity of content producers. The transition from scheduled, linear viewing to on-demand, personalized experiences has dramatically altered the relationship between audiences and the television medium. While this transformation has brought about considerable benefits, including unprecedented access to diverse content and tailored viewing experiences, it has also presented new challenges. The industry is actively grappling with issues such as content fragmentation, subscription fatigue, and the ethical implications of AI-powered personalization. The future of television will likely depend on navigating these complexities while continuing to innovate and adapt to the ever-changing landscape of media consumption. The core of television – its ability to entertain, inform, and connect – remains constant, even as the way we access and experience it continues to evolve at an astonishing rate. The coming years will undoubtedly witness further transformations, with technological innovations and evolving consumer habits driving the industry toward new, unforeseen forms of television. The ongoing convergence of technology and storytelling promises an exciting, though unpredictable, future for television.

The Future of Television Content Delivery Trends and Predictions

The convergence of several technological advancements is poised to reshape the television landscape in profound ways. The continued expansion of high-speed internet access, particularly in regions currently underserved, will be a critical factor. Broadband penetration remains a significant barrier to widespread adoption of streaming services in many parts of the world. As internet infrastructure improves, more viewers will gain access to the vast libraries of on-demand content offered by streaming platforms, potentially leading to a dramatic shift in viewing habits globally. This expansion will also necessitate the development of more robust and resilient streaming infrastructure capable of handling the increased demand. Investment in content delivery networks (CDNs) and other technologies designed to optimize streaming performance will be crucial to ensure a seamless viewing experience for a growing global audience. The need for low-latency streaming, minimizing buffering and lag, will become increasingly important as viewers demand higher-quality video formats and interactive features.

Furthermore, the ongoing development of 5G and other next-generation wireless technologies will play a critical role. 5G's higher bandwidth and lower latency capabilities will allow for the delivery of higher-resolution video streams, including 8K and beyond, as well as more interactive and immersive viewing experiences. This will open up new possibilities for mobile streaming, allowing viewers to access high-quality content on their smartphones and tablets with minimal buffering or interruption. The increasing prevalence of mobile viewing will necessitate the development of user interfaces and applications tailored to smaller screens and mobile devices, optimizing the viewing experience on the go. The combination of improved internet infrastructure and advanced wireless technologies will create a more versatile and accessible viewing environment, making television content available virtually anywhere.

The evolution of television screens themselves will also impact content delivery. The transition from standard definition to high definition and now to ultra-high definition (4K and 8K) has already begun to transform the viewing experience. As screen resolutions continue to improve, content producers will need to adapt, creating content that takes full advantage of the enhanced visual fidelity. This will require significant investments in high-resolution cameras, editing software, and other production technologies. The increasing adoption of larger screens, including giant-screen televisions and projection systems, will further enhance the immersive viewing experience, leading to a corresponding increase in demand for high-quality, high-resolution content. This shift toward higher resolutions will also require significant advancements in video compression technologies, enabling efficient delivery of large video files without compromising quality or increasing bandwidth requirements. Finding a balance between image quality and efficient data transmission will be a key challenge for content providers and technology developers.

The increasing sophistication of artificial intelligence (AI) will significantly influence both the production and consumption of television content. AI-powered tools are already being used in various aspects of television production, from automated editing and special effects to content creation and personalized recommendations. The future will likely see an even greater reliance on AI for tasks such as scriptwriting, character design, and scene generation. While this raises concerns regarding the role of human creativity and potential job displacement, it also promises to enhance efficiency and reduce production costs, potentially leading to more diverse and innovative content. The ethical implications of AI-generated content will need careful consideration, addressing issues such as bias, authenticity, and the potential for misuse. The development of ethical guidelines and regulatory frameworks will be crucial to ensure the responsible development and use of AI in television production.

AI's impact on content consumption is equally transformative. AI-powered recommendation algorithms will become increasingly sophisticated, providing viewers with ever-more tailored content suggestions. This level of personalization will enhance the viewing experience by ensuring a continuous supply of engaging content, but it also raises concerns about "filter bubbles" and the potential for echo chambers. The development of algorithms that promote diversity and exposure to different perspectives will be crucial to mitigate these risks. AI can also personalize the user interface and viewing experience, adapting to individual preferences and viewing habits, making the navigation of large content libraries more intuitive and efficient. This will involve the development of sophisticated user profiles and machine learning models capable of understanding and responding to individual viewer behavior.

The integration of virtual reality (VR) and augmented reality (AR) technologies holds immense potential for revolutionizing the television viewing experience. VR can create immersive, interactive environments that place viewers directly into the world of their favorite shows and movies. This technology can be used to create highly engaging and interactive games, simulations, and other forms of entertainment, transforming passive viewing into an active and participatory experience. AR, on the other hand, can overlay digital information onto the real world, enriching the viewing experience by providing context, background information, and interactive elements. The use of AR can enhance the viewing of live sports events, documentaries, and other programs by providing additional information and insights, making it a more engaging and educational experience. The integration of VR and AR requires significant advancements in hardware and software, including the development of high-resolution displays, responsive tracking systems, and intuitive user interfaces. The cost and accessibility of these technologies will also influence their widespread adoption.

The future of television content delivery will likely involve a hybrid model, combining traditional broadcast television, streaming services, and new interactive technologies. Broadcast television may continue to play a role in delivering live events and news, while streaming services will dominate on-demand viewing. The rise of personalized and interactive experiences will blur the lines between television and other forms of media, creating a more seamless and integrated entertainment ecosystem. The convergence of different technologies and platforms will create new opportunities for content creators and distributors, leading to the development of novel forms of storytelling and interactive experiences. The industry will need to adapt to the changing landscape, developing sustainable business models that balance consumer preferences with the need for innovation and profitability. This will likely involve innovative approaches to advertising, subscription models, and content monetization.

However, several challenges lie ahead. Concerns regarding data privacy and the ethical use of AI will need to be addressed to ensure the responsible development and implementation of new technologies. The potential for misinformation and the spread of harmful content through online platforms also require careful attention. Regulatory frameworks and ethical guidelines will be essential to address these challenges and ensure a responsible and sustainable future for the television industry. The industry will need to navigate the complexities of copyright and intellectual property rights in a rapidly evolving digital environment, ensuring fair compensation for content creators and protecting the rights of copyright holders. International collaborations and agreements will be essential to harmonize regulations and standards across different countries and regions.

The future of television is dynamic and uncertain, but one thing is certain: the medium will continue to evolve, driven by technological innovation and changing consumer expectations. The interplay between technology and storytelling will continue to shape the future of television, offering viewers new and innovative ways to engage with their favorite programs and discover new content. The next decade will likely witness further consolidation within the streaming industry, as companies seek to build scale and achieve profitability. This consolidation may lead to the emergence of a few dominant players, controlling a significant share of the market. However, it may also lead to increased innovation, as companies compete to attract and retain subscribers through offering unique and high-quality content. The future of television is a complex tapestry woven from technological advancements, evolving consumer behaviors, and the ongoing creative drive of content creators. The convergence of these forces promises a vibrant, yet unpredictable, future for the medium.

The Introduction of HighDefinition Television Enhanced Visuals

The transition to high-definition television (HDTV) marked a significant turning point in the history of the medium, fundamentally altering the viewing experience for millions. While standard definition television had offered a glimpse into a world of moving images, HDTV ushered in an era of unprecedented visual fidelity, sharpness, and detail. This wasn't simply a gradual improvement; it was a quantum leap, comparable to the shift from black and white to color television. The enhanced visuals, with their significantly increased resolution, dramatically improved the realism and immersion of televised content. Suddenly, viewers could see textures, subtle expressions, and intricate details that were previously lost in the blurriness of standard definition.

The technological underpinnings of HDTV involved a significant advancement in both the broadcasting and receiving ends of the television system. The core change was a substantial increase in the number of pixels used to create the image. Standard definition television typically used a resolution of 720 x 480 pixels (for NTSC in the US and similar standards elsewhere) resulting in a relatively coarse, pixelated image. HDTV, on the other hand, offered a vastly superior resolution, initially with 720p (720 lines of progressive scan) and 1080i (1080 lines of interlaced scan), later evolving to 1080p (1080 lines of progressive scan), offering considerably more detail and smoother motion. This increased pixel count meant that images could be displayed with much finer detail, leading to a more natural and realistic representation of the visual world.

The impact on viewer experience was profound. The enhanced clarity and sharpness of HDTV made watching television a much more immersive and engaging experience. Sports broadcasts, once characterized by blurred motion and indistinct details, suddenly became incredibly lifelike. Viewers could see the sweat on the athletes' brows, the texture of the playing field, and the nuances of their movements with remarkable precision. Similarly, movies and television dramas benefited greatly from the increased resolution. Facial expressions became more expressive, fabrics appeared more realistic, and scenes were rendered with far greater visual richness. The improved image quality breathed new life into established genres and paved the way for entirely new artistic approaches to filmmaking and television production.

However, the transition to HDTV was not without its challenges.

The higher resolution and improved picture quality demanded a significant investment in new infrastructure and equipment.

Broadcasters needed to upgrade their transmission facilities, investing in new cameras, editing equipment, and transmission towers capable of handling the increased data flow. This substantial cost proved to be a significant hurdle, especially for smaller broadcasters and those in developing countries. Viewers, too, had to invest in new HDTV-compatible television sets and, in many cases, high-definition receivers or set-top boxes, effectively creating a technological divide. This disparity created a two-tiered system: viewers with access to HDTV enjoyed a superior viewing experience, while those without were left behind with the older, inferior technology. This created a significant social and economic divide as early adopters gained access to superior quality while many others did not.

The rollout of HDTV was a complex and multifaceted process.

Different countries adopted different standards, further complicating the transition. For instance, while the United States largely adopted the ATSC standard, other regions adopted different systems, sometimes creating compatibility issues. This led to a period of uncertainty and confusion as consumers and broadcasters navigated the intricacies of different technical specifications and standards. The development and standardization of high-definition formats was crucial for ensuring the smooth transition. Various formats, with different resolutions and frame rates, existed for a period, creating complexity and confusion for both viewers and broadcasters. Only through significant industry collaboration and standardization were these issues eventually resolved.

Moreover, the increased data requirements of HDTV presented significant challenges for transmission and distribution. The higher bandwidth necessitated by the larger image files required broadcasters to re-evaluate their transmission methods. This led to advancements in compression technologies, allowing for the efficient transmission of high-resolution video signals without compromising image quality. The development of new compression algorithms, such as MPEG-2 and later H.264 and HEVC, was critical in managing this bandwidth increase while maintaining acceptable picture quality. The development of efficient compression techniques proved crucial in achieving a balance between image quality and the efficient use of bandwidth, making it economically viable for broadcasters to adopt the new technology.

Beyond the technical aspects, the transition to HDTV also prompted a shift in content creation. Filmmakers and television producers needed to adapt to the enhanced capabilities of HDTV. High- definition cameras and editing software became essential tools, and the production process needed to be adapted to take full advantage of the enhanced visual capabilities. The increase in resolution required a greater emphasis on visual details, both in terms of setting design and performance. It also led to creative experimentation with visual effects and special effects that were previously constrained by the limitations of standard definition.

The impact of HDTV extended beyond just the quality of the image. The shift to digital broadcasting, which often accompanied the introduction of HDTV, opened the door to interactive features and a more engaging viewing experience. Digital television signals allowed for the inclusion of interactive elements, such as subtitles, closed captions, and electronic program guides. The digital platform became a conduit for additional information and features, enhancing the overall viewing experience.

The adoption of HDTV also played a significant role in the eventual decline of analog broadcasting. As HDTV became increasingly prevalent, the demand for analog broadcasts decreased. Countries around the world eventually switched over to digital broadcasting completely, making HDTV the standard mode of television transmission. This transition marked not just a change in technology, but also a shift in the overall television landscape, paving the way for the next generation of innovations.

In retrospect, the introduction of HDTV represents a crucial phase in the evolution of television. It significantly elevated the visual quality, significantly improving viewer experience and ushering in a new era of realism and immersion. While the transition had its challenges, overcoming these obstacles led to significant advancements in both broadcasting technology and content creation, paving the way for the even higher resolutions we see today in 4K and 8K television. The success of HDTV's adoption demonstrates the power of technological innovation to transform a widely used medium and reshape how we interact with and experience the visual world. This success laid the groundwork for further innovation, propelling the industry towards even higher levels of visual fidelity and technological advancement. The legacy of HDTV is not simply about better picture quality; it's about a paradigm shift in television's potential to deliver a richer and more immersive viewing experience.

K and K Resolution UltraHigh Definition Television

The success of HDTV paved the way for an even more dramatic leap in visual fidelity: the arrival of ultra-high definition (UHD) television, encompassing 4K and 8K resolutions. This represented not just an incremental improvement, but another quantum leap, pushing the boundaries of what was previously considered possible in home viewing. While HDTV offered a significant improvement over standard definition, the jump to 4K and beyond offered a level of detail and realism that transformed the viewing experience once again.

4K resolution, also known as Ultra High Definition (UHD) TV, boasts a resolution of 3840 x 2160 pixels, representing four times the number of pixels found in 1080p HDTV. This dramatic increase in pixel density resulted in images with significantly enhanced sharpness, clarity, and detail. Subtle textures, fine lines, and intricate patterns, previously lost in the lower resolution displays, became readily visible, resulting in a far more immersive and lifelike viewing experience. The impact was particularly noticeable in scenes with complex details or intricate textures, such as nature documentaries showcasing vibrant landscapes or action films filled with fast-paced movement.

The increased pixel count wasn't simply about making things sharper; it allowed for a more nuanced and accurate representation of colors and contrast. The richer color palette and improved contrast ratios created a far more realistic and vibrant image, enhancing the overall viewing experience. This resulted in a more believable portrayal of the scenes and characters, enhancing the emotional impact and viewer engagement. Darker scenes, previously prone to crushing of blacks or loss of detail, became significantly improved with better delineation of shadows and highlights, allowing for a more dynamic and detailed image.

The introduction of 4K technology required substantial upgrades across the entire television ecosystem. Camera technology advanced to capture the increased resolution, requiring higher quality sensors and lenses capable of resolving finer details. Post-production workflows had to adapt to handle the larger files sizes and increased computational demands of 4K video editing. Broadcasters and streaming services needed to upgrade their infrastructure, including transmission networks and content delivery systems, to handle the higher bandwidth requirements.

Despite the significant technological challenges, the advantages of 4K were readily apparent. The enhanced detail and visual fidelity enhanced the viewer experience across various forms of content.

From sporting events where the expression on an athlete's face became crystal clear, to documentaries where the textures of ancient artifacts were vividly portrayed, to feature films where the cinematography was breathtakingly realistic, the impact of 4K on the viewing experience was undeniable. The improvement was so substantial that it often resulted in a sense of presence, making viewers feel as if they were directly participating in the events on the screen.

The introduction of High Dynamic Range (HDR) technology further enhanced the capabilities of 4K displays. HDR technology expands the range of colors and brightness, allowing for a wider spectrum of shades and tones, resulting in images with improved contrast, depth, and realism. The richer, more vibrant colors and improved contrast provided by HDR dramatically improved the visual impact of 4K content. Scenes with bright highlights and deep shadows, previously exhibiting washed-out or crushed details, became significantly improved, leading to a more realistic and immersive viewing experience. HDR's ability to display a wider range of luminance gave images a more natural and lifelike appearance, noticeably enhancing the quality of both entertainment and informative content.

However, the adoption of 4K technology, while significant, was not without its challenges. The increased resolution demanded higher bandwidths for both broadcasting and streaming. This necessitated upgrades to both the infrastructure and the content delivery networks. The significantly larger file sizes of 4K content also placed greater demands on storage capacity and processing power.

This created a need for improved compression algorithms to maintain acceptable transmission speeds without severely compromising image quality. The higher cost of 4K displays also served as a barrier to adoption, initially making the technology available only to a more affluent segment of the consumer market.

The progression didn't stop at 4K. The next logical step, 8K, with a resolution of 7680 x 4320 pixels, represents yet another significant leap forward. Offering sixteen times the pixel density of 1080p HDTV, 8K displays boast exceptional clarity and detail, surpassing even the impressive visuals of 4K. The increased resolution brings the viewer even closer to a photorealistic experience, resulting in an unparalleled level of immersion. While the adoption of 8K technology has been slower compared to 4K, driven by factors such as higher costs, limited content availability, and the relatively less significant visual improvement over 4K on screens with conventional viewing distances, it represents the continued pursuit of higher fidelity in home entertainment.

8K technology presents even greater challenges in terms of bandwidth, storage, and processing power. The sheer volume of data associated with 8K necessitates significant advancements in compression technologies and content delivery systems. While the content creation process also requires specialized high-resolution cameras and editing software, the potential benefits are considerable. In professional applications such as medical imaging or scientific visualization, the exceptional detail offered by 8K can be transformative. Within the realm of entertainment, though the benefits might not be as dramatic as the leap from standard definition to HD, or from HD to 4K on consumer-grade screens, the enhanced clarity and realism continue to push the boundaries of immersive visual experiences, creating a new benchmark in visual fidelity for home viewers.

The continued advancement in resolution brings with it both excitement and challenges. The increasing resolution demands necessitate further advancements in compression technologies, efficient streaming protocols, and content delivery networks. The cost of 8K displays and the lack of readily available 8K content remain significant hurdles. However, the trend towards higher resolutions demonstrates a persistent drive to improve the viewer's experience, pushing the boundaries of what's possible in the realm of home entertainment. The ongoing evolution is a testament to the innovative spirit driving the television industry and its commitment to continuously refining and enhancing the viewing experience for generations to come. The journey from the grainy images of early television to the breathtaking realism of 8K represents an incredible technological achievement, continuously reshaping how we engage with visual storytelling and the world beyond our screens. The future of television resolution undoubtedly holds further advancements, promising even more immersive and engaging viewing experiences, but the path forward will require continued technological innovation, improved infrastructure, and a sustained commitment to delivering high-quality content to meet the demands of these ever-evolving display technologies. The potential impact on everything from high-end film production to everyday home viewing is truly vast, making this area of television technology a fascinating area for continued observation and analysis.

The Impact of High Resolution on Content Production

The shift to high-definition television, and subsequently, ultra-high definition (4K and 8K), fundamentally altered the landscape of content production. The increased pixel density didn't simply mean sharper images; it necessitated a complete overhaul of the entire content creation pipeline, from camera acquisition to post- production workflows and distribution methods. The cost implications were significant, requiring substantial investments in new equipment, software, and infrastructure.

Cameras designed for high-resolution capture needed significantly more advanced sensors and lenses. These sensors, capable of resolving finer details and capturing a broader range of light, were more expensive to manufacture and required more sophisticated processing capabilities. The lenses themselves needed to meet the demands of these higher-resolution sensors, ensuring that they could effectively resolve the increased level of detail without introducing distortion or other optical artifacts. This meant a significant increase in the cost of camera equipment, pushing it beyond the reach of many independent filmmakers and smaller production companies.

Post-production workflows underwent a similar transformation. The vastly larger file sizes associated with 4K and 8K video footage demanded more powerful editing systems, capable of handling the increased computational load associated with rendering and exporting high-resolution video. This meant investing in high-end workstations with substantial processing power, ample RAM, and extensive storage capacity. The software used for editing, color grading, visual effects, and audio post-production also needed to be upgraded to handle the increased complexity and detail of higher-resolution video. This resulted in a rise in post-production costs, particularly for projects aiming for the highest visual fidelity.

The increased demands on storage and processing power extended beyond post-production. Archiving and distributing high-resolution video content also became considerably more challenging. The storage requirements for 4K and 8K footage are vastly greater than those of standard or high-definition video, leading to increased costs for storage solutions. Distribution, whether through broadcast, streaming, or physical media, demanded significant upgrades to infrastructure to handle the larger bandwidth requirements.

Streaming platforms, for example, needed to enhance their servers and networks to accommodate the increased data flow.

Broadcasters needed to invest in updated transmission technologies to deliver high-resolution content to viewers without significant lag or compression artifacts.

The cost implications were not limited to hardware and software.

The increased complexity of high-resolution workflows also necessitated a more skilled workforce. Editors, colorists, and other post-production professionals needed to be trained in the use of new tools and technologies, adding to the overall cost of production. Furthermore, the increased demand for high-quality content drove up the prices of services, creating further pressure on budgets. As a result, the production of high-resolution video content became significantly more expensive, potentially excluding smaller productions or independent filmmakers who lacked access to the necessary resources.

However, the investment in higher resolutions was not solely a matter of cost; it represented a significant advancement in storytelling potential. The improved detail allowed for a more nuanced and immersive viewing experience. Subtle facial expressions, intricate textures, and environmental details previously lost in lower resolutions became readily apparent, enriching the narrative and emotional impact. In documentaries, the increased resolution allowed for a more detailed exploration of the subject matter, capturing fine details that enhanced viewers' understanding and appreciation. In feature films, high-resolution imagery allowed filmmakers to create more visually stunning and realistic scenes, pushing the boundaries of cinematic artistry.

The realism offered by higher resolutions allowed for a deeper connection between the viewer and the content. Viewers could feel more immersed in the story, as if they were present in the scene itself. This enhanced immersion added a new layer of emotional depth to the viewing experience, creating a more profound impact on audiences. This realism, however, demanded more attention to detail during the creation process. Set design, lighting, and costume design needed to be of the highest caliber to take full advantage of the improved resolution. Any imperfections or inconsistencies would become immediately apparent, demanding a greater level of precision and professionalism in all aspects of production.

The move to higher resolutions also impacted the creative process itself. Filmmakers had to consider the implications of increased detail on their storytelling. Close-ups, for instance, became more impactful, capable of revealing subtle nuances in characters' emotions. Wide shots gained a new richness, revealing previously unseen details of the environment. The increased resolution demanded a more sophisticated approach to cinematography, requiring careful consideration of composition, lighting, and framing to maximize the impact of the higher resolution. The result was a more deliberate and refined artistic approach to filmmaking, driven by the enhanced capabilities of high-resolution technology.

The transition to high-resolution video also presented new opportunities for innovation in visual effects and animation. The increased detail provided a richer canvas for creating realistic and believable special effects. The ability to render and composite images with finer detail enhanced the believability of visual effects, blurring the lines between reality and imagination. The same was true for animation, where higher resolutions enabled animators to create more detailed and expressive characters, enhancing the emotional connection between the audience and the animated world.

In conclusion, the impact of high resolution on content production was transformative. While it necessitated significant investments in technology and skilled personnel, the benefits were undeniable. The enhanced detail, realism, and immersion provided by high- resolution video opened up new creative possibilities for filmmakers, animators, and content creators across various genres.

The journey from standard definition to 4K and 8K marked a profound evolution in visual storytelling, enhancing the viewer experience and pushing the boundaries of what's possible in the realm of visual media. The evolution continues, with advancements in display technology and content creation pushing the limits of visual fidelity even further, promising even more immersive and engaging experiences for viewers in the years to come. The challenge remains to ensure that the benefits of this technological advancement are accessible to a wider range of creators, fostering innovation and creativity across the entire media landscape.

The Consumer Adoption of HighResolution Television

The transition to high-definition television (HDTV) marked a significant turning point in the history of the medium, but its widespread adoption wasn't a seamless process. While the enhanced visual quality offered by HDTV was undeniably appealing, several factors influenced the rate at which consumers embraced this new technology. Cost, infrastructure limitations, and a lack of readily available high-definition content all played significant roles in shaping the consumer adoption curve.

One of the most significant barriers to early adoption was the expense of HDTV sets. In the early years of HDTV's rollout, these sets were considerably more expensive than their standard- definition counterparts. This price disparity limited access to the technology, primarily confining it to early adopters with higher disposable incomes. The higher cost reflected not only the advanced technology incorporated into the displays but also the limited manufacturing scale and economies of scale that hadn't yet been achieved. Consequently, the market for HDTVs was initially segmented, with a disproportionately high concentration of sales among affluent consumers.

The lack of readily available high-definition content further hampered widespread adoption. While broadcasters began transitioning to HDTV broadcasts, the process was gradual. Initially, much of the content available was still in standard definition, upscaled to fit the higher-resolution screens. This meant that consumers who invested in expensive HDTV sets didn't always experience the full visual benefits of their purchase, leading to some dissatisfaction and potentially dampening the market's growth. The development of high-definition content required investment in new cameras, editing equipment, and post-production workflows, adding to the overall cost of production. This cost barrier slowed the transition to a fully high-definition content ecosystem.

Infrastructure limitations also posed significant challenges. The transmission of high-definition signals required greater bandwidth compared to standard-definition broadcasts. This meant that existing broadcast infrastructure in many regions needed upgrading to accommodate the increased data flow. Cable companies and broadcasters faced the daunting task of upgrading their networks to support the demands of high-definition television. This involved substantial investments in new equipment, such as improved transmission towers, updated cable systems, and enhanced network infrastructure. The rollout of digital terrestrial television (DTT) also played a critical role, offering a path towards high-definition broadcasting over the air. However, the transition to DTT was itself a complex process, influenced by factors like government regulations, licensing agreements, and the availability of set-top boxes for receiving DTT signals. In areas with limited or underdeveloped infrastructure, the adoption of HDTV proceeded more slowly.

Consumer behavior also played a crucial role in shaping the adoption curve. Early adopters, often tech enthusiasts or individuals with higher disposable incomes, readily embraced HDTV, attracted by the promise of a superior viewing experience. However, the wider market required a more gradual process of education and persuasion. Marketing campaigns played a significant role in promoting the benefits of HDTV, emphasizing the improvements in picture quality, clarity, and overall viewing experience. However, these campaigns needed to effectively address the cost concerns and the lack of readily available high-definition content to effectively persuade a larger segment of the population.

Furthermore, the perception of value played a critical role.
Consumers needed to be convinced that the higher price of HDTV sets was justified by the benefits they would receive. The improved picture quality had to be significantly superior to warrant the increased cost, considering that many viewers were accustomed to the acceptable quality of standard-definition television. The transition to a fully high-definition ecosystem, therefore, required a concerted effort from manufacturers, broadcasters, and content creators to ensure a compelling value proposition for consumers.

The pace of adoption varied across different geographical regions and demographic groups. In developed countries with more advanced infrastructure and higher disposable incomes, the adoption rate was generally faster than in developing countries, where cost and infrastructure limitations were more significant obstacles. Similarly, younger demographics, generally more technologically inclined, adopted HDTV at a higher rate compared to older generations who were less likely to invest in new technology.

Market trends revealed an interesting interplay of technological advancements and consumer behavior. The initial high price point of HDTV sets created a niche market dominated by early adopters. As manufacturing techniques improved and economies of scale were achieved, the price of HDTV sets gradually decreased, making them more accessible to a wider range of consumers. The increased availability of high-definition content, driven by both broadcasters and streaming services, further fueled the adoption curve.

Streaming services, in particular, played a significant role in accelerating the transition to high-definition viewing, offering consumers a convenient and relatively inexpensive way to access a growing library of high-resolution content. Consequently, the market for HDTVs expanded dramatically, shifting from a niche market to a mainstream consumer product.

Looking towards the future, the trajectory of the HDTV market is closely tied to advancements in display technology. The emergence of ultra-high definition (4K and 8K) television sets presents new opportunities for enhancing the viewing experience. However, the adoption curve for these higher-resolution sets is likely to follow a similar pattern to that of HDTV. The initially high cost will create a niche market before gradually decreasing prices and increasing content availability bring it into the mainstream. The demand for higher resolution content and improved image processing will continue to drive innovation in the television industry, ensuring that the evolution of this medium continues. The ongoing interplay of technological advancements, cost considerations, infrastructure limitations, and consumer behavior will shape the future of television technology and its widespread adoption for many years to come. The integration of internet connectivity and smart features further complicates the picture, as consumers' choices are now influenced by factors beyond mere image resolution.

The Future of Visual Experience in Television Predictions and Trends

The evolution of television technology shows no signs of slowing.

While the widespread adoption of high-definition television represented a monumental leap forward, the quest for an even more immersive and realistic viewing experience continues to drive innovation. The future of visual experience in television promises a dramatic departure from the familiar, blurring the lines between the screen and the viewer's reality. Several key trends are shaping this future, promising a revolution in how we consume television content.

One of the most immediate advancements is the continued push towards ever-higher resolutions. While 4K and 8K televisions are already making inroads into the market, the potential for even higher resolutions, perhaps exceeding 16K, remains a significant area of development. These ultra-high-definition displays promise an unprecedented level of detail and clarity, bringing viewers closer to the feeling of actually being present in the scene depicted on screen. However, the realization of this potential hinges on several factors. Firstly, the development of content capable of taking full advantage of these resolutions is crucial. Producing and distributing such high-resolution video requires significant investment in equipment and infrastructure, particularly in terms of storage, bandwidth, and processing power. Secondly, the cost of these ultra-high-definition displays needs to decrease to make them accessible to a broader consumer base. Currently, these advanced displays occupy a niche market, typically catering to early adopters and affluent consumers.

Beyond resolution, the integration of new display technologies is transforming the television landscape. Advances in OLED (Organic Light Emitting Diode) and MicroLED technologies offer superior contrast ratios, deeper blacks, and wider color gamuts compared to traditional LCD displays. These improvements translate to more vibrant and realistic images, enhancing the overall viewing experience significantly. Furthermore, the development of flexible and transparent displays opens up possibilities for entirely new forms of television, envisioning screens that can be rolled up or integrated seamlessly into various environments. Imagine a television screen that can be embedded in a window, offering a breathtaking view of a virtual landscape alongside the real world, or a flexible screen that can be adjusted to any shape or size. The limitations of conventional rigid screens will soon become a thing of the past.

The convergence of television and other technologies, such as virtual reality (VR) and augmented reality (AR), is poised to revolutionize the viewing experience. VR headsets offer the potential for truly immersive experiences, transporting viewers directly into the world of their favorite shows. Imagine watching a documentary about the Amazon rainforest and feeling like you are actually traversing the jungle floor or experiencing a historical drama as if you were present during those significant events. The level of immersion afforded by VR promises to redefine the relationship between the viewer and the content.

However, VR's adoption faces challenges. The need for specialized equipment, the potential for motion sickness in some users, and the cost of high-quality VR content are significant hurdles that need to be addressed. Augmented reality, on the other hand, offers a different, yet equally compelling, path towards a more interactive viewing experience. AR technology overlays digital information onto the real world, enabling interactive elements within the television viewing environment. Imagine a sports broadcast where AR overlays provide real-time statistics, player information, and replay angles directly onto the screen, augmenting the broadcast with valuable context without disrupting the viewing experience. AR could also provide viewers with additional information about the actors, directors, or plotlines of a show by simply pointing a smartphone or tablet at the screen.

The integration of artificial intelligence (AI) is transforming television in several ways. AI-powered recommendation systems already personalize viewing experiences by suggesting content based on individual viewing habits and preferences. In the future, AI could play a far more significant role, enabling more sophisticated content creation, personalized interactions with the content, and even the adaptation of content in real-time based on viewer response. Imagine a show where the narrative changes based on your choices, or a personalized news broadcast that prioritizes the information relevant to your location and interests. This potential for personalized content creation and adaptive narratives promises a more engaging and interactive television experience.

The future of television viewing also includes the evolution of the user interface. The traditional remote control is likely to be supplanted by more intuitive and user-friendly interfaces, such as voice control, gesture recognition, and brain-computer interfaces. Imagine controlling your television simply by speaking your commands or using simple hand gestures, or even directly influencing the action on screen with your thoughts. These advancements will make the interaction with television more seamless and intuitive.

The increasing integration of internet connectivity and smart features in television sets further complicates the picture. The lines between traditional broadcasting and streaming services are becoming increasingly blurred, with televisions evolving into sophisticated entertainment hubs that provide access to a vast library of content from multiple sources. This convergence of platforms offers viewers unprecedented choices, but it also creates challenges in terms of navigation, organization, and access to content. AI-powered recommendation systems and more intuitive user interfaces will become increasingly critical in navigating this expanding landscape of entertainment options.

The energy efficiency of television sets will also play an increasingly important role in their design and adoption. With growing awareness of environmental concerns, consumers are likely to prioritize energy-efficient television models, pushing manufacturers to develop more sustainable technologies. The adoption of more efficient display technologies and power management systems will be crucial in meeting this demand.

The development of holographic displays holds the potential for a truly revolutionary change in television technology. Holographic displays can project three-dimensional images that appear to float in the air, creating an incredibly immersive and realistic viewing experience. While the technology is still in its early stages of development, holographic televisions could eventually become a staple of home entertainment systems. The challenge lies in making this technology affordable and accessible to the average consumer.

However, the future of television is not without challenges. The issue of accessibility, particularly for individuals with disabilities, requires careful consideration. Television technology should be designed to be inclusive and usable by everyone, regardless of their physical limitations. Subtitles, audio descriptions, and other accessibility features need to be seamlessly integrated into the design of future television sets. Furthermore, the ethical implications of AI-powered personalization and content creation need to be carefully addressed. The potential for bias, manipulation, and the creation of filter bubbles requires careful oversight and regulatory frameworks.

The future of visual experience in television will be shaped by a complex interplay of technological advancements, consumer demand, economic factors, and regulatory landscapes. While predicting the precise trajectory of this evolution is impossible, one thing is certain: the television of the future will offer a viewing experience far beyond anything we can imagine today. The convergence of higher resolutions, innovative display technologies, immersive VR and AR experiences, AI-powered personalization, intuitive user interfaces, and considerations for accessibility and sustainability will fundamentally change how we consume television content and integrate it into our daily lives. The journey continues, and the next chapter in this ever-evolving story is sure to be as fascinating and transformative as the chapters that have come before.

Interactive Television Features Early Innovations

The seeds of interactive television were sown long before the advent of the internet and smart TVs. While the early days of television offered a largely passive viewing experience, a gradual evolution towards interactivity began with seemingly simple innovations that fundamentally changed the relationship between the viewer and the screen. One of the earliest and most impactful of these was the introduction of the remote control. Before the ubiquitous remote, viewers were tethered to their television sets, forced to physically approach the device to change channels or adjust the volume. This seemingly minor inconvenience drastically impacted viewing habits, limiting spontaneous channel surfing or quick adjustments during commercials.

The development of the remote control wasn't a single eureka moment but rather a process of incremental improvements. Early versions were often wired, limiting their range and convenience. Zenith Electronics introduced the first truly wireless remote control, the "Flash-Matic," in 1955, utilizing ultrasonic technology to transmit signals. This innovation, though plagued by interference issues and a limited range, marked a crucial turning point. The subsequent evolution of infrared (IR) technology in the 1980s significantly improved reliability and range, making the remote control a standard feature in almost every household. This simple device, while seemingly insignificant in isolation, profoundly impacted the viewing experience, transforming it from a stationary activity to a more dynamic and personalized engagement. Viewers could now effortlessly explore a wider variety of channels, adjust the volume discreetly, and even access simple functions without leaving their viewing position. This increased ease of use led to longer viewing sessions and a more relaxed interaction with the technology.

Beyond the remote, the development of on-screen menus added another layer of interactivity. Early television sets displayed limited information, primarily channel numbers and basic volume indicators. The introduction of on-screen menus, however, allowed viewers to access a much wider range of information and functions directly through the television interface. This functionality evolved alongside the increasing processing power of television sets, allowing for the inclusion of electronic program guides (EPGs), parental controls, and access to various setup options. The EPG, in particular, revolutionized television viewing by allowing users to easily browse through upcoming programs, set reminders, and even search for specific content. While rudimentary in its early forms, the introduction of on-screen menus represented a crucial step towards a more user-friendly and personalized television experience.

Further enhancing the interactive capabilities of television were the early attempts at incorporating interactive games. These early games were often simple, utilizing limited graphics and basic input mechanisms, often through a wired keypad or a rudimentary remote control. Despite their technological limitations, these early interactive gaming experiences demonstrated the potential of television as a platform for entertainment beyond passive viewing. Games like "Pong" in the 1970s, initially intended for arcades, were eventually adapted for home television sets, becoming a surprising success. These early iterations, while limited by the processing power of home consoles and television sets, captured the imaginations of millions and proved the marketability of interactive elements within a television viewing context. This laid the groundwork for the future development of sophisticated game consoles and interactive television experiences.

However, the early innovations in interactive television were not without their limitations. The resolution of television screens was significantly lower than contemporary standards, limiting the visual quality of interactive games and on-screen menus. The processing power of early television sets was also limited, resulting in sluggish responses and occasional glitches. Furthermore, the limited bandwidth of early broadcast systems created challenges in delivering interactive content efficiently. These technological limitations constrained the sophistication and complexity of interactive features, impacting the overall user experience. The cost of incorporating these interactive features was also a factor, making them initially inaccessible to a broad consumer base.

Despite these constraints, the introduction of remote controls, on-screen menus, and interactive games profoundly impacted the societal perception of television. Television became a more personalized and engaging medium, blurring the lines between passive consumption and active participation. The convenience of the remote control allowed for a more relaxed and flexible viewing experience, fostering a more intimate relationship between viewers and their television sets. On-screen menus empowered viewers with greater control over their viewing environment and allowed for a more customized experience. Interactive games broadened the appeal of television, attracting a wider audience and laying the foundations for the future convergence of television and video gaming.

The societal impact was further amplified by the emergence of specialized channels dedicated to interactive television services. These channels introduced viewers to interactive game shows, quizzes, and voting mechanisms, further integrating the audience into the broadcasting experience. Viewers were no longer passive observers but active participants in the content, shaping the direction of the show or influencing the outcome. This engagement fostered a sense of community and collective participation, further solidifying the transformation of television from a one-way broadcast to a more bidirectional communication channel.

The early history of interactive television, though marked by technological limitations, showcases the relentless drive towards a more dynamic and engaging television experience. The seemingly minor innovations of the remote control, on-screen menus, and early interactive games collectively laid the groundwork for the sophisticated interactive technologies we enjoy today. The lessons learned from these early attempts—the importance of user-friendliness, the limitations of existing technology, and the societal impact of improved interactivity—shaped the future trajectory of television development and continue to inform innovations in the field. The path from the simple act of changing channels with a cumbersome dial to the sophisticated personalized entertainment experiences of today is a testament to both human ingenuity and the ever-evolving demand for a more interactive and immersive viewing experience. This early phase of interactive television demonstrates not only technological progress but also a crucial shift in the social contract between broadcasters and viewers, paving the way for the ubiquitous interactive television landscape of the present day. The analysis of these early innovations serves as a crucial foundation for understanding the subsequent evolution of interactive television, highlighting the continuous interplay between technological advancements, user expectations, and the socio-cultural impact of this transformative medium.

The Evolution of Interactive Features From Basic to Advanced

The next significant leap in interactive television came with the advent of video on demand (VOD). While early attempts at providing on-demand content existed, the widespread adoption of VOD was largely fueled by the rise of digital cable and satellite services. These services, with their increased bandwidth and storage capacity, enabled the delivery of a vast library of programs that viewers could access at their convenience. No longer were viewers constrained to predetermined broadcast schedules; they could now select and watch their preferred programs anytime, anywhere, representing a fundamental shift in the television viewing paradigm. This freedom extended beyond mere scheduling; viewers could choose from a greater variety of content, accessing niche programming and international films that were previously unavailable through traditional broadcast channels.

The implementation of VOD necessitated significant technological advancements. The development of digital compression techniques was crucial in efficiently storing and transmitting large volumes of video data. This allowed for a greater number of channels and on-demand options within the existing bandwidth constraints.

Furthermore, the development of sophisticated server infrastructure and content delivery networks (CDNs) ensured the reliable and efficient streaming of content to millions of viewers simultaneously. The user interface also underwent a transformation, moving from simple channel selectors to intuitive menus and search functions allowing users to easily navigate and discover content within the extensive VOD libraries.

Personalization further enhanced the interactive capabilities of VOD services. Early VOD systems offered limited personalization options, primarily through basic genre selection. However, as data collection and analytical techniques advanced, VOD services began to offer increasingly personalized content recommendations. Algorithms analyzed viewing history, preferences, and even demographic data to suggest programs tailored to individual tastes, creating a more targeted and engaging viewing experience. This personalized approach significantly improved user satisfaction and increased viewing time as users discovered new content aligned with their interests. The development of sophisticated recommendation engines was pivotal to this personalization, utilizing machine learning and artificial intelligence to improve the accuracy and relevance of recommendations over time.

Beyond VOD, the integration of social media into the television viewing experience marked another pivotal moment in interactive television. Early attempts involved basic viewer interaction during live broadcasts, often limited to text-based polls or simple feedback mechanisms. However, with the widespread adoption of social media platforms, television began to fully integrate these social elements, enabling real-time interactions and discussions among viewers. Viewers could now share their opinions, reactions, and thoughts directly on social media during live broadcasts, creating a dynamic and engaging shared viewing experience. This integration was facilitated by the development of companion apps and second-screen technologies, which allowed viewers to access social media feeds and interact with other viewers on their smartphones or tablets while simultaneously watching television.

The integration of social media also fostered a new form of content creation and engagement. Television programs began to incorporate social media challenges, contests, and even viewer-generated content directly into their broadcasts. Viewers could actively participate in shaping the narrative, influencing plot developments, or even having their own creations featured on television. This level of interactivity blurred the lines between passive consumption and active participation, fostering a more intimate connection between viewers and the content they were consuming. The widespread adoption of social media further amplified the reach and influence of television programs, creating viral trends and expanding the audience beyond traditional viewerships.

Another significant advance in interactive television is the emergence of interactive advertising. Early forms of interactive advertising involved simple clickable banners or links within commercials. However, advancements in technology enabled more sophisticated forms of interactive ads, including personalized ads based on viewer data, interactive games embedded within commercials, and even the ability to purchase products directly from the television screen. This development transformed the advertising experience, moving beyond simple exposure to a more engaging and responsive model. The development of targeted advertising based on viewer data proved effective in increasing advertising ROI while also enhancing the overall user experience by offering relevant and personalized advertising messages. These targeted advertisements were often less intrusive and even perceived as helpful by viewers, providing direct access to relevant products or services during their viewing experience.

The rise of smart TVs has fundamentally reshaped the interactive television landscape. Smart TVs offer a seamless integration of various interactive features, including access to streaming services, applications, and online content, all through a unified interface. This central access point eliminates the need for multiple devices, simplifying the user experience and consolidating the various interactive elements of television into a singular point of access. The development of intuitive operating systems for smart TVs was crucial in delivering this user-friendly experience, making it effortless to navigate and access the wide range of content and features.

Further enhancing the capabilities of smart TVs is the incorporation of voice control and artificial intelligence. Viewers can now use voice commands to control their television sets, access content, and even interact with applications through natural language processing. AI-powered features, such as personalized content recommendations and automated recording capabilities, further enhance the convenience and user experience. The integration of AI is also transforming the accessibility of television for viewers with disabilities, offering voice-activated navigation, captioning, and personalized audio settings.

The evolution of interactive television continues at a rapid pace, with ongoing advancements in areas such as augmented reality (AR) and virtual reality (VR). AR applications overlay digital content onto the real world, potentially enhancing the viewing experience by incorporating interactive elements directly into the viewer's environment. VR, on the other hand, offers a fully immersive viewing experience, potentially transforming television into a more participatory and engaging form of entertainment. The use of these technologies is still in its early stages, but their potential to revolutionize the way we consume television is undeniable.

Looking ahead, the future of interactive television promises an even greater level of personalization, immersion, and engagement. Advancements in artificial intelligence, machine learning, and data analytics will further enhance personalized content recommendations, tailoring the viewing experience to individual preferences with unprecedented accuracy. The integration of AR and VR technologies has the potential to blur the lines between the physical and digital worlds, creating immersive and interactive viewing experiences that transcend the limitations of traditional television. The continued development of high-resolution displays, like 8K technology, further enhances the visual fidelity of the content, immersing viewers in a more realistic and engaging experience.

The trajectory of interactive television suggests that the passive viewer is becoming a thing of the past. The future of television is one of active participation, personalized experiences, and immersive entertainment. As technology continues to advance, the lines between traditional television, gaming, and social media will become increasingly blurred, resulting in a more integrated and seamless entertainment ecosystem. This ever-evolving landscape promises a future where the television screen acts as a gateway to a personalized world of entertainment, tailored to individual preferences and desires, providing not just passive consumption, but active participation and immersive engagement in a truly personalized and interconnected experience.

The Impact of Interactive Television on the Viewing Experience

The integration of interactive elements into television has profoundly altered the viewing experience, moving it from a primarily passive activity to one involving active participation and engagement. This shift has had a demonstrable impact on viewer behavior, creating both opportunities and challenges for broadcasters and content creators. One of the most significant changes is the increase in viewer control over their viewing experience. With features like video on demand (VOD), viewers are no longer beholden to rigid broadcast schedules. They can select programs based on their individual preferences and watch them at their convenience, leading to a more personalized and satisfying viewing experience. This freedom has also contributed to increased viewing time, as viewers are more likely to watch shows when it best suits their schedule. The ability to pause, rewind, and fast-forward further enhances control, allowing viewers to engage with content at their own pace. This level of control stands in stark contrast to the traditional television experience, where viewers were largely passive recipients of pre-programmed content.

The rise of interactive features has also led to a notable increase in viewer engagement. The ability to participate in polls, quizzes, and social media discussions during live broadcasts fosters a sense of community and shared experience among viewers. Interactive advertising, while sometimes controversial, has also increased viewer engagement by offering more personalized and relevant ads.

These interactive elements encourage active participation, transforming the viewer from a passive observer into an active participant. This increased engagement is reflected in higher viewership figures and greater audience loyalty for programs that effectively utilize interactive features. However, the effectiveness of these features is contingent upon their seamless integration into the viewing experience; poorly designed interactive elements can prove disruptive or even frustrating for the viewers.

Viewer satisfaction has also been positively impacted by interactive television. Personalized content recommendations, powered by AI and machine learning algorithms, offer viewers access to programs and content that align with their tastes and preferences. This targeted approach improves the likelihood of viewers discovering new content they enjoy, ultimately increasing their satisfaction with the viewing experience. The ability to create personalized profiles and save preferred settings further enhances viewer satisfaction by providing a tailored and convenient experience. Conversely, poorly implemented interactive features, such as intrusive advertising or complex user interfaces, can detract from the overall viewing experience, leading to decreased satisfaction and potentially viewer frustration. The success of interactive television hinges upon delivering a balanced and well-integrated experience that enhances rather than detracts from viewer enjoyment.

The opportunities presented by interactive television are substantial. For broadcasters and content creators, interactive features offer an avenue for increased audience engagement and monetization. Interactive advertising allows for more targeted and effective advertising campaigns, yielding higher returns on investment while delivering a less disruptive experience to the viewer. The ability to gather data on viewer preferences through interactive elements allows for a greater understanding of audience demographics and viewing habits, helping broadcasters refine programming and content strategies. Furthermore, interactive television presents an opportunity to cultivate a stronger sense of community amongst viewers by providing platforms for interaction and discussion. Social media integration, for example, can foster a sense of shared experience among viewers, thereby increasing their loyalty to particular programs or channels.

However, the adoption of interactive television also presents certain challenges. One significant challenge is the creation of user-friendly and intuitive interfaces. Complex or poorly designed interactive features can frustrate viewers, leading to decreased engagement and satisfaction. The challenge lies in balancing innovative features with ease of use, creating an experience that is both engaging and accessible to a wide range of viewers, regardless of their technical skills or prior experience with interactive technologies.

Another challenge is ensuring data privacy and security. The collection of viewer data, while essential for personalized content recommendations and targeted advertising, raises concerns about privacy and the potential for misuse of personal information.

Maintaining viewer trust requires transparent data handling practices and robust security measures. Balancing the benefits of data collection with the imperative for data privacy is a crucial ethical and practical concern. Striking a balance between providing personalized experiences and protecting user privacy remains a significant ongoing challenge for the industry.

The potential for increased advertising revenue, through interactive advertising, presents both an opportunity and a challenge. The need for innovative advertising formats that are both engaging and not intrusive must be carefully considered. Finding the optimal balance between generating revenue through advertising and maintaining an enjoyable and undistracting viewing experience for viewers will require a careful approach. Overly aggressive or intrusive interactive advertising can lead to negative user experiences, potentially undermining the entire purpose of implementing these features in the first place.

Finally, the ever-evolving technological landscape presents an ongoing challenge. Keeping up with the rapid pace of technological advancements and integrating new features seamlessly into the viewing experience requires significant investment and ongoing innovation. The need for constant upgrades and adaptation to accommodate new technologies requires substantial resources and ongoing commitment.

In conclusion, the impact of interactive television on the viewing experience has been profound and multifaceted. While it has led to increased viewer control, engagement, and satisfaction, it also presents challenges related to user interface design, data privacy, advertising strategies, and the pace of technological change. The future of television will likely involve an even greater degree of personalization, interactivity, and integration with other digital platforms. Success in this evolving landscape will depend on the ability of broadcasters and content creators to navigate these opportunities and challenges effectively, offering viewers engaging and user-friendly experiences that respect their privacy while enhancing their overall enjoyment of television. The ultimate goal is to strike a balance between innovation and usability, creating a television viewing experience that is both entertaining and enriching.

The Future of Interactive Television Predictions and Potential

The trajectory of interactive television points towards a future brimming with possibilities, driven by the convergence of several powerful technological trends. Artificial intelligence (AI), already making inroads into personalized content recommendations and targeted advertising, is poised to revolutionize the viewing experience even further. Imagine a television system that not only anticipates your preferences but also actively adapts to your moods and emotional responses. AI algorithms could analyze your viewing history, facial expressions captured by the television's camera, even your heart rate (via a smart wearable), to curate a truly personalized viewing experience. This hyper-personalization could extend beyond simple content recommendations, encompassing dynamic adjustments to the audio and visual elements of a program, optimizing the viewing environment for your individual comfort and engagement.

However, the implementation of AI in interactive television presents significant challenges. The ethical implications of AI-driven personalization are paramount. Concerns about data privacy and the potential for algorithmic bias must be addressed proactively. Transparency in data collection and use, coupled with robust safeguards against discriminatory outcomes, are crucial for ensuring responsible AI integration. The potential for manipulation through personalized advertising, subtly influencing viewer choices, requires careful consideration and regulation. Striking a balance between leveraging AI's capabilities for enhanced personalization and mitigating its potential risks will require a collaborative effort between technology developers, broadcasters, regulators, and consumers.

Beyond AI, the convergence of television with virtual and augmented reality (VR/AR) technologies opens up exciting new avenues for interactive entertainment. VR headsets could transport viewers into the worlds of their favorite shows, offering immersive experiences that blur the lines between reality and fiction. Imagine watching a historical drama and being able to virtually "walk" through the depicted city, interacting with digital representations of the characters. Or consider the possibilities for interactive gaming, where viewers become active participants in the narrative, shaping the storyline through their choices and actions. AR, meanwhile, could overlay digital information onto the real-world viewing experience, enriching the content with interactive elements. A sports broadcast, for instance, could utilize AR to display real-time player statistics and interactive maps, enhancing the viewer's understanding and engagement.

Yet, the integration of VR and AR into interactive television faces considerable hurdles. The high cost of VR headsets and the need for sufficient processing power to support immersive experiences may limit their widespread adoption. The potential for motion sickness and the physical limitations imposed by VR headsets could deter some viewers. Furthermore, the development of compelling VR/AR content that is both immersive and user-friendly requires significant investment and innovation. Striking a balance between creating a truly engaging experience and ensuring accessibility and comfort for all viewers will be a key challenge.

The increasing interconnectedness of devices promises to fundamentally change the interactive television experience. The"smart home" concept, with its network of interconnected devices, offers the potential for seamlessly integrated entertainment experiences. Imagine a system where your television, smart speakers, lighting system, and even your thermostat work together to optimize the viewing environment. The lights dim automatically as the show begins, the temperature adjusts to your preference, and a smart speaker provides voice-controlled access to various interactive features. Such seamless integration could lead to a more immersive and personalized viewing experience, enhancing both convenience and entertainment.

However, the complexity of integrating various devices and platforms raises considerable challenges. Ensuring interoperability between different devices and operating systems will be crucial. Robust security measures are necessary to prevent unauthorized access and protect user data. The potential for system failures and the difficulties of troubleshooting technical issues must also be addressed. The success of interconnected television hinges upon creating a user-friendly system that is both robust and reliable, offering a seamless and trouble-free experience for viewers.

The future of interactive television will undoubtedly involve a greater emphasis on personalized content delivery. AI-powered recommendation systems will continue to improve, offering increasingly nuanced and relevant suggestions based on individual preferences and viewing habits. However, these systems must be designed to avoid creating "filter bubbles," where users are only exposed to content that reinforces their existing beliefs and perspectives. Algorithmic transparency and the ability for viewers to customize their recommendation settings will be crucial in ensuring a diverse and enriching viewing experience.

Furthermore, the future of interactive television will likely involve greater integration with social media platforms. Live broadcasts will incorporate more interactive elements, encouraging viewers to participate in real-time discussions and polls. Social media integration could enhance the sense of community among viewers, fostering a more engaging and interactive viewing experience.

However, the potential for online harassment and the spread of misinformation must be addressed through effective moderation and content management strategies.

In conclusion, the future of interactive television is a dynamic and ever-evolving landscape shaped by rapid technological advancements and shifting consumer preferences. While the integration of AI, VR/AR, and interconnected devices promises to revolutionize the viewing experience, addressing ethical concerns, ensuring user-friendliness, and mitigating potential risks will be paramount. Success in this evolving landscape hinges on striking a balance between technological innovation and responsible implementation, prioritizing user experience, data privacy, and the overall enhancement of the viewing experience. The next generation of interactive television must not only be technologically advanced but also ethically sound and genuinely enriching for viewers. The challenge lies in creating a future where technological innovation serves to enhance, not diminish, the joy and value of the television viewing experience. The future is not just about enhancing technology, but about intelligently integrating it into a cohesive and enriching user experience.

The Role of Artificial Intelligence in Shaping Interactive Television

The integration of artificial intelligence (AI) into interactive television represents a profound shift in how we consume and engage with this medium. Beyond simply offering personalized recommendations, AI is poised to fundamentally reshape the entire viewing experience, from content creation to audience participation. The algorithms powering today's recommendation engines are already learning our preferences, analyzing viewing habits to suggest shows, movies, and even specific scenes within programs that align with our established tastes. This level of personalization is just the beginning. Future iterations will delve deeper into understanding our emotional responses to content.

Imagine a system that detects signs of boredom or frustration through facial recognition technology incorporated into the television itself or via connected devices like smart wearables. This data, combined with viewing history and other contextual information, will allow the AI to dynamically adjust the viewing experience in real-time. A show deemed too intense might subtly shift its pacing or tone, while a slow-moving documentary could be supplemented with interactive elements to maintain engagement.

This hyper-personalized approach promises to tailor the viewing experience to each individual's unique needs and preferences, creating a level of immersion previously unattainable.

However, this level of personalization brings with it a complex set of ethical considerations. The collection and use of personal data are central to AI-driven personalization. To function effectively, these systems require access to a vast amount of viewer data, including viewing habits, demographic information, and potentially even biometric data reflecting emotional responses. The potential for misuse of this sensitive information is significant. Concerns about data privacy, algorithmic bias, and the potential for manipulative advertising techniques are paramount. Algorithmic bias, a well-documented problem in AI systems, could lead to discriminatory outcomes, potentially reinforcing existing societal biases through personalized content delivery. For example, an AI system trained on biased data might disproportionately recommend certain types of content to specific demographics, leading to a skewed and potentially harmful viewing experience. The lack of transparency in how these algorithms operate further exacerbates these concerns, making it difficult for viewers to understand how their viewing experience is shaped and to challenge potentially unfair or discriminatory outcomes.

The potential for manipulation through personalized advertising also demands careful consideration. Targeted advertising, already a prevalent feature of online platforms, could be amplified in the context of AI-driven interactive television. AI systems could analyze viewer responses in real-time, adjusting advertising strategies to maximize their impact. This raises concerns about the potential for subtle influence and manipulation, particularly for vulnerable populations. For instance, children or individuals with pre-existing mental health conditions could be particularly susceptible to manipulative advertising techniques. The development of ethical guidelines and regulatory frameworks to govern the use of AI in personalized advertising is crucial to prevent exploitation and protect viewers' autonomy.

Beyond personalized recommendations, AI is also playing an increasingly important role in content creation itself. AI-powered tools can assist writers and directors in various stages of the production process, from scriptwriting and storyboarding to editing and post-production. AI algorithms can analyze existing scripts and identify patterns and themes, suggesting plot points or dialogue options. They can also assist in generating different versions of a script, allowing writers to explore various creative options. In post-production, AI can automate tasks such as color grading, sound mixing, and special effects, improving efficiency and reducing production costs. However, the use of AI in content creation also raises questions about the nature of creativity and authorship. The extent to which AI can be considered a creative partner, as opposed to a mere tool, remains a subject of ongoing debate.

The impact of AI extends to audience engagement as well. Interactive television experiences are increasingly incorporating AI-powered features to enhance audience participation. Live broadcasts, for example, could utilize AI to analyze viewer comments and questions in real-time, allowing producers to tailor the program's content to reflect the audience's interests. AI-powered chatbots could provide viewers with instant access to information or interact with them in a personalized way, creating a more immersive and engaging viewing experience. Interactive games and quizzes, powered by AI, could offer viewers opportunities to participate actively in the show's narrative, shaping its outcome through their choices and actions. However, the potential for misuse of these interactive features, such as the spread of misinformation or the facilitation of online harassment, needs careful consideration. Robust moderation and content management strategies are essential to ensure a safe and positive viewing environment.

The future of AI in interactive television hinges on the responsible development and deployment of these technologies. Transparency in data collection and usage practices is crucial. Viewers should have clear understanding of how their data is being collected, used, and protected. Robust safeguards against algorithmic bias and discriminatory outcomes must be implemented. Ethical guidelines and regulatory frameworks are necessary to govern the use of AI in personalized advertising and content creation. A collaborative effort involving technology developers, broadcasters, regulators, and consumers is essential to ensure that the benefits of AI-driven personalization are realized without compromising user privacy, autonomy, or well-being. The goal is not simply to enhance the technological capabilities of interactive television but to create an experience that is both engaging and ethically sound, serving to enrich rather than diminish the value of television as a medium.

The challenge lies in striking a balance between leveraging the immense potential of AI to enhance the viewer experience and mitigating the significant ethical risks inherent in its deployment. Only through thoughtful consideration and proactive measures can we ensure that the future of interactive television is one that is both technologically advanced and ethically responsible. The ultimate success will depend on prioritizing user experience, data privacy, and the overall enhancement of the viewing experience, ensuring that technological innovation serves to enhance, not diminish, the enjoyment and value of television for all viewers.

The Emergence of Smart TVs Internet Connectivity and Functionality

The transition from traditional television to the era of smart TVs marked a significant turning point in the history of the medium. The integration of internet connectivity fundamentally altered the television viewing experience, transforming it from a primarily passive activity into an interactive and personalized one. No longer confined to broadcast schedules and limited channel selections, smart TVs opened up a universe of on-demand content, interactive applications, and personalized experiences that redefined the relationship between viewers and their television sets.

The advent of broadband internet access played a pivotal role in enabling the widespread adoption of smart TVs. The increasing availability of high-speed internet connections, capable of delivering high-definition video streams, provided the necessary infrastructure to support the bandwidth-intensive nature of online video content. This development was a crucial catalyst, paving the way for the seamless integration of internet capabilities into television sets. Early attempts at internet-enabled televisions often relied on cumbersome external devices or limited functionalities, but the convergence of robust internet infrastructure and increasingly sophisticated television technology made smart TVs a truly viable and appealing proposition.

One of the most significant features of smart TVs is the ability to access a wide range of streaming services. Platforms such as Netflix, Hulu, Amazon Prime Video, Disney+, and countless others offer vast libraries of movies, television shows, and documentaries, providing viewers with an unparalleled selection of on-demand content. This shift from scheduled broadcast television to on- demand streaming fundamentally changed the way people consume television, allowing viewers to watch what they want, when they want, without being bound by traditional broadcast schedules. The convenience and personalization offered by these streaming services proved immensely popular, contributing substantially to the rapid rise in the adoption of smart TVs.

Beyond streaming services, smart TVs offer a plethora of other functionalities, enriching the viewing experience in numerous ways. Web browsing capabilities, often integrated directly into the smart TV's interface, allow users to access the internet directly from their television set. This expands the possibilities of the television beyond mere entertainment, enabling viewers to access news, social media, and other online resources directly on the large screen. This convergence of television and internet technologies blurs the lines between traditional media consumption and the broader online experience.

App integration further enhances the functionality of smart TVs. Similar to smartphones and tablets, smart TVs can download and run a wide variety of applications, each offering unique functionalities. These apps range from fitness and wellness applications to educational programs, games, and social networking platforms. The app ecosystem for smart TVs is constantly evolving, with new apps and services continually emerging, expanding the scope of what's possible on the television screen. This makes the smart TV a versatile home entertainment hub that can cater to a broad range of interests and preferences.

The integration of voice assistants represents another major advancement in the evolution of smart TVs. Voice-activated control features, often powered by virtual assistants like Amazon Alexa or Google Assistant, allow viewers to control their televisions using voice commands. This hands-free operation simplifies the user interface, making it easier for viewers to navigate menus, search for content, and adjust settings. The convenience and intuitive nature of voice-controlled interfaces have significantly enhanced the user-friendliness of smart TVs, contributing to their widespread adoption.

However, the rise of smart TVs has also raised concerns regarding data privacy and security. Smart TVs, being connected to the internet, collect data about user viewing habits and preferences. This information is often used by manufacturers and streaming services to personalize content recommendations and target advertisements. The collection and use of this data have sparked concerns regarding potential breaches of user privacy and the possibility of data misuse. Transparency and user control over data collection practices remain significant challenges in the smart TV landscape.

Furthermore, the increasing sophistication of smart TVs has also raised concerns about the potential for security vulnerabilities. The connectivity that makes smart TVs so versatile also makes them vulnerable to cyberattacks. Hackers could potentially gain access to user data or even remotely control the television set. The development of robust security measures to protect against such threats is essential to ensuring the safe and reliable operation of smart TVs.

The integration of smart TV technology into the broader landscape of the Internet of Things (IoT) presents further challenges and opportunities. Smart TVs are increasingly capable of interacting with other smart home devices, such as smart lighting, thermostats, and security systems. This interconnectedness can enhance the overall home entertainment and automation experience, creating a truly immersive and personalized environment. However, the interconnectedness of these devices also poses additional security risks. A vulnerability in one smart home device could potentially compromise the security of other connected devices, including the smart TV.

The economic impact of smart TVs has been substantial. The growth of the smart TV market has spurred innovation and competition within the television manufacturing industry. The availability of a diverse range of smart TVs from different manufacturers at varying price points has made this technology accessible to a broad segment of the population. The shift to streaming services and on-demand content has also had a significant impact on the entertainment industry, transforming the landscape of content creation and distribution. The rise of smart TVs has undeniably reshaped the entire ecosystem of television and entertainment.

In conclusion, the emergence of smart TVs marks a pivotal moment in the history of television. The integration of internet connectivity has fundamentally transformed the viewing experience, offering a wealth of features and functionalities that enhance personalization, interactivity, and convenience. While concerns remain regarding data privacy, security, and the ethical implications of data collection, the pervasive adoption of smart TVs points to their undeniable impact on the way we consume and interact with this medium. The ongoing evolution of smart TV technology, coupled with the continuous growth of the IoT, promises to further transform the way we interact with our homes and entertainment, making the television set a central hub in the connected home environment. The future of television will undoubtedly be shaped by the continued integration and expansion of smart TV capabilities.

Smart TVs and the Internet of Things IoT Connected Devices

The seamless integration of smart TVs into the burgeoning Internet of Things (IoT) ecosystem represents a significant and ongoing evolution of the television medium. This interconnection transforms the television from a standalone entertainment device into a central node within a broader network of smart home appliances, creating opportunities for enhanced functionality and personalized experiences, but also presenting new challenges related to security and privacy.

One of the most visible examples of this integration is the rise of voice control. Smart TVs, increasingly equipped with built-in microphones and sophisticated voice recognition software, allow users to interact with their televisions using natural language commands. This capability, often powered by virtual assistants like Amazon Alexa or Google Assistant, significantly enhances user experience. Instead of navigating complex on-screen menus, users can simply ask their TV to change channels, search for specific content, adjust the volume, or launch specific applications. This intuitive and hands-free control method simplifies the user interface, making smart TVs more accessible to a wider range of users, including those with limited dexterity or technological proficiency. Moreover, the capability to control other IoT devices through voice commands further underscores the centrality of the smart TV in the connected home. Imagine commanding the TV to turn on the lights, adjust the thermostat, or lock the doors – all without lifting a finger. This level of seamless integration creates a truly immersive and convenient smart home experience.

Home automation, another key aspect of the IoT, is profoundly impacted by the integration of smart TVs. Many smart TVs offer functionalities that allow them to interact with other smart home devices, such as smart lighting systems, thermostats, and security cameras. This interoperability enables advanced control and automation scenarios, further enriching the user experience. For instance, a smart TV might automatically dim the lights in the room when a movie starts, adjust the thermostat to a comfortable viewing temperature, and even display a live feed from a security camera on the screen. This coordinated control of different devices creates a more immersive and personalized entertainment experience, tailored to the user's preferences and the context of the viewing environment. Moreover, the capacity to monitor and control various aspects of the home through the smart TV centralizes control, simplifying the management of a complex smart home system. This eliminates the need to navigate multiple apps and interfaces, providing a unified and intuitive control point.

However, this increased connectivity and interoperability also raises significant concerns regarding data security and privacy. The more devices that are connected to the network, the larger the potential attack surface becomes. A vulnerability in one device could potentially compromise the security of other connected devices, creating a cascading effect that could impact the entire smart home ecosystem. Smart TVs, being central nodes in this network, become especially vulnerable. They collect substantial amounts of data on user viewing habits, preferences, and interactions with various applications. This data, if compromised, could lead to identity theft, financial fraud, or other serious security breaches. Therefore, robust security measures are crucial to protect the privacy and safety of users within the IoT landscape.

Furthermore, the proliferation of smart TVs and IoT devices raises important questions about data privacy. Manufacturers and service providers collect extensive data on user viewing habits, preferences, and interactions with their devices. This data is often used for targeted advertising, personalized recommendations, and product development. While this can lead to a more tailored user experience, it raises ethical concerns about the collection and use of personal information without informed consent. Transparency and user control over data collection practices are paramount. Users should have the right to understand what data is being collected, how it is being used, and how to limit its collection and dissemination. Stronger regulatory frameworks and industry standards are essential to address these concerns and ensure the responsible use of personal data within the smart home ecosystem.

The economic impact of the integration of smart TVs into the IoT is also profound. The growth of the smart TV market has driven significant innovation and competition within the television manufacturing industry. The increasing demand for smart TVs with advanced features and capabilities has spurred manufacturers to develop more sophisticated and feature-rich products, driving down costs and increasing accessibility. This has resulted in a diverse range of smart TVs available to consumers at varying price points, catering to different budgets and needs. Moreover, the integration of smart TVs into the IoT has created new market opportunities for manufacturers of other smart home devices, fostering growth and innovation across the entire ecosystem. The expanding network of interconnected devices creates an ecosystem where different products complement and enhance each other, driving increased consumption and demand.

The influence of smart TVs on the entertainment industry is equally significant. The shift towards streaming services and on-demand content has transformed how content is created, distributed, and consumed. The accessibility of vast libraries of movies, TV shows, and other content on smart TVs has changed viewer habits, fostering a culture of personalized entertainment consumption. This shift has also had a profound impact on content creators, challenging traditional business models and prompting the development of innovative approaches to content production and distribution. Moreover, the integration of smart TVs into the IoT opens up new opportunities for interactive and personalized entertainment experiences. The potential for immersive and engaging entertainment experiences, driven by the integration of various smart home devices, is transforming the way we interact with the entertainment medium.

However, the rapid development and widespread adoption of smart TVs and IoT devices have also raised concerns about the potential for social and cultural impacts. The increasing reliance on technology for entertainment and home management has prompted discussions about the potential for social isolation, decreased physical activity, and the erosion of traditional forms of social interaction. The constant flow of information and entertainment available through smart TVs and other connected devices can lead to information overload and reduced attention spans. The ethical considerations surrounding data privacy, algorithmic bias, and the potential for manipulation through personalized recommendations require careful attention and ongoing scrutiny. The development and implementation of responsible and ethical guidelines for the design and use of smart technologies are crucial to mitigate potential negative impacts.

In conclusion, the integration of smart TVs into the IoT represents a significant technological and societal shift. The interconnectedness of smart TVs with other home devices creates a more immersive and personalized home entertainment and automation experience, offering substantial benefits in terms of convenience, control, and entertainment options. However, this interconnectedness also introduces new challenges related to security, privacy, and ethical considerations. Addressing these challenges and developing robust security measures, transparent data practices, and ethical guidelines is crucial to harnessing the full potential of smart TVs within the IoT ecosystem while mitigating potential risks and ensuring responsible innovation. The future of television, and indeed the connected home, will be profoundly shaped by the ongoing evolution and integration of these technologies. The responsible development and deployment of these advancements will be crucial in shaping a future where technology enhances our lives without compromising our privacy, security, or well-being.

The Impact of Smart TVs on Content Consumption A Changing Viewing Experience

The advent of smart TVs has profoundly altered how we consume television content, ushering in an era of personalized viewing experiences unlike anything seen before. The shift from traditional broadcast schedules to on-demand streaming has fundamentally reshaped viewing habits, granting audiences unprecedented control over what they watch, when they watch it, and how they watch it. This transformation is driven by the seamless integration of internet connectivity, providing access to vast libraries of content through streaming services like Netflix, Hulu, Amazon Prime Video, and Disney+, among countless others. No longer are viewers tethered to rigid broadcast schedules; instead, they curate their own viewing experiences, choosing from a seemingly infinite array of options tailored to their individual preferences.

This personalized approach to content consumption is further enhanced by the sophisticated recommendation algorithms employed by many streaming platforms. These algorithms analyze viewing history, preferences, and even social media activity to suggest content that aligns with individual tastes. This personalized curation, while convenient and often effective, also raises questions about algorithmic bias, filter bubbles, and the potential for echo chambers that limit exposure to diverse viewpoints. The curated nature of these recommendations might inadvertently limit viewers' exposure to content that falls outside their established preferences, potentially narrowing their cultural horizons and hindering the exploration of new genres or perspectives. The algorithms themselves are often opaque, making it difficult for users to understand how recommendations are generated, creating a sense of unease and a lack of transparency.

Beyond the algorithmic curation of content, smart TVs also empower viewers to engage with television in ways previously unimaginable. Interactive features, such as polls, quizzes, and social media integration, enhance audience participation and foster a sense of community among viewers. These interactive elements transform the passive act of watching television into an active and engaging experience. Live sports broadcasts, for example, now often incorporate interactive elements, allowing viewers to participate in polls, share their opinions on social media, and even receive real-time updates and statistics directly on their screens. This heightened interactivity creates a more dynamic and engaging viewing experience, blurring the lines between audience and participant.

However, this personalized and interactive approach to television consumption also presents new challenges. The sheer volume of content available on streaming platforms can lead to "choice overload," a phenomenon where the abundance of options paradoxically results in decision paralysis and a feeling of dissatisfaction. Viewers may find themselves spending more time searching for something to watch than actually watching anything, leading to a frustrating and unproductive experience. This abundance of choice might ironically diminish overall satisfaction, highlighting the paradoxical nature of increased choice in a digital age.

The accessibility of on-demand content has also significantly impacted the viewing experience itself. No longer constrained by commercial breaks or predetermined broadcast schedules, viewers can now consume content at their own pace, pausing, rewinding, and fast-forwarding as they see fit. This control over the viewing experience offers flexibility and convenience, allowing viewers to tailor their consumption to their own schedules and preferences.

However, this also potentially reduces the sense of shared experience associated with traditional broadcast television. The communal experience of watching a program simultaneously with a large audience, experiencing the collective reaction to pivotal moments, is arguably diminished in the fragmented world of on-demand viewing. While social media offers some avenues for shared commentary, it still lacks the spontaneous and unified engagement of a live broadcast.

Smart TVs also significantly impact how we consume news and information. With multiple news channels and online news sources readily available at the touch of a button, viewers can easily access news from various perspectives and geographical locations. This increased accessibility is essential for informed citizenship in an increasingly globalized world. However, this abundance of information also presents challenges related to source credibility and the spread of misinformation. The ease with which unsubstantiated claims and fake news can proliferate online necessitates media literacy skills and critical evaluation of information sources. Viewers must be equipped to discern credible sources from unreliable ones to ensure they are consuming factual and accurate information. Smart TVs, while providing access to a wealth of news, also highlight the critical need for media literacy and critical thinking skills to navigate the complexities of the digital information landscape.

Furthermore, the integration of smart TV features with other smart home devices creates a holistic and immersive viewing experience. Smart lighting systems can automatically adjust the ambient lighting to complement the viewing experience, while smart sound systems enhance the audio quality, creating a more immersive cinematic environment. This seamless integration of smart TV with other smart home appliances contributes to a more personalized and controlled entertainment environment, further enhancing the viewing experience. However, this integration also introduces potential vulnerabilities in terms of data privacy and security, necessitating careful consideration of the potential risks and the implementation of robust security measures. The convenience and immersive quality of this interconnected ecosystem must be balanced with the imperative of protecting user privacy and data security.

The economic impact of smart TV's effect on content consumption is substantial. The rise of streaming services has disrupted the traditional broadcasting model, forcing networks and studios to adapt to the changing landscape. Subscription-based models have emerged as a dominant revenue stream, replacing the traditional advertising-based model of broadcast television. This has led to significant changes in the production and distribution of content, impacting budgets, creative processes, and the types of programs produced. The competition among streaming services has also increased, leading to a proliferation of high-quality content in a bid to attract and retain subscribers. This increased competition is generally viewed as beneficial for consumers, offering a wider range of content choices and potentially driving down costs in the long run.

Finally, the sociological implications of smart TV's impact on content consumption are profound. The ease of access to a vast library of content can lead to increased screen time and potential for decreased social interaction. The fragmentation of viewing habits, with each individual consuming personalized content, may lead to a decline in shared cultural experiences and a diminished sense of community. This shift away from shared viewing experiences necessitates a critical evaluation of potential negative consequences and the exploration of methods to mitigate them. The cultivation of media literacy and the promotion of mindful media consumption are vital to counteract these potential negative impacts. Encouraging opportunities for shared viewing and facilitating discussions about the content consumed are essential to preserving the social aspects of the television-watching experience in the age of personalized content. The evolution of smart TVs and their impact on content consumption present both significant opportunities and considerable challenges, necessitating careful consideration of their social, economic, and cultural implications. The ongoing evolution of this technology necessitates continuous adaptation and careful consideration of both its potential benefits and its potential drawbacks.

The Security and Privacy Concerns of Smart TVs Challenges and Solutions

The seamless integration of the internet into our television sets, while offering unprecedented convenience and entertainment options, introduces a new layer of complexity: security and privacy. Smart TVs, by their very nature, collect and transmit data, raising concerns about the potential misuse of personal information and the vulnerability of these devices to hacking and malicious attacks. Understanding these risks and implementing appropriate safeguards is crucial for enjoying the benefits of smart TV technology without compromising personal security.

One of the primary concerns revolves around data collection. Smart TVs, like many internet-connected devices, collect a substantial amount of data about their users. This data can include viewing habits – what shows are watched, how long they are watched for, and at what times – input data from voice commands and searches through smart assistants (like Amazon Alexa or Google Assistant), the use of connected apps, and even the unique identification number of the TV itself. This information, while seemingly innocuous on its own, can be aggregated to build a detailed profile of a user's viewing preferences, interests, and even lifestyle. The potential for this data to be used for targeted advertising is obvious, and the lack of transparency surrounding how this data is collected, used, and protected raises legitimate concerns.

Many smart TV manufacturers have privacy policies outlining their data collection practices. However, these policies are often lengthy, complex, and difficult for the average user to understand fully. The sheer volume of information and legal jargon can make it challenging to grasp the extent of data collection and the potential implications for user privacy. Moreover, these policies may not always reflect the actual practices of the manufacturers, leaving users vulnerable to data collection beyond what is explicitly stated. The issue is further complicated by the fact that many users simply accept the default settings of their smart TVs without reviewing or understanding the privacy implications. This lack of informed consent significantly contributes to the vulnerability of users' personal data.

Beyond the issue of data collection itself, there is the significant concern of data security. Smart TVs, being connected devices, are susceptible to hacking and malware attacks. If a smart TV is compromised, hackers could potentially access personal data stored on the device, including viewing history, login credentials for other accounts, and potentially even information from other connected devices on the home network. This vulnerability extends beyond the device itself; a compromised smart TV could serve as an entry point for hackers to access other parts of the home network, potentially compromising other smart devices and personal computers.

The vulnerability of smart TVs is exacerbated by the fact that many users fail to update the software on their devices. Software updates frequently include security patches that address known vulnerabilities and improve the overall security of the device. However, many users either fail to update their TVs regularly or are unaware of the importance of these updates. This negligence significantly increases the risk of security breaches and compromises. Manufacturers, in turn, often struggle to incentivize users to perform these updates, resulting in a persistent security risk for a large number of smart TVs in use.

Another factor contributing to the security vulnerabilities of smart TVs is the use of third-party applications. Many smart TVs offer access to various apps, including streaming services, games, and other entertainment options. However, not all these apps adhere to the same security standards, and some may contain malware or vulnerabilities that can compromise the security of the smart TV. Users should exercise caution when installing apps on their smart TVs, making sure to only download apps from reputable sources and avoiding those that seem suspicious or have poor reviews.

The use of voice assistants integrated into smart TVs also raises privacy concerns. While voice assistants offer convenience and hands-free control, they constantly listen for voice commands, collecting audio data that could contain sensitive information. While manufacturers typically state that voice data is anonymized, the possibility of this data being used for other purposes remains a concern, especially considering the potential for unintended activation or accidental recording of conversations. Users need to understand how their voice data is handled and be aware of the privacy implications of using these features.

Solutions to address these security and privacy concerns are multifaceted. Firstly, users must be proactive in understanding their smart TV's privacy settings and adjusting them accordingly. This involves carefully reviewing the privacy policy, disabling unnecessary data collection features, and opting out of data sharing wherever possible. Updating the smart TV's software regularly is also crucial, ensuring that any known vulnerabilities are patched.

Secondly, manufacturers need to take responsibility for improving the security and privacy of their smart TVs. This involves implementing stronger security protocols, encrypting data transmissions, and regularly conducting security audits. Greater transparency regarding data collection practices is also needed, with clear and concise privacy policies that are easy for users to understand. Moreover, manufacturers should provide users with more control over data collection and sharing, empowering them to make informed choices about their privacy.

Thirdly, governments and regulatory bodies have a role to play in establishing clear standards and regulations for the security and privacy of smart TVs. This could involve mandating minimum security standards for manufacturers, requiring transparency in data collection practices, and providing consumers with redress mechanisms in case of data breaches. Furthermore, initiatives to educate consumers about the security and privacy risks associated with smart TVs are necessary to empower them to make informed choices and protect their personal data.

Finally, the development and implementation of robust security solutions for smart TVs are crucial. This includes advancements in encryption technology, improved intrusion detection systems, and the development of secure software development practices to mitigate vulnerabilities from the outset. Furthermore, research into privacy-preserving technologies, such as differential privacy and federated learning, can help to enable the benefits of data collection without compromising user privacy. Continuous innovation in security technology is paramount to keeping pace with the evolving threats in the connected environment of smart TVs.

In conclusion, the security and privacy concerns surrounding smart TVs are significant and require a multi-pronged approach. Users, manufacturers, governments, and researchers all have a responsibility to address these issues and ensure that the benefits of smart TV technology can be enjoyed without compromising personal security and privacy. By implementing robust security measures, promoting transparency, and educating users about the potential risks, we can work towards a safer and more privacy-respecting ecosystem for smart TVs and the broader Internet of Things. The future of smart television hinges on addressing these concerns effectively, ensuring that this technology remains a valuable and secure component of our digital lives.

The Future of Smart TVs and the IoT Integration and Innovation

The convergence of smart TVs and the Internet of Things (IoT) represents a significant technological leap, promising a future where our home entertainment systems are seamlessly integrated with a vast network of interconnected devices. This integration offers a tantalizing array of possibilities, from personalized content recommendations tailored to individual viewing habits and smart home automation triggered by television viewing patterns to proactive troubleshooting and enhanced accessibility features. However, realizing this potential requires overcoming significant technological, security, and user experience hurdles.

One key area for future development lies in enhancing the personalization and intelligence of smart TVs. Current smart TV platforms already offer personalized recommendations based on viewing history, but future iterations could leverage more sophisticated AI algorithms to offer even more nuanced and accurate suggestions. These algorithms could analyze not just viewing history, but also metadata associated with content, such as genre, actors, directors, and even viewer sentiment expressed on social media platforms. This granular level of analysis could lead to a more refined understanding of individual preferences and allow for the development of hyper-personalized content recommendations that are far more effective than current offerings. This level of personalization could extend beyond simple program recommendations to encompass curated content playlists, customized user interfaces, and even the ability to automatically adjust settings such as picture quality and sound based on individual preferences and the environment.

Furthermore, advancements in AI could dramatically improve the accessibility of smart TVs for users with disabilities. AI-powered voice assistants are already making strides in providing voice control and captioning features, but future developments could include advanced real-time translation capabilities, personalized audio descriptions for visually impaired users, and sophisticated gesture recognition for users with limited motor skills. These advancements have the potential to make smart TVs a truly inclusive medium, accessible to a wider audience than ever before.

The integration of smart TVs with other IoT devices offers a wealth of opportunities for creating a more seamless and intuitive home entertainment experience. Imagine a future where your smart TV automatically dims the lights, adjusts the thermostat, and even shuts off other devices when you begin watching a movie, creating the perfect ambient atmosphere for viewing. Or envision a system where your smart TV can seamlessly integrate with your smart speakers to provide a multi-room audio experience or with your smart home security system to trigger alerts based on specific viewing activities. These are just a few examples of how the integration of smart TVs with the IoT can enhance the overall user experience.

However, realizing this vision requires overcoming significant challenges. One of the primary hurdles is interoperability.

Currently, there is a lack of standardization across different IoT platforms and protocols, making it difficult for smart TVs to communicate effectively with other devices. Developing universal standards and protocols is crucial to ensuring seamless integration and avoiding the fragmentation that could hinder the widespread adoption of these technologies. This includes developing more robust and secure communication protocols that can handle the increased data traffic generated by a large number of interconnected devices.

Another significant challenge is data security and privacy. As smart TVs become more integrated with the IoT, the amount of data they collect and transmit increases exponentially, raising concerns about the potential misuse of personal information and the vulnerability of these devices to hacking and malicious attacks. The issue of data security extends beyond the device itself. A compromised smart TV could serve as a gateway for attackers to access other devices on the home network, compromising personal computers and other smart home appliances. Addressing these concerns requires a multi-pronged approach, including the development of more robust security protocols, enhanced encryption techniques, and greater transparency regarding data collection practices. Users need to be more involved in understanding their data privacy and security settings and to maintain updated software on their devices.

The user experience is another critical aspect to consider. As the number of features and functionalities of smart TVs increases, ensuring a seamless and intuitive user interface becomes increasingly challenging. Overly complex interfaces with too many options can overwhelm users, leading to frustration and dissatisfaction. Future smart TV designs must prioritize simplicity and ease of use, making it easy for users to navigate the various functionalities and access the content they want without unnecessary complexity. The intuitive design of the interface must also be sensitive to the evolving user preferences. This will require robust user testing and feedback mechanisms to ensure that the design remains user-friendly.

Further technological advancements will undoubtedly drive the future of smart TVs. Higher resolutions, such as 8K and beyond, will offer an even more immersive viewing experience, while improvements in display technology, such as OLED and MicroLED, will lead to enhanced picture quality and better energy efficiency. Advances in audio technology, including the adoption of immersive sound formats like Dolby Atmos, will further enhance the overall sensory experience. The development of more sophisticated AI-powered features will continue to improve personalization, accessibility, and convenience.

Moreover, the advent of new display technologies like microLED could revolutionize the viewing experience, offering higher contrast ratios, wider color gamuts, and improved brightness compared to current OLED displays. These advancements will lead to a more vivid, realistic, and immersive viewing experience. Furthermore, the use of AI-powered upscaling algorithms could improve the quality of lower-resolution content, making it appear sharper and more detailed on high-resolution displays.

Looking ahead, the integration of smart TVs with augmented and virtual reality technologies presents exciting possibilities. Imagine a future where you can interact with your favorite TV shows in a more immersive way, or use your smart TV as a portal to explore virtual worlds. However, the seamless integration of these technologies presents significant technological challenges, such as overcoming latency issues and ensuring compatibility across different devices and platforms. The processing power of the smart TV devices will need to improve to handle the high data requirements of VR and AR applications.

Despite the significant advancements in technology, the ethical implications of the ever-increasing data collection and the potential for misuse of that data remain a significant concern. It's crucial that manufacturers, developers, and regulators work together to establish clear guidelines and regulations that protect user privacy and security. Transparency and user control over data collection and sharing are paramount in building trust and ensuring responsible innovation. This includes creating privacy policies that are easily understandable and providing users with clear choices regarding data sharing.

In conclusion, the future of smart TVs and the IoT is bright, promising a more personalized, immersive, and integrated home entertainment experience. However, realizing this potential requires overcoming significant challenges in terms of interoperability, security, privacy, and user experience. By focusing on these key areas, developers and manufacturers can unlock the full potential of smart TVs and the IoT, creating a truly transformative experience for consumers. The key lies in a collaborative effort between manufacturers, developers, and regulators to ensure a future where technological innovation and ethical considerations are closely intertwined. Only then can we fully harness the power of smart TV technology to enhance our lives without compromising our privacy and security.

AIPowered Recommendations Personalized Content Experiences

The evolution of television viewing habits has been dramatically reshaped by the advent of personalized content recommendations, a development largely driven by the power of artificial intelligence.

No longer are viewers passively subjected to a pre-determined broadcast schedule; instead, AI algorithms curate content tailored to individual preferences, creating a deeply personalized viewing experience. This shift represents a fundamental change in the relationship between viewer and content, moving away from a one-to-many broadcast model towards a more individualized, one-to-one interaction.

This personalization is achieved through sophisticated algorithms that analyze vast amounts of data. This data includes viewing history, which provides a clear record of the types of programs a viewer enjoys. For example, if a viewer consistently watches crime dramas, the algorithm will prioritize suggesting similar shows, potentially identifying lesser-known titles within the same genre.

Going beyond simple genre classification, these algorithms also analyze metadata, which includes details such as actors, directors, writers, and even specific themes or plot points within a program. A viewer who enjoys the work of a particular director might be presented with a list of their other films, even if they fall outside the viewer's usual genre preferences. This nuanced approach allows for a deeper understanding of individual tastes, moving beyond superficial categorization.

Furthermore, the analysis extends beyond the viewer's direct engagement with content. AI algorithms can incorporate data from social media platforms, analyzing viewer comments, reviews, and ratings to gauge audience sentiment toward specific shows. A positive response to a particular actor or storyline, expressed across various social media channels, could significantly boost that show's prominence in the viewer's recommendation feed. Conversely, negative feedback, even if only a small fraction of the overall response, can be factored in to avoid recommending potentially disliked content. This sophisticated data aggregation provides a more complete and nuanced picture of the viewer's preferences.

The impact of these AI-powered recommendation systems extends beyond simply suggesting new programs. They play a significant role in shaping the overall user experience. By tailoring the content presented, these systems increase viewer engagement and satisfaction, keeping viewers invested in the platform. This is particularly crucial in the current streaming landscape, where viewers are presented with an overwhelming amount of choices. AI helps to navigate this deluge, presenting viewers with a manageable selection of relevant and engaging content, effectively maximizing their enjoyment and retention on the platform. The result is a more efficient and satisfying viewing experience, fostering greater user loyalty.

However, the implementation of these AI-powered recommendation systems is not without its challenges. One major consideration is the potential for filter bubbles and echo chambers. By constantly prioritizing content that aligns with a viewer's existing preferences, these algorithms can limit exposure to diverse perspectives and viewpoints. This can lead to a skewed understanding of the world, reinforcing existing biases and potentially isolating viewers within a narrow ideological or cultural bubble. Mitigating this risk requires careful algorithm design, incorporating features that introduce viewers to diverse content and actively challenge their existing preferences.

Another significant concern is the issue of data privacy. The vast amount of data collected to power these recommendation systems raises legitimate concerns about the potential for misuse and the ethical implications of data handling. Transparency and user control are paramount. Viewers need to have clear understanding of what data is being collected, how it is being used, and the ability to control the extent of data collection. This requires not only robust privacy policies but also user-friendly interfaces that make it easy for viewers to understand and manage their data preferences.

The development of AI-powered recommendation systems is an ongoing process, with constant improvements and refinements being made. One area of active research is the development of more sophisticated algorithms that can anticipate viewer preferences more accurately. This includes exploring techniques such as natural language processing to better understand the nuances of viewer feedback, and machine learning to identify patterns and correlations that would be difficult for human analysts to spot.

Furthermore, research is ongoing into creating more ethical algorithms that mitigate biases and promote diverse content recommendations, thereby combating the formation of echo chambers.

Beyond individual viewers, AI-powered recommendation systems also impact the television industry as a whole. These systems provide valuable data for content creators, providing insights into viewer preferences that can inform the production of new programs and potentially shape future trends. Understanding viewer demand allows broadcasters and production companies to allocate resources more efficiently, focusing on content that is more likely to resonate with the audience and be commercially successful. This data-driven approach leads to a more efficient and effective use of resources in the content creation and distribution process.

Moreover, AI can automate various aspects of the television production pipeline. This includes tasks such as content tagging and metadata generation, which are currently labor-intensive processes. Automation allows for a more streamlined workflow, reducing production costs and accelerating the delivery of content to viewers.

AI also plays a crucial role in content discovery and distribution, helping to ensure that programs reach their intended audience efficiently.

Looking ahead, the integration of AI in television will likely become even more pervasive. We can expect to see even more sophisticated recommendation systems that provide more personalized and insightful content suggestions. The integration of other technologies, such as virtual and augmented reality, will further enhance the viewing experience, creating new opportunities for engagement and interaction. The ongoing evolution of AI promises to continue to transform the way we consume television content, leading to new and innovative ways of interacting with this fundamental medium.

Ultimately, the impact of AI-powered recommendations on television is multifaceted and far-reaching. While offering significant benefits in terms of personalized viewing experiences and efficient content creation, it also raises important ethical and privacy considerations. Navigating these challenges will require a collaborative effort between technology developers, content creators, policymakers, and viewers themselves, ensuring a future where technological advancements are aligned with the interests and well-being of both individuals and society as a whole. Only through careful consideration of these ethical implications can we fully harness the potential of AI to enhance the television viewing experience for all. The future of television is not just about the technology itself; it's about the responsible use of that technology to serve the needs of its viewers.

AI in Content Creation Automation and Enhanced Production

The transformative potential of AI extends beyond personalized recommendations; it is profoundly reshaping the very process of television content creation. The industry is witnessing a surge in AI-powered tools designed to automate and enhance various stages of production, from initial script development to final post-production polishing. This technological shift promises to increase efficiency, reduce costs, and potentially unlock new creative avenues, although it also raises important questions about the role of human creativity and the potential for bias in AI-generated content.

One of the most significant impacts of AI is in scriptwriting. While AI cannot yet replace the imaginative spark and nuanced understanding of human writers, it can assist in several crucial aspects of the process. AI tools can analyze existing scripts, identifying successful narrative structures, character archetypes, and dialogue patterns. This data can inform the writing process, suggesting plot points, character developments, or dialogue options that have historically proven effective with audiences. This isn't about replacing human writers; instead, it's about providing them with powerful analytical tools to refine their work and explore new creative possibilities. Imagine a screenwriter struggling with a particular plot point; AI could analyze thousands of scripts to suggest alternative resolutions, drawing upon a vast database of narrative techniques. This can significantly accelerate the writing process and potentially lead to more compelling and engaging narratives.

Furthermore, AI is making significant inroads in the editing process. Automated editing tools can analyze footage, identifying scenes that are too long, poorly paced, or lacking visual interest. They can also flag continuity errors or inconsistencies in sound design, allowing editors to focus their attention on more complex creative decisions. These AI-powered assistants don't replace the artistic judgment of a human editor; rather, they streamline the workflow, freeing up valuable time for more nuanced creative tasks. Think of the time saved in identifying jump cuts or audio glitches—tasks that are often tedious and time-consuming for human editors. This automation allows for faster turnaround times and increased productivity, which can be particularly beneficial in the fast-paced world of television production.

The impact of AI extends beyond scripting and editing; it also plays a crucial role in post-production. AI-powered tools can enhance audio and video quality, automatically correcting imperfections and enhancing visual effects. For instance, AI can automatically upscaling lower-resolution footage to higher resolutions, improving the overall visual appeal of older programs or content filmed with less advanced equipment. AI can also automate color grading, ensuring consistent visual tone and style across the entire production. These capabilities can save significant time and resources, allowing post-production teams to focus on the more creative aspects of their work. Consider the complexities of color correction in a large-scale television production. Manually adjusting the color balance for hundreds of hours of footage is a daunting task, prone to inconsistencies. AI can automate this process, ensuring a consistent and visually appealing final product.

However, the integration of AI in content creation is not without its challenges. One major concern is the potential for bias. AI algorithms are trained on existing data, and if this data reflects societal biases, the AI-generated content may perpetuate and even amplify these biases. For example, if an AI is trained on scripts that predominantly feature male characters in leading roles, it may be more likely to generate scripts that also feature predominantly male characters. Addressing this issue requires careful attention to the datasets used to train AI models, ensuring that they are diverse and representative of the broader population. This necessitates a critical examination of the data itself, a proactive effort to mitigate bias, and ongoing monitoring of the output to ensure fairness and inclusivity. The development of AI tools for content creation must prioritize ethical considerations and actively work towards mitigating potential biases.

Another critical aspect is the potential impact on human employment. As AI takes over some aspects of content creation, there is a legitimate concern about the displacement of human workers. However, it's important to recognize that AI is more likely to augment human creativity rather than replace it entirely. The role of human writers, editors, and post-production professionals will likely evolve, shifting towards more creative and strategic tasks, while AI handles the more repetitive and technical aspects of the process. This transition necessitates proactive retraining and upskilling programs to equip the workforce with the skills needed to thrive in this evolving landscape. The focus should be on collaboration between humans and AI, leveraging the strengths of both to create higher quality content more efficiently.

Moreover, the creative potential of AI in content creation remains largely untapped. While current applications focus primarily on automating existing processes, there is a potential for AI to inspire new forms of storytelling and creative expression. AI could generate entirely new narrative structures, develop unique character archetypes, or even compose original music scores. Exploring these possibilities requires a shift in mindset, moving beyond the current focus on automation towards a more collaborative and experimental approach. The creative potential of AI is not limited to simply replicating existing forms of storytelling; it offers the possibility of entirely new forms of narrative and artistic expression. This requires a willingness to experiment and embrace the unknown, exploring the intersection of human creativity and artificial intelligence.

The ethical considerations extend beyond bias and employment. Questions about ownership and copyright of AI-generated content are still being debated. If an AI generates a script or a musical score, who owns the copyright? Is it the developer of the AI, the user who prompted the AI, or the AI itself? These legal and ethical questions require careful consideration and a thoughtful approach to intellectual property rights in this rapidly evolving field. The legal framework surrounding AI-generated content is still in its infancy, and clear guidelines are needed to protect the rights of all stakeholders.

The future of AI in television content creation is undeniably bright, but it is crucial to approach this technological revolution with both enthusiasm and caution. By prioritizing ethical considerations, investing in retraining initiatives, and fostering a collaborative approach between humans and AI, the television industry can harness the transformative power of artificial intelligence to create more efficient, creative, and inclusive content for audiences worldwide. The challenge lies in navigating the complexities of this rapidly changing landscape, ensuring that the integration of AI benefits both the industry and its viewers, fostering a future where technology enhances, rather than diminishes, the human creative spirit. The success of this integration will depend on careful consideration of ethical implications, proactive planning for workforce adaptation, and a commitment to leveraging AI as a tool to amplify, not replace, human creativity.

AIDriven Interactive Features Enhancing Viewer Engagement

The integration of artificial intelligence (AI) is not merely automating tasks within television production; it's fundamentally altering the viewer experience. We've explored AI's role in streamlining content creation, but its impact on viewer engagement through interactive features is equally transformative. This represents a paradigm shift, moving beyond the passive consumption of pre-programmed content towards a more dynamic, personalized, and participatory viewing experience. AI is the engine driving this transformation, enabling a level of interactivity previously unimaginable.

One of the most visible impacts is the rise of AI-powered voice assistants integrated into smart TVs. These assistants, powered by natural language processing (NLP) and machine learning (ML), allow viewers to control their television sets using voice commands. This simple yet profound change enhances accessibility, especially for viewers with disabilities. Commands like "Play the latest episode of [show name]" or "Turn on the subtitles" eliminate the need for complex remote controls, creating a more intuitive and user- friendly experience. Moreover, voice assistants are becoming increasingly sophisticated, understanding nuanced requests and responding in more natural and human-like ways. This goes beyond simple commands; it opens up possibilities for interactive storytelling and personalized recommendations. Imagine asking, "What's a similar show to this one?" and receiving recommendations based not only on genre but also on your past viewing habits and preferences, learned through AI's analysis of your viewing data.

Beyond basic control, AI is enriching interactive television with personalized game experiences. We are moving beyond static advertisements and into a realm of dynamic, interactive engagement. Imagine a scenario where a viewer is watching a sports game and can, via voice command or a dedicated app, participate in a real-time prediction game against other viewers, winning prizes or virtual rewards based on their accuracy. The AI engine powering this system analyzes the game in real-time, adjusting the odds and difficulty levels based on viewers' performance and the unfolding events. This transforms passive viewing into an active, competitive experience, fostering a deeper connection with the content and creating a sense of community among viewers. Similarly, AI can personalize educational programs, adapting the pace and complexity of the content to the individual viewer's learning style and comprehension level. Quizzes and interactive exercises can be tailored in real-time, providing immediate feedback and adjusting the curriculum to optimize the learning experience.

Another exciting development is the use of AI to create personalized content recommendations. While recommender systems are not entirely new, AI-powered systems are significantly more sophisticated, employing advanced algorithms that analyze viewing habits, preferences, and even emotional responses to tailor recommendations with impressive accuracy. This means viewers are less likely to encounter irrelevant or uninteresting content, increasing their overall satisfaction and engagement. This goes beyond simple genre classifications; AI can analyze the nuances of a viewer's tastes, recommending shows based on specific actors, directors, themes, or even subtle stylistic elements they favor. Imagine an AI system analyzing not just what you watched but *how* you reacted to it – detecting moments of laughter, suspense, or boredom through subtle changes in viewing patterns. This level of granularity allows for extremely personalized content recommendations, fostering a deeper connection between viewer and content.

Moreover, AI is enabling the creation of truly interactive narratives. Imagine watching a crime drama where the viewer, through their smart TV or a companion app, can influence the storyline by making critical decisions on behalf of the protagonist. The AI engine seamlessly integrates the viewer's choices into the narrative, creating a unique and personalized experience each time the show is watched. This could transform episodic viewing into a series of branching storylines, where each viewer's journey through the story is distinct and their choices have meaningful consequences. This is not just enhancing passive consumption; it's forging a new collaborative relationship between viewers and content creators.

However, this increased interactivity brings its own set of challenges. Privacy concerns are paramount. AI systems that analyze viewers' preferences and emotional responses collect substantial amounts of personal data. The ethical implications of collecting and utilizing this data need careful consideration, with robust mechanisms in place to protect viewer privacy and ensure compliance with data protection regulations. Transparency is key; viewers need to understand what data is being collected, how it's being used, and have the option to control their data sharing preferences.

The potential for bias in AI-powered recommendation systems is another critical consideration. If the algorithms are trained on biased data, they may perpetuate and even amplify existing societal biases, leading to unfair or discriminatory outcomes. For example, a system trained predominantly on data from a specific demographic might recommend similar content disproportionately to viewers from that group, excluding other demographics from a wider range of content. Addressing this requires careful curation of training datasets, ensuring they are diverse and representative, and ongoing monitoring of the algorithms for any signs of bias.

Furthermore, the increasing complexity of interactive features poses challenges for accessibility. While AI-powered voice assistants enhance accessibility for some, the sophisticated interactive narratives and personalized game experiences can inadvertently create new barriers for viewers with disabilities. The design of these features needs to be inclusive, ensuring that they are accessible to all viewers regardless of their abilities. This includes considering alternative input methods, providing clear and concise instructions, and offering adjustable difficulty levels.

The cost of developing and maintaining AI-powered interactive features is another factor. Creating sophisticated AI algorithms, integrating them into television platforms, and ensuring their ongoing performance requires significant financial investment. This raises concerns about affordability and accessibility for both broadcasters and viewers, particularly in regions with limited resources. There needs to be a careful balance between innovation and affordability, ensuring that these technologies are accessible to a broad audience.

Finally, the technological infrastructure needs to support these advancements. AI-powered interactive features require significant bandwidth and processing power, which could pose challenges in regions with limited internet access or older television infrastructure. The rollout of these features needs to be carefully planned and phased, taking into account the technological capabilities of various regions and ensuring a smooth and equitable transition.

The future of television is inextricably linked to the continued development and implementation of AI-powered interactive features. This technology is not merely enhancing the viewing experience; it's fundamentally reshaping it, creating a more dynamic, personalized, and participatory form of entertainment and information dissemination. However, realizing this future requires careful navigation of the ethical, accessibility, and infrastructure challenges. A collaborative effort between technologists, broadcasters, regulators, and viewers is crucial to ensure that AI is used responsibly and equitably to create a truly engaging and inclusive television experience for all. The journey towards this future is one of continuous innovation, adaptation, and careful consideration of the implications of this powerful technology. The success of this transition hinges on prioritizing user experience, addressing ethical concerns, and ensuring inclusivity throughout the process.

Ethical Considerations of AI in Television Bias Privacy and Transparency

The integration of AI into television, while promising a more personalized and engaging viewing experience, necessitates a careful examination of its ethical implications. The power of AI to analyze viewing habits, predict preferences, and even infer emotional responses raises significant concerns about privacy, bias, and transparency. The sheer volume of data collected by AI- powered recommendation systems and interactive features presents a considerable challenge to data protection regulations. Viewers are often unaware of the extent of data collection, the specific data points being tracked, and how this data is being used to shape their viewing experience. This lack of transparency undermines trust and raises justifiable concerns about potential misuse of personal information. Therefore, establishing clear and transparent data policies, readily accessible to viewers, is crucial. These policies must detail what data is collected, why it's collected, how it's used, and what security measures are in place to protect it. Moreover, viewers must be given explicit control over their data, with the ability to opt out of data collection or request deletion of their data. This requires the development of user-friendly interfaces and easily accessible mechanisms for managing data privacy settings. The implementation of robust data anonymization and encryption techniques is also paramount to minimizing the risk of data breaches and unauthorized access.

Furthermore, the algorithms driving AI-powered systems are not immune to bias. If the training data reflects existing societal biases, the resulting AI system will inevitably perpetuate and even amplify these biases in its recommendations and interactions. For example, an AI-powered recommendation system trained primarily on data from a specific demographic might overwhelmingly recommend content that aligns with the preferences of that group, effectively excluding other demographics from a wider range of viewing choices. This can lead to the reinforcement of stereotypes and the marginalization of underrepresented groups. To mitigate this risk, significant effort must be invested in creating diverse and representative training datasets. This involves careful selection of data sources, ensuring a balanced representation of different demographics, viewpoints, and cultural backgrounds. Moreover, ongoing monitoring and auditing of the algorithms are essential to detect and address any signs of bias that might emerge over time. Independent audits by external experts can provide an objective assessment of the fairness and equity of AI-powered systems, ensuring that they are not perpetuating harmful biases.

Transparency in algorithmic design and decision-making processes is also key to fostering accountability and building public trust.

The issue of algorithmic transparency is multifaceted. While some argue for complete transparency in the algorithms themselves, making them fully open-source, this approach faces practical challenges. Complex algorithms can be difficult to understand even for experts, making full transparency difficult to achieve and potentially exposing the system to manipulation. A more pragmatic approach involves providing users with explanations of how the algorithms arrive at their recommendations, highlighting the key factors and data points influencing their decisions. This can be achieved through easily understandable summaries and visual representations of the decision-making process, allowing users to understand the rationale behind the recommendations and identify any potential biases. This level of transparency empowers users to make informed decisions about the content they consume and participate more actively in shaping the algorithms' behavior through feedback mechanisms.

Another critical ethical consideration is the potential for AI to manipulate viewers' emotions and behavior. AI-powered systems can analyze viewers' emotional responses in real-time, adjusting content delivery to maximize engagement and influence their choices. This capability raises concerns about the potential for manipulative advertising techniques and the erosion of viewers' autonomy. The use of AI to personalize advertising, while effective in targeting specific demographics, raises concerns about the potential for creating echo chambers and reinforcing existing biases. The use of subliminal messaging or manipulative emotional cues in advertising, facilitated by AI, raises significant ethical questions. The development of ethical guidelines and regulations is crucial to prevent the misuse of AI for manipulative purposes, ensuring that viewers are not subjected to unethical or coercive practices. This requires a collaborative effort between technologists, regulators, and ethicists to establish clear standards for responsible AI use in advertising and content creation.

The accessibility of AI-powered interactive features also demands careful consideration. While AI can enhance accessibility for some viewers, such as those with disabilities, the complexity of interactive features can inadvertently create new barriers for others. The design of these features needs to prioritize inclusivity, ensuring they are usable and enjoyable by viewers of all abilities. This includes offering alternative input methods, providing clear and concise instructions, and offering adjustable difficulty levels.

Furthermore, the cost of accessing and utilizing these features needs to be considered, ensuring equitable access for viewers from all socioeconomic backgrounds. The development of cost-effective solutions and the promotion of affordable access to these technologies are crucial to prevent the creation of a digital divide that excludes certain segments of the population from the benefits of AI-powered television experiences.

The responsible development and implementation of AI in television necessitates a multi-stakeholder approach. Collaboration between technologists, broadcasters, regulators, and viewers is crucial to ensure that AI is used ethically and responsibly. This includes establishing clear ethical guidelines, implementing robust data protection measures, and promoting transparency in algorithmic design and decision-making processes. Open dialogue and public engagement are vital to building trust and ensuring that the benefits of AI are shared equitably across the population.

Regulators must play a key role in developing and enforcing appropriate regulations, ensuring that AI-powered systems are held accountable and comply with ethical standards. Industry self-regulation, while important, cannot fully address the complex ethical challenges posed by AI, necessitating the involvement of independent oversight bodies and regulatory frameworks.

In conclusion, the ethical considerations surrounding the use of AI in television are complex and multifaceted, requiring careful attention from all stakeholders. Balancing the promise of personalized and engaging viewing experiences with the potential risks to privacy, fairness, and autonomy demands a proactive and collaborative approach. The development of robust ethical guidelines, transparent data practices, and inclusive design principles is crucial to ensure that AI is used responsibly and equitably in the television industry, creating a more enriching and accessible viewing experience for all. The ongoing dialogue between technologists, policymakers, and the public is essential to navigate the challenges and realize the full potential of AI in this rapidly evolving media landscape. The future of television, deeply intertwined with the advancement of AI, rests on our ability to address these ethical concerns proactively and responsibly.

The Future Role of AI in Television Predictions and Challenges

The integration of AI into television is still in its nascent stages, yet its potential to revolutionize the industry is undeniable. Looking ahead, we can anticipate several key developments, each presenting both exciting opportunities and significant challenges. One of the most transformative areas will be in content creation. AI-powered tools are already being used to assist with scriptwriting, editing, and even the generation of entirely new storylines. While concerns exist about the potential displacement of human creatives, the reality is likely to be more nuanced. AI is more likely to act as a powerful collaborative tool, augmenting human creativity rather than replacing it entirely. Imagine AI assisting screenwriters by generating plot options, suggesting dialogue, or even creating initial drafts based on specified parameters. This could significantly speed up the production process and allow for exploration of more diverse and innovative storylines. For example, AI could analyze vast datasets of existing television scripts to identify successful narrative structures and tropes, providing insights that could enhance the storytelling process. However, the reliance on AI in creative writing also raises concerns about originality and the potential homogenization of narratives. Safeguarding against algorithmic biases in content generation will also be paramount, ensuring diverse and representative portrayals in television shows. The development of robust ethical guidelines for AI-assisted content creation will be crucial to mitigate these risks.

Beyond creative writing, AI is poised to play a major role in production. AI-powered tools can optimize camera angles, lighting, and sound mixing, resulting in higher-quality productions with potentially reduced costs. Imagine AI analyzing a director's visual style to automatically adjust camera movements and lighting during filming, offering real-time feedback and suggesting improvements.

This could greatly enhance the efficiency and effectiveness of the production process. Furthermore, AI can improve the process of post-production editing, automatically detecting errors, cleaning up audio, and even suggesting optimal cuts and transitions. This would allow editors to focus on the more creative aspects of their work, leading to higher-quality final products. Yet, this also raises concerns about the potential for job displacement among editors and other production staff. The industry needs to adapt and retrain its workforce to leverage AI's capabilities alongside human expertise to ensure a smooth transition.

The distribution of television content will also undergo a significant transformation through AI. AI-powered recommendation systems are already widely used by streaming platforms, but future iterations will become even more sophisticated and personalized.

They will go beyond simply recommending shows based on past viewing habits; they will anticipate viewers' preferences based on a range of factors, including contextual information, mood, and even real-time emotional responses. This will lead to a highly tailored viewing experience, where each viewer receives a unique stream of content perfectly aligned with their individual preferences. This raises privacy concerns, however, as these systems will collect vast quantities of personal data, requiring robust data protection measures to safeguard user privacy. Transparency in how these systems operate will also be critical, empowering viewers to understand the rationale behind recommendations and control the data collected.

Beyond recommendations, AI will also revolutionize the way television content is delivered. Adaptive bitrate streaming, powered by AI, will ensure seamless and high-quality playback regardless of network conditions. AI will dynamically adjust the video and audio quality to optimize for the viewer's network bandwidth, preventing buffering and ensuring a smooth viewing experience. Furthermore, AI can optimize content delivery networks, routing content efficiently to reduce latency and improve overall streaming performance. The challenge here will be ensuring equitable access to high-speed internet for all viewers, preventing a digital divide where some segments of the population are excluded from the benefits of AI-powered streaming. Investment in infrastructure and initiatives to bridge the digital divide will be crucial to ensure inclusive access to this technology.

The consumption of television will also be dramatically altered by AI. Interactive television experiences, powered by AI, will allow viewers to actively participate in the narrative, influencing the plot and characters in real time. Imagine viewers voting on plot choices, influencing the direction of a story or even choosing their own personalized endings. AI-powered chatbots could provide interactive companions during viewing, answering questions, providing context, and even engaging in dialogue related to the content. This would create immersive and engaging viewing experiences that go beyond passive consumption. This also raises accessibility concerns. Interactive features need to be designed inclusively, considering the needs of viewers with disabilities to ensure that all viewers can enjoy the enhanced engagement.

However, the increasing sophistication of AI in television also presents a number of challenges. The potential for algorithmic bias is a significant concern. AI systems are only as good as the data they are trained on, and if this data reflects existing societal biases, the resulting AI systems will inevitably perpetuate and even amplify those biases. This could lead to biased content recommendations, perpetuating stereotypes and marginalizing underrepresented groups. Careful attention must be paid to the design of AI systems to ensure fairness and mitigate the risk of bias. This involves the careful selection of training data, ensuring diverse representation, and continuous monitoring and auditing of algorithms to detect and address potential biases. The development of standardized methodologies for assessing algorithmic fairness will be crucial to ensuring accountability.

Another critical challenge is the potential misuse of AI for manipulative purposes. AI systems can be used to analyze viewer emotions and behavior in real time, tailoring content and advertising to maximize engagement and influence viewer choices.

This raises serious ethical concerns about the potential for manipulation and the erosion of viewer autonomy. The development of robust ethical guidelines and regulations will be crucial to prevent the misuse of AI for manipulative purposes. This includes setting clear standards for transparency in data collection and use, as well as guidelines for responsible content creation and advertising.

Finally, the integration of AI into television raises crucial questions about privacy and data security. AI-powered systems collect vast quantities of personal data about viewers' viewing habits, preferences, and emotional responses. Protecting this data from unauthorized access and misuse is critical. Robust data security measures, including encryption and anonymization techniques, will be essential. Furthermore, transparent data policies that clearly articulate what data is collected, how it is used, and what security measures are in place are crucial to building trust with viewers. Giving viewers explicit control over their data, allowing them to opt out of data collection or request data deletion, is equally important.

In conclusion, the future of AI in television is full of both immense promise and significant challenges. The potential to create more personalized, engaging, and accessible television experiences is undeniable, but careful consideration must be given to the ethical implications. Addressing concerns about bias, manipulation, privacy, and accessibility will be crucial to ensuring that AI is used responsibly and equitably in the television industry. A collaborative effort involving technologists, broadcasters, regulators, and viewers is essential to navigate these challenges and harness the transformative power of AI to create a more enriching and inclusive television landscape for all. The future of television, deeply intertwined with the advancement of AI, hinges on our ability to address these concerns proactively and responsibly, ensuring that technology serves humanity rather than the other way around.

The Integration of Social Media into the Television Experience

The rise of social media has fundamentally altered how we consume and interact with television. No longer is the viewing experience confined to the living room; it's now a shared, multi-platform event unfolding across screens and social networks. Viewers simultaneously engage with the program and with each other, creating a vibrant, dynamic ecosystem of commentary, analysis, and even collective viewing experiences. This integration of social media into television viewing is a complex phenomenon with far-reaching consequences, impacting everything from audience engagement to content creation and even the future of television itself.

One of the most visible ways social media has changed television is through the creation of "second screens." While watching a show, many viewers simultaneously use their smartphones, tablets, or laptops to engage on platforms like Twitter, Facebook, Instagram, or dedicated forums and online communities. This allows for real-time reactions, discussions, and the creation of a shared viewing experience that transcends geographical boundaries. During popular shows, particularly live events like award ceremonies or sporting events, social media platforms become virtual water coolers, buzzing with commentary and opinions. The hashtag () has become a crucial tool for aggregating conversations around a specific show or event, transforming social media into a live, interactive extension of the program itself.

The impact of these second-screen interactions is significant. For viewers, it offers a sense of community and shared experience, enhancing their engagement with the program. They can connect with like-minded individuals, share opinions, and engage in lively discussions, enriching their viewing experience beyond the confines of the broadcast. The immediacy of social media allows for spontaneous reactions and interpretations, fostering a sense of collective interpretation and engagement. For example, during a live sporting event, fans can instantly share their excitement or disappointment, creating a collective emotional landscape that enhances the overall viewing experience for all participants. Similar collective responses and discussions are observed during reality TV shows or highly anticipated dramas, where real-time reactions and speculation fuel further engagement.

For broadcasters and content creators, the integration of social media provides valuable insights into audience engagement and preferences. By monitoring social media conversations, producers and marketers can gauge viewer reactions in real-time, understanding what resonates and what doesn't. This real-time feedback loop is invaluable for shaping future content, adapting to audience preferences, and even influencing the direction of a show during production. For instance, a trending hashtag related to a character's death might influence the producers' decisions for subsequent episodes. This data-driven approach to content creation allows for a more dynamic and audience-centric approach to television programming.

However, the relationship between television and social media is not always harmonious. The rise of "spoiler culture" is one notable consequence of this integration. The speed and accessibility of social media mean that plot twists and critical moments can be instantly disseminated, potentially ruining the viewing experience for those watching the show later or on a delayed schedule. This has led to a growing awareness and concern amongst broadcasters and viewers regarding the need for responsible social media engagement and spoiler avoidance. Attempts to control the flow of information, however, often prove futile, showcasing the inherent challenges in managing information dissemination in the digital age.

Moreover, the constant influx of social media commentary can be overwhelming and even distracting for some viewers. The need to constantly check social media for reactions and opinions can detract from the enjoyment of the television program itself. This constant multi-tasking can lead to fragmentation of attention and a less immersive viewing experience. Furthermore, negative or toxic social media conversations can cast a shadow over the enjoyment of a program, potentially leading to decreased viewership and negative sentiment.

The integration of social media has also impacted advertising and marketing strategies. Television commercials are no longer the sole domain of the television screen; they extend to social media platforms, leveraging the potential for targeted advertising and viral marketing campaigns. Social media campaigns can complement traditional television advertisements, broadening the reach and impact of marketing efforts. Furthermore, social media can be utilized to engage with potential viewers before and after the broadcast, cultivating anticipation and prolonging the conversation. This integrated approach offers a more holistic and multi-platform strategy for reaching audiences, maximizing the impact of advertisement spending, and fostering a stronger connection with consumers.

However, the use of social media in advertising and marketing also presents potential pitfalls. Negative comments or criticisms can quickly spread through social media, damaging a brand's image and reputation. The potential for mismanaged or poorly executed social media campaigns can significantly impact the effectiveness of advertising, highlighting the need for careful planning and moderation. The speed and reach of social media necessitate a more responsive and adaptable marketing strategy, requiring real-time monitoring of public sentiment and audience feedback.

Looking ahead, the relationship between television and social media will likely become even more intertwined. The emergence of interactive television experiences, where viewers can influence the narrative in real-time through social media interactions, is already under development. This blurring of lines between viewer and participant could revolutionize how we engage with television content. Moreover, the continued advancement of AI-powered algorithms and personalized content recommendations will further customize and enhance the social media integration, leading to a more dynamic and tailored viewing experience.

However, ethical concerns and challenges related to data privacy and the spread of misinformation will require careful consideration and addressal. Protecting user data, ensuring the authenticity of information, and mitigating the potential for manipulation are crucial aspects of responsible social media integration. The development of robust regulations and guidelines will be necessary to ensure responsible use of this technology and to protect the integrity of both the television broadcast and the social media platforms. The need for transparency and accountability, and empowering viewers to make informed choices about their online interactions, is equally important.

In conclusion, the integration of social media into the television viewing experience has profoundly altered how we consume and interact with television. While this integration has brought about many positive developments, including enhanced audience engagement, valuable audience feedback, and innovative marketing strategies, it also presents challenges related to spoiler culture, information overload, and the potential for negative or toxic social media interactions. Successfully navigating these challenges will require a collaborative effort amongst broadcasters, content creators, and viewers. A future where responsible and ethical use of social media complements and enhances the television viewing experience is achievable, but only through thoughtful consideration, transparent practices, and the development of comprehensive guidelines to address the ethical and practical concerns that arise.

The integration of social media into television is not just a technological development; it's a societal one, and its impact on how we watch, engage, and interpret the stories presented to us will continue to unfold in the years to come.

Social TV Live Tweeting Hashtags and Interactive Engagement

The convergence of television and social media has created a new form of viewing experience, often termed "social TV." This phenomenon transcends the passive consumption of content, transforming television into a dynamic, interactive, and communal event. Live tweeting, the use of hashtags, and other interactive engagement features have significantly altered how audiences connect with television programs, fostering a sense of shared experience and collective interpretation.

The rise of live tweeting, the practice of posting real-time comments and reactions on Twitter during a television broadcast, has arguably been the most significant factor in the growth of social TV. Viewers no longer simply watch; they actively participate in a running conversation alongside the program itself. This simultaneous engagement creates a virtual water cooler effect, where individuals across geographical locations can share their thoughts, opinions, and analyses instantaneously. The immediacy of this interaction makes it feel as though viewers are collectively watching and experiencing the program together, building a sense of community around a shared cultural moment.

Hashtags play a crucial role in organizing and aggregating these conversations. They act as digital signposts, allowing viewers to easily find and join the discussions surrounding a specific show. Producers and networks actively encourage the use of show-specific hashtags, promoting participation and amplifying the social media buzz. The effectiveness of a hashtag can be measured by the number of times it's used, the reach of the conversations it generates, and the overall tone and sentiment of the comments. A successful hashtag can transform a show's viewing experience, turning it into a national or even global conversation. The volume of commentary and engagement generated by a well-chosen hashtag can significantly boost a show's visibility and influence its popularity.

The impact of live tweeting and hashtags extends beyond the viewers' individual experience. For television networks and producers, social media engagement provides valuable, real-time feedback on audience reactions. By monitoring the volume, sentiment, and topics discussed under a specific hashtag, producers can gain crucial insight into which aspects of a show are resonating with viewers and which are falling flat. This data allows for course corrections during production, more targeted marketing campaigns, and even the potential to directly incorporate audience feedback into future storylines. The ability to adapt in response to immediate audience feedback significantly changes the relationship between content creators and their audience, fostering a more symbiotic and dynamic exchange.

Consider the example of the widely popular reality competition show *Survivor* . Each season generates massive online conversation, with viewers live-tweeting their reactions to tribal councils, strategic alliances, and surprise eliminations. The official show hashtag becomes a hub for speculation, predictions, and passionate debates among viewers. The producers actively monitor this conversation, gaining valuable insight into the audience's emotional responses and preferred storylines. This real-time feedback informs their editing choices, promotional strategies, and even influences the direction of future seasons.

However, not all social TV interactions are positive. The immediacy of social media can also lead to negative consequences, such as the rapid spread of spoilers. The ability to instantly share plot twists and significant events can disrupt the viewing experience for those who haven't yet watched the episode, highlighting the challenges of managing information flow in a digitally connected world. This has prompted discussions surrounding the ethics of social media engagement during television broadcasts, with calls for responsible use and increased awareness of the impact of spoiler culture. The desire for real-time reaction often conflicts with the need to preserve the viewing experience for all, creating a tension inherent to social TV.

Beyond spoilers, the sheer volume of social media commentary can be overwhelming for some viewers. The constant influx of opinions and reactions might distract from the actual television program, leading to a less immersive viewing experience. The constant need to check social media during a show can fragment attention and lessen the enjoyment of the broadcast itself. Furthermore, the presence of negative or toxic comments can negatively impact the overall viewing experience, contributing to a less enjoyable and more stressful engagement with the program.

The integration of social media also impacts television advertising and marketing strategies. Networks often use social media to promote shows, engage with viewers, and extend the reach of their advertising campaigns. Interactive contests and giveaways, utilizing hashtags and social media challenges, can further amplify engagement and extend the life of an advertisement. The ability to target specific demographics through social media advertising allows for more precise marketing efforts, maximizing the impact of ad spending and improving return on investment. The use of social media can also enhance the lifespan of a TV program, as engagement can extend long after the final credits roll. Social media allows viewers to continue their discussions, theories, and analysis, prolonging the program's relevance and impact.

Despite the benefits, the use of social media in advertising presents potential drawbacks. Negative feedback or critical comments can rapidly spread across social media platforms, impacting the brand's image and damaging its reputation. A poorly executed or controversial social media campaign can undermine the effectiveness of marketing efforts, highlighting the need for careful planning and monitoring of online sentiment. The speed and virality of social media necessitate a quick and responsive strategy, enabling brands to address criticisms and engage with users promptly and effectively.

The future of social TV is likely to involve even deeper integration of social media into the viewing experience. Interactive television technologies are under development, offering viewers the ability to directly influence storylines and character arcs through real-time social media interaction. This signifies a move from passive consumption to active participation, potentially revolutionizing how television content is created and consumed. AI-powered algorithms and personalized content recommendations will further enhance the social media integration, tailoring the viewing experience to individual user preferences. However, this increased personalization raises concerns about data privacy and the potential for algorithmic bias.

The success of social TV hinges on responsible use of social media platforms. Protecting viewer data, combating misinformation, and mitigating the potential for online harassment are crucial for ensuring a positive and enriching viewing experience. The development of robust guidelines and ethical frameworks will be vital in navigating the complexities of social media integration, balancing the benefits of interactive engagement with the need to protect user privacy and maintain a healthy online environment.

The future of social television will rely on a collaborative effort between content creators, viewers, and policymakers to ensure that social TV remains an enriching and enjoyable experience for all.

The Influence of Social Media on Television Programming Trends and Feedback

The rise of social media has fundamentally reshaped the television landscape, moving beyond the simple act of broadcasting to create a dynamic, interactive ecosystem. No longer are viewers passive recipients of content; they are active participants, shaping narratives, influencing programming decisions, and even dictating the future of their favorite shows. This symbiotic relationship between television and social media, a phenomenon often described as "social TV," is a powerful illustration of how technology transforms media consumption and production.

One of the most significant impacts of social media is its ability to provide television producers with real-time audience feedback. Pre-social media, gauging audience reaction primarily relied on delayed metrics like Nielsen ratings, providing only a broad overview of viewership and often lagging behind the actual broadcast. Social media, in contrast, offers a continuous stream of data, allowing producers to monitor reactions in real-time. The immediate feedback loop is invaluable, offering insights into what resonates with viewers, what falls flat, and even identifying potential plot points or character arcs that might be particularly successful or controversial.

Analyzing the volume, sentiment, and topics trending under relevant show hashtags allows for a granular understanding of audience engagement. Positive comments indicate elements viewers appreciate, prompting producers to emphasize similar themes or storylines in future episodes. Conversely, negative feedback highlights aspects that need adjustment or improvement. This can translate into direct changes within a series, such as altering a character's arc, refining the narrative's pacing, or even adjusting the overall tone and style of the show to better align with audience expectations. The immediacy of this process allows for swift course corrections, adapting to the ever-evolving preferences of the audience throughout a season rather than waiting for the delayed feedback of traditional rating systems.

The impact extends beyond immediate adjustments. Social media trends often inform long-term strategic decisions. A show's successful incorporation of social media trends can lead to increased viewership, improved brand recognition, and ultimately, stronger profitability. Producers actively monitor social media conversations to identify potential storylines, character developments, or even guest appearances that are likely to resonate with their audience and drive online engagement. For example, a trending topic on social media relating to a particular social issue might inspire a storyline directly addressing that topic, incorporating audience-driven themes into the program's narrative. This demonstrates the remarkable power of social listening in shaping television programming.

The effectiveness of this feedback loop is particularly evident in reality TV shows. Competitions like *Survivor*, *The Bachelor*, and *Big Brother* thrive on social media engagement. Viewers passionately debate strategies, discuss favorite contestants, and predict outcomes, generating a massive online conversation surrounding each episode. Production teams actively monitor these discussions, gaining valuable insights into which contestants are resonating with the audience, what aspects of the competition are most engaging, and what storylines are eliciting the strongest emotional responses.

This information is directly applied to subsequent seasons, modifying casting strategies, tweaking challenges, and even shaping the narrative arcs of individual competitors to capitalize on audience preferences gleaned from social media.

However, the influence of social media is not solely confined to reality television. Scripted dramas and comedies are equally susceptible to, and influenced by, audience reaction on social media. A widely-discussed online opinion about a character's actions or a plot development can prompt showrunners to recalibrate storylines or alter character behavior in subsequent episodes. This demonstrates a significant shift in the power dynamic between creators and audiences; the audience's voice, once relegated to the margins, now holds a central position in shaping the narrative arc of a television show. The ability for producers to adapt and respond to these trends demonstrates a far more dynamic and responsive relationship with viewers.

The impact extends beyond program content to promotional strategies. Social media platforms offer unparalleled opportunities for targeted advertising and fan engagement. Television networks utilize social media to promote shows, generating buzz, increasing anticipation, and expanding their viewership reach. This includes interactive contests, giveaways, and behind-the-scenes content that further engages viewers and keeps them invested in the show beyond the broadcast. The use of hashtags, targeted advertising campaigns, and influencer marketing expands the reach of promotional materials significantly, extending the program's influence beyond its core viewing audience.

This digital integration, however, is not without its challenges. The immediacy of social media also brings the risk of negative feedback, online criticism, and even the rapid spread of damaging rumors or spoilers. The speed at which information disseminates online can create significant challenges for producers, demanding a robust and responsive strategy to manage online perceptions and address critical comments. Furthermore, the prevalence of online negativity and the potential for social media to become a platform for harassment necessitate strategies to manage and mitigate such situations.

Furthermore, the sheer volume of social media commentary can be overwhelming, potentially disrupting the viewing experience itself. The constant stream of opinions, reactions, and debates can distract viewers from the actual program, leading to a fragmented and less immersive experience. The temptation to constantly check social media during a broadcast can impact the enjoyment and focus of viewers, creating a tension between real-time engagement and active viewing.

The future of social TV promises even deeper integration, blurring the lines between passive consumption and active participation. Interactive television technologies are being explored, offering opportunities for real-time audience input that directly affects storylines and character arcs. AI-powered algorithms could personalize the viewing experience, tailoring content recommendations and creating more targeted, engaging content.

However, these advancements raise concerns about data privacy, algorithmic bias, and the potential for manipulative practices.

The ongoing evolution of the relationship between television and social media highlights the complexities of a rapidly changing media landscape. The potential benefits of real-time engagement and feedback are immense, offering viewers a greater sense of agency and participation in the creative process. Yet, the potential risks associated with online negativity, misinformation, and privacy concerns require careful navigation. The future success of social TV hinges on a collaborative effort between broadcasters, producers, and viewers, working together to establish ethical guidelines and responsible practices that protect viewers and enrich the viewing experience for everyone. This requires a delicate balance between exploiting the opportunities of social media engagement and mitigating the associated risks. The ongoing dialogue between the technology, the content creators, and the audience will determine the future trajectory of television.

Social Media and the Television Industry Marketing Promotion and Brand Building

The symbiotic relationship between television and social media extends far beyond influencing content; it has revolutionized how television programs are marketed, promoted, and ultimately, how brands are built. The traditional methods of television advertising, relying heavily on costly broadcast spots and print media, have been augmented, and in many cases superseded, by the targeted, cost-effective, and highly engaging strategies offered by social media platforms. This shift has empowered television networks and production companies to reach audiences with unprecedented precision and efficiency.

One of the most significant changes is the ability to engage in highly targeted advertising. Unlike traditional television advertising, which casts a broad net, social media allows for the precise targeting of specific demographic groups, based on factors such as age, gender, location, interests, and even viewing habits. This granular level of targeting ensures that promotional materials reach the individuals most likely to be interested in a particular program, maximizing the effectiveness of advertising spend and minimizing wasted impressions. For instance, a new crime drama could target viewers who have previously engaged with similar genre content on streaming platforms or followed related accounts on social media. This precision significantly improves the return on investment (ROI) compared to traditional broadcast advertising, where the reach is inherently less focused.

Social media campaigns have become an integral part of the pre-launch buzz for new television shows and the ongoing promotion of existing ones. These campaigns often involve a coordinated strategy across multiple platforms, using a consistent brand voice and visual identity. This integrated approach maximizes the impact of promotional materials, reinforcing the show's branding and maintaining audience engagement across all channels. A successful campaign might utilize teaser trailers released on platforms like YouTube and TikTok, followed by interactive polls and Q&A sessions on Twitter and Instagram, engaging potential viewers and building anticipation for the show's premiere.

Influencer marketing plays a significant role in this process.

Partnering with influential figures on social media, individuals with established followings and credibility within specific niches, provides a powerful way to reach a wider audience. Influencers can organically introduce television shows to their followers, providing authentic endorsements that resonate more strongly than traditional advertising. The authenticity of influencer-driven content is a crucial factor. Viewers are more likely to trust a recommendation from a trusted source, particularly when the influencer demonstrates genuine enthusiasm for the program. This approach extends the reach beyond the network's primary promotional efforts, leveraging existing relationships and trust established within the influencer's community.

The strategies employed often go beyond simple promotional announcements. Television networks frequently utilize interactive contests and giveaways to engage their audience on social media. This interactive approach fosters a sense of community and allows viewers to actively participate in the promotional campaign.

Contests might involve predicting plot points, sharing favorite scenes using specific hashtags, or creating user-generated content related to the show. The use of hashtags is particularly effective in organizing and amplifying online conversations around the program. By incorporating user-generated content into the overall campaign, networks foster a sense of ownership and involvement, strengthening audience loyalty and building a more engaged community.

Community building is a crucial aspect of social media-driven promotion. Networks actively cultivate online communities surrounding their television shows by responding to comments, engaging in discussions, and creating content that encourages interaction. This can involve live Q&A sessions with cast and crew members, behind-the-scenes glimpses into the production process, or even online polls that allow viewers to influence future storylines. This direct interaction cultivates a loyal audience that feels connected to the show beyond simply watching the episodes. This sense of participation and connection is particularly effective in driving viewership and promoting the show within the online community.

However, the utilization of social media in marketing television programs also presents unique challenges. The immediacy of social media means that negative feedback or controversies can spread rapidly, potentially harming a show's reputation. Crisis communication strategies are therefore crucial in mitigating potential damage. A prompt and thoughtful response to negative feedback, addressing concerns and acknowledging criticism, can effectively manage online perceptions. Furthermore, the potential for misinformation and the spread of rumors requires a proactive approach to managing the narrative surrounding the show. This necessitates a strong social media presence that actively engages with audiences and refutes inaccurate information promptly.

Moreover, the sheer volume of data generated by social media platforms presents its own challenges. Analyzing and interpreting this vast amount of information to extract meaningful insights requires sophisticated tools and a skilled team capable of discerning meaningful trends from noise. The temptation to focus solely on quantitative metrics, such as follower counts and engagement rates, should be tempered with an understanding of qualitative data, including the sentiment and tone of audience feedback. Balancing quantitative and qualitative analysis is crucial for a comprehensive understanding of audience perception.

The strategic use of paid social media advertising is also an important aspect of a comprehensive marketing strategy. While organic reach is valuable, paid advertising campaigns allow networks to precisely target specific demographic segments and amplify their message. The ability to tailor advertising content to different platforms and optimize campaigns based on performance data enhances the ROI of this investment significantly. This requires a well-defined budget and meticulous tracking of campaign performance to optimize the effectiveness of paid social media advertising.

Furthermore, the integration of social media into television programming itself is constantly evolving. Interactive elements, such as live polls and quizzes during broadcasts, are becoming increasingly common. This deeper integration creates a more engaging viewing experience, blurring the lines between passive consumption and active participation. The ability for audiences to directly influence storylines, vote for contestants, or even shape character arcs enhances their sense of ownership and participation in the show.

Finally, measuring the effectiveness of social media marketing campaigns for television programs is paramount. While traditional metrics such as Nielsen ratings still hold importance, social media analytics provide a granular view of audience engagement, allowing for a deeper understanding of the campaign's impact. Key metrics to track include reach, engagement, sentiment analysis, website traffic driven by social media, and ultimately, a correlation between social media activity and viewership numbers. By meticulously analyzing these data points, networks can optimize their strategies for future campaigns.

In conclusion, social media has fundamentally reshaped the television industry's approach to marketing, promotion, and brand building. The precision of targeting, the potential for engagement, and the efficiency of social media campaigns offer a significant advantage over traditional methods. However, the challenges of managing online perceptions, navigating the complexities of social media analytics, and developing effective crisis communication strategies cannot be overlooked. A sophisticated and nuanced approach, integrating organic and paid social media strategies, interactive elements, and robust analytics, is crucial for maximizing the impact of social media in the ever-evolving landscape of television. The ongoing dialogue and innovation in this space will continue to redefine how television programs are brought to, and engaged with, audiences worldwide.

The Future of Television and Social Media Enhanced Integration and Engagement

The convergence of television and social media is not a static phenomenon; it's a dynamic, rapidly evolving relationship that promises even deeper integration in the years to come. We've already witnessed the transformative impact of social media on television marketing and promotion, but the future holds possibilities that extend far beyond mere advertising. The next generation of television viewing will likely be characterized by a seamless blend of passive consumption and active participation, a fusion driven by advancements in technology and a more demanding, interactive audience.

One of the most significant predicted trends is the expansion of interactive television experiences. While rudimentary forms of interactivity, such as live polls and quizzes during broadcasts, are already commonplace, future iterations will be far more sophisticated. Imagine a scenario where viewers can influence storylines in real-time through social media platforms, directly impacting the narrative unfolding on their screens. This could involve voting on crucial plot points, choosing character actions, or even submitting ideas for future episodes. Such interactive narratives would foster a deeper sense of immersion and ownership, transforming viewers from passive observers into active participants in the storytelling process. The technical challenges involved in seamlessly integrating real-time social media input into broadcast television are significant, requiring robust infrastructure and sophisticated algorithms to manage the volume of data and ensure smooth integration. However, the potential rewards, in terms of enhanced audience engagement and a more dynamic viewing experience, are substantial, pushing innovation in this domain.

Furthermore, the rise of personalized television experiences will be significantly amplified by the data-driven insights gleaned from social media. Television networks and streaming platforms are already utilizing social media data to understand viewer preferences, tailor recommendations, and customize content. This trend will intensify, leading to the creation of highly personalized viewing experiences, where algorithms curate content specifically tailored to individual tastes and preferences based on social media activity, viewing history, and other data points. This level of personalization will require sophisticated data analysis techniques and robust privacy protocols, ensuring that viewers' data is protected while their viewing experience is enhanced. The ethical considerations of personalized content delivery, particularly with respect to data privacy and algorithmic bias, will require ongoing discussion and careful consideration as these technologies mature.

The use of augmented reality (AR) and virtual reality (VR) technologies promises to further enhance the television viewing experience. Imagine watching a sporting event and having AR overlays providing real-time statistics, player information, and interactive analyses directly on your screen. Or consider experiencing a documentary or historical drama through VR, allowing viewers to immerse themselves in the events being portrayed. The combination of television content with AR/VR technologies could redefine how we interact with and understand information, opening new avenues for storytelling and education. The integration of these immersive technologies requires significant advancements in both hardware and software, and the accessibility of such technologies will need to be considered for wider adoption.

However, the potential to create truly engaging and memorable viewing experiences is undeniable.

Social media platforms themselves will continue to evolve as vital extensions of the television experience. We can anticipate more integrated viewing parties and virtual communities forming around specific shows and events. These online spaces will serve as extensions of the television broadcast, offering opportunities for real-time discussion, fan interaction, and the creation of shared experiences. This creates a more robust community around television programs, strengthening engagement and expanding the reach beyond the traditional broadcast audience. Managing the vast amount of data generated by such interactive online platforms, ensuring a secure environment, and addressing potential issues of online toxicity will be crucial in maximizing the benefits of these platforms.

The future integration of television and social media also presents the opportunity to enhance accessibility for viewers with disabilities. Social media platforms can incorporate features such as live captioning, sign language interpretation, and audio descriptions, extending the viewing audience to include those who might otherwise have limited access. Furthermore, the integration of social media data can inform the creation of television programming that is more inclusive and representative of diverse communities. This emphasis on accessibility will become increasingly important as television programming becomes more interactive and personalized, ensuring that the benefits of these technological advances are shared by everyone.

However, the ongoing convergence of television and social media also raises important concerns. Data privacy and security will remain paramount issues, necessitating robust safeguards to protect viewer information and prevent misuse. The potential for algorithmic bias, where algorithms used to personalize content inadvertently discriminate against certain groups, will require careful monitoring and mitigation strategies. Furthermore, the ease with which misinformation can spread on social media platforms necessitates the development of effective strategies for combating disinformation and promoting media literacy among viewers. The constant need to adapt to new platforms and technological advancements will be a significant challenge for both television networks and social media companies.

Another critical consideration is the potential impact on the creative process. While interactive elements can enhance storytelling and viewer engagement, they also introduce new complexities and constraints for television writers and producers.
Striking a balance between creative freedom and the need to incorporate viewer participation will require a thoughtful and innovative approach. Furthermore, the potential for audience feedback to directly influence storylines could lead to creative compromises or potentially stifle artistic innovation, posing challenges that need to be thoughtfully addressed.

In conclusion, the future of television and social media will be defined by a deep and seamless integration, transforming how we consume and interact with television content. Interactive experiences, personalized viewing, augmented and virtual reality applications, and expanded online communities will shape the landscape of the future. However, this convergence also presents significant challenges, particularly concerning data privacy, algorithmic bias, misinformation, and the impact on the creative process. Addressing these challenges responsibly while harnessing the transformative potential of this convergence will be crucial to ensuring a vibrant and engaging future for television and social media. The ongoing conversation and innovation surrounding this interconnected landscape will continuously redefine how television programs are presented and engaged with on a global scale, fundamentally altering the very nature of the viewing experience.

This requires a multi-faceted approach, involving collaboration between television networks, social media platforms, policymakers, and viewers themselves, ensuring that the benefits of this technological convergence are realized while mitigating the potential risks. The next chapter in the evolution of television promises to be one of profound change and exciting possibilities, but success depends on a careful and considered approach to the numerous challenges that lie ahead.

International Television Markets Diversity of Content and Formats

The global television landscape is far from monolithic. While advancements in technology have fostered a degree of homogenization, with certain formats and genres transcending national borders, significant diversity persists in content and formats across international markets. This diversity is deeply rooted in cultural nuances, societal values, regulatory frameworks, and the unique historical trajectories of each nation's broadcasting industry.

Examining these differences reveals a fascinating tapestry of television experiences worldwide.

One key aspect of this diversity lies in the types of programming favored by different audiences. In many Western European countries, for instance, a strong emphasis is placed on high-quality drama series, often featuring intricate plots, complex characters, and sophisticated production values. Shows like "Stranger Things" (US) and "The Crown" (UK), while finding international success, demonstrate the appeal of such narrative structures, though adaptations and local variations often emerge to cater to specific cultural contexts. In contrast, some Asian markets show a greater preference for lighter, more comedic programming, or for serialized dramas that run for hundreds of episodes, offering a different kind of sustained viewing experience. Japanese television, for example, has long been known for its unique blend of anime, variety shows, and highly stylized dramas, often incorporating elements of fantasy or surrealism. The success of Korean dramas ("K-dramas") globally highlights the potential for specific cultural styles to become globally appreciated but also highlights the nuances of adaptation for international audiences. While the format— episodic serialized drama—is globally exportable, the specific cultural elements of each drama heavily influence its global success.

The prevalence of news and current affairs programming also varies considerably. In some countries, public broadcasters play a dominant role, providing in-depth coverage and analysis that prioritizes journalistic integrity and public service. In others, commercial channels prioritize sensationalism and ratings, potentially compromising journalistic standards to capture a wider audience. This difference is reflected not only in the content of news broadcasts, but also in their presentation style, tone, and perceived role within the broader media ecosystem. The contrast between the BBC's news output and that of some American cable news networks clearly illustrates the varying approaches to presenting news within different political and social contexts.

Further, the influence of government censorship or regulation significantly impacts the content and framing of news broadcasts, with countries like China maintaining strict control over information disseminated via their media platforms, contrasting sharply with the generally freer press found in many Western democracies.

Furthermore, the regulatory frameworks governing television broadcasting differ greatly across countries. Some nations favor a heavily regulated system, with public broadcasters holding a significant share of the market and strict rules governing content and advertising. This is often the case in countries with a strong public broadcasting tradition, such as those in many European nations. Other countries have more deregulated markets, with a greater emphasis on commercial broadcasting and less government intervention. This often leads to a more competitive landscape, but can also result in concerns about media concentration, the proliferation of low-quality programming, and a lack of diversity in ownership. The United States, with its mix of public broadcasting and a highly competitive commercial sector, demonstrates this regulatory model. Brazil provides another example, as a nation with historically complex media policies that reflect the country's socioeconomic divisions and political landscapes.

Viewing habits also differ significantly. In some countries, viewers favor linear television, watching scheduled broadcasts on traditional channels. In others, on-demand streaming services have become increasingly popular, allowing viewers to watch what they want, when they want. This shift is influenced by factors such as internet penetration, the availability of streaming platforms, and cultural preferences. The rapid adoption of streaming services in many Asian markets contrasts with the continued popularity of linear television in certain parts of Europe and Africa, reflecting differences in technological infrastructure and consumer behavior.

The formats of television programming also show remarkable international variation. Reality television, for example, has experienced a global boom, but its manifestations differ substantially from one country to another. Reality shows in the US often prioritize drama, conflict, and sensationalism, while those in some European countries may emphasize interpersonal relationships and character development. Game shows, too, exhibit significant diversity, with formats being adapted and customized to appeal to local tastes and cultural values. The popularity of particular formats varies widely; the success of singing competitions, for example, differs greatly in various nations.

The rise of international co-productions adds another layer to the global television landscape. Increasingly, television programs are produced through collaborations between broadcasters and production companies from different countries. This allows for the sharing of creative resources and expertise, and helps to reach broader audiences. However, co-productions also present challenges in terms of balancing creative visions, navigating cultural differences, and addressing logistical hurdles. Such collaborations often reveal insights into how various cultures intersect and influence the aesthetic and thematic choices in productions. The popularity and success of international co-productions underscore the growing interdependence of the global television market.

The impact of globalization on the television industry is a complex issue. While global distribution platforms have allowed for greater accessibility of content, they have also raised concerns about cultural homogenization and the dominance of certain production centers. Striking a balance between cultural exchange and the preservation of local identities is an ongoing challenge that needs careful consideration. The potential for cultural appropriation in international co-productions, for instance, is a risk that must be managed thoughtfully through collaborations that incorporate diverse voices from both local communities and international markets.

Furthermore, the rise of niche television channels and streaming services has enabled smaller markets to access more diverse programming and to nurture their own creative industries.

However, these same platforms can also further marginalize smaller, local productions that may lack the resources and market reach to compete effectively.

The future of international television markets will likely be shaped by the ongoing convergence of technology and culture. The increasing availability of high-speed internet access, combined with the rise of new streaming platforms and immersive technologies like virtual and augmented reality, will offer new possibilities for content creation and distribution. The ability to tailor content to increasingly diverse audiences while celebrating and supporting local cultural production will remain a central challenge for the industry. The interplay of globalization and localization, of technology and culture, will continue to define the dynamic and ever-evolving global television landscape. The next decade will witness a continuous reshaping of this landscape, demanding ongoing observation and critical analysis to comprehend its full complexity and impact. The ongoing evolution necessitates a flexible and adaptable approach from broadcasters, producers, and regulators alike to ensure that the industry thrives and continues to provide rich and diverse viewing experiences to audiences worldwide. This calls for sustained conversations that foster collaboration and innovation, building bridges between cultural traditions and celebrating the universal power of storytelling through the medium of television.

Global Television Production Collaboration and Distribution

The increasing interconnectedness of the global television market has fostered a new era of international collaboration in television production. This collaboration manifests in various forms, from co-productions involving multiple countries to the strategic distribution of content across international platforms. The rise of streaming services has been particularly instrumental in facilitating these cross-border collaborations, bypassing traditional geographical limitations and expanding the potential audience for television programs exponentially. Netflix, for example, has invested heavily in international productions, commissioning series and films from various countries and making them available globally through its platform. This strategy has not only broadened the range of content available to viewers worldwide but has also empowered local creative industries in countries that might not have had access to such significant funding or distribution channels otherwise. The success of shows like "Squid Game" (South Korea) and "Money Heist" (Spain), both initially produced for domestic markets but achieving global popularity through Netflix, underscores the potential for international collaboration to unearth and amplify previously untapped creative talent and storytelling traditions.

However, international co-productions are not without their complexities. Negotiating creative differences between partners from diverse cultural backgrounds requires considerable sensitivity and diplomacy. The balancing of national interests, budgetary concerns, and creative visions can be challenging, particularly when dealing with varying regulatory frameworks and broadcasting standards across countries. For instance, censorship regulations, broadcast standards, and even differing production techniques and technologies can pose significant hurdles. A co-production between a European broadcaster known for its commitment to sophisticated, character-driven narratives and an American network focused on faster-paced, action-oriented programming would necessitate careful planning and compromise to ensure a product that satisfies the expectations of both partners and their target audiences. These challenges often necessitate skilled international production teams capable of navigating the complexities of diverse cultural contexts and regulatory environments. The success of such ventures hinges on effective communication, a deep understanding of the nuances of different cultural markets, and a willingness to adapt creative approaches to resonate with a global audience.

Another critical aspect of global television production involves the distribution of content. The traditional model of broadcasting, where programs were transmitted via terrestrial channels to a predominantly domestic audience, has been significantly disrupted by the rise of satellite and cable television, followed by the even more radical shift brought about by streaming services. This transformation has led to a more fragmented but significantly broader television landscape, presenting both opportunities and challenges for producers and distributors. While streaming platforms provide unprecedented reach, they also increase competition for viewers' attention. The sheer volume of content available means that programs must be highly compelling to stand out in a crowded marketplace. This competitive environment has driven innovation in content marketing and distribution strategies, with producers increasingly relying on data analytics and sophisticated marketing techniques to reach and engage target audiences across borders. Moreover, the ability to tailor content to specific regional markets, incorporating localized elements such as dubbing, subtitles, and even plot adaptations to better reflect cultural norms and preferences, has become increasingly crucial to achieving international success.

The economic implications of global television production are significant. International co-productions can inject substantial funds into the economies of participating countries, creating jobs and fostering growth in local creative industries. This is particularly valuable in emerging markets where the television industry may still be developing. However, the concentration of production in certain global hubs, such as Hollywood or certain cities in India or South Korea, also raises concerns about economic inequality and the potential marginalization of smaller production centers. Finding a sustainable model for global collaboration that balances the benefits of international co-productions with the need to support local industries is an ongoing challenge. The influence of multinational media conglomerates also affects this economic landscape, potentially limiting the diversity of voices and content within the global television market.

Beyond the economic dimensions, the cultural impact of global television production is arguably even more profound. The widespread dissemination of television programs across borders has accelerated the exchange of ideas, values, and cultural practices. While this cultural exchange can enrich global understanding and foster greater appreciation of diverse cultures, it can also raise concerns about cultural homogenization and the potential erosion of local identities. The risk of cultural appropriation, where elements of a culture are adopted without proper understanding or respect, is a significant ethical consideration for those involved in international co-productions. Consequently, ethical considerations are increasingly important in the production and distribution of television across borders. Collaborations that prioritize authenticity, mutual respect, and a deep engagement with the cultural nuances of participating countries are crucial for ensuring that these collaborations are enriching and beneficial to all involved.

Furthermore, the rise of digital platforms and the associated metadata capabilities present both challenges and opportunities for content producers. While the ability to track viewing habits and tailor content to specific audiences allows for more efficient targeting, it also raises privacy concerns. The ethical use of data and the protection of viewers' privacy are important issues that require careful consideration by those involved in global television production. The increasing use of artificial intelligence (AI) in content creation, distribution, and marketing also presents ethical challenges that need to be addressed proactively. Balancing the potential benefits of AI with the need to prevent bias and maintain human control over creative decision-making requires a nuanced and forward-thinking approach.

In conclusion, the global television landscape is a dynamic and multifaceted environment, constantly evolving in response to technological advancements and shifting cultural trends.

International collaboration and content distribution are key drivers of this evolution, presenting both remarkable opportunities and significant challenges. Successfully navigating this complex landscape requires a sophisticated understanding of cultural dynamics, economic forces, and the ethical considerations inherent in cross-border production and distribution. The future of global television will undoubtedly be shaped by the ability of the industry to balance the demands of globalization with the importance of fostering diverse cultural voices and ensuring ethical practices in content creation and distribution. The ongoing conversation around these issues is vital for the continued growth and sustainability of the global television industry, ensuring it continues to provide engaging and meaningful content to viewers worldwide.

The Influence of Globalization on Television Content Cultural Exchange and Adaptation

The proliferation of global television networks and streaming platforms has fundamentally altered the landscape of television content creation and consumption. No longer are national borders the primary determinant of what viewers see on their screens. Instead, a complex interplay of cultural exchange, adaptation, and commercial strategies shapes the programming available worldwide. This globalization of television content has led to both exciting opportunities for creative collaboration and significant challenges in navigating diverse cultural sensitivities and commercial interests.

One of the most striking aspects of this globalization is the increased flow of cultural ideas and narratives across borders. Shows originally produced for a domestic audience in one country can achieve international success, often exceeding their initial expectations. The South Korean thriller "Squid Game," for example, transcended linguistic and cultural barriers to become a global phenomenon on Netflix. Its success highlights the universal appeal of certain themes – in this case, the desperation faced by those trapped in a system of immense economic inequality – and the power of compelling storytelling to resonate with audiences worldwide. The show's visual style, its suspenseful plot, and its exploration of societal pressures captivated viewers worldwide, demonstrating the potential for non-English language programming to achieve global dominance. This success prompted a surge in interest in South Korean dramas and films, leading to increased investment in the Korean entertainment industry and inspiring similar productions in other countries.

However, the international success of a show like "Squid Game" is not simply a matter of luck. The strategic distribution by Netflix played a critical role. The platform's global reach and sophisticated marketing strategies ensured the show's exposure to a vast international audience. Furthermore, the show's underlying themes of social inequality and competition resonate with a global audience facing similar anxieties and struggles. While the specific cultural context of South Korea informed the show's unique aesthetic and narrative, its core themes transcended cultural boundaries, striking a chord with viewers worldwide. This successful global launch demonstrated the potential for non-English language shows to dominate the global television landscape, a remarkable feat previously less common.

The global success of "Squid Game" also spurred a wave of imitations and adaptations, highlighting the tension between cultural exchange and homogenization. While some productions attempted to replicate the show's format and style, many others were inspired to explore similar themes and narratives within their own unique cultural contexts. This showcases both the powerful influence of a globalized media landscape and the resilience of local cultural identities. The phenomenon revealed that while global audiences appreciate certain universal themes, successful international content often requires a careful balance between adapting to global tastes and retaining the authenticity and cultural specificity that made the original work compelling.

Another impactful example of global television's influence is the adaptation of successful formats across national borders. Reality TV shows, particularly, demonstrate the adaptability and commercial viability of certain formats in diverse cultural contexts. The "Big Brother" franchise, for instance, has been adapted for numerous countries, each tailoring the show to suit local sensibilities and cultural norms. While the core concept of individuals living together under constant surveillance remains consistent, variations in the casting process, the types of challenges presented, and even the overall tone of the show reflect the unique characteristics of each national adaptation. This adaptation process underscores the intricate balance between global format standardization and local cultural specificity. It also highlights the importance of understanding local markets, local cultural values, and viewer expectations to achieve success in international markets. The success of these localized adaptations underscores the notion that global audiences crave familiarity within the context of cultural specificity.

Beyond reality TV, successful drama series have also been adapted and reimagined for international audiences. While adapting successful drama formats requires meticulous work to retain the essence of the original while tailoring it to a new cultural context, these adaptations demonstrate the power of cross-cultural collaboration and the enduring appeal of compelling stories. The challenge lies in navigating the nuances of language, cultural references, and social conventions, ensuring that the adaptation resonates authentically with its new target audience without losing the essence of the original. This delicate process necessitates a deep understanding of both the original source material and the cultural context of the target audience, requiring skillful localization that extends beyond simple translation.

The process of adaptation often involves not just translating dialogue but also modifying storylines, characters, and even the overall tone of the show to better reflect the cultural norms and expectations of the target audience. Sometimes, this involves adding or removing scenes, adjusting character relationships, or even changing the setting or timeframe of the narrative. This adaptability showcases the dynamic nature of global television and the creativity involved in bridging cultural divides. These adaptations highlight that successful globalization in television is not about homogenization but about creating a nuanced bridge between global appeal and cultural specificity.

However, this global exchange of television content is not without its critics. Concerns about cultural homogenization and the erosion of local identities remain prevalent. The dominance of Western media, particularly American productions, in global television markets has raised concerns about the potential marginalization of other cultures and the imposition of Western values and perspectives. This uneven power dynamic raises questions about the fairness and equity of global television's influence and calls for a more balanced and representative media landscape. The fear is that the overwhelming influence of a limited number of cultural narratives may lead to a reduction in diversity and originality. The challenge then becomes how to foster a global television landscape that celebrates cultural diversity while also ensuring that global audiences have access to a wide range of high-quality programming.

The economic implications of this globalization are equally significant. The increased production and distribution of television programs across borders create both opportunities and challenges for national television industries. While international co- productions can inject substantial capital into local economies and foster the growth of local creative industries, they can also lead to a concentration of production in certain global hubs, leaving smaller production centers marginalized. The balancing act between global production efficiency and the support of local talent and industries continues to be a critical issue shaping the future of global television. A careful examination of the economic consequences is vital for developing policies that promote sustainable growth and equitable distribution of resources.

In conclusion, globalization's influence on television content is a complex and multifaceted phenomenon. It represents a fascinating exchange of cultural ideas and creative approaches, showcasing the power of storytelling to transcend national borders. However, the challenges associated with cultural adaptation, economic inequality, and concerns about cultural homogenization demand careful consideration. The future of global television hinges on a balanced approach that fosters cross-cultural collaboration, respects local identities, and promotes equitable access to global markets while encouraging diversity and originality in television content worldwide. The ongoing evolution of global television will undoubtedly shape how we understand and engage with narratives, cultures, and the very fabric of the world around us.

The Role of Streaming Services in the Global Television Market Accessibility and Reach

The rise of streaming services has fundamentally reshaped the global television landscape, dramatically altering the accessibility and reach of television content. Before the widespread adoption of streaming, access to international programming was often limited by geographical restrictions, broadcast schedules, and the availability of specific channels. International programming relied heavily on syndication deals and carefully curated selections offered by national broadcasters, resulting in a somewhat fragmented and limited viewing experience for global audiences. Streaming platforms, however, have dismantled many of these geographical and logistical barriers, creating a truly globalized television market.

Netflix, arguably the pioneer in this revolution, demonstrated the power of a subscription-based model to deliver a vast library of content to consumers worldwide. Its early success in establishing a global footprint paved the way for other streaming giants like Amazon Prime Video, Disney+, HBO Max, and Apple TV+, each bringing its own unique catalog and strategic approach to the international market. These platforms bypass traditional broadcast distribution chains, delivering content directly to viewers through internet-connected devices. This direct-to-consumer model has significantly increased the accessibility of international programming, allowing viewers to access shows and movies from around the world with unprecedented ease.

One of the key aspects that sets streaming services apart is their ability to transcend linguistic barriers. While dubbed or subtitled content has always existed, streaming services have invested heavily in providing viewers with options that cater to their preferred language. Netflix, in particular, has been a leader in supporting multilingual content, offering a wide range of shows and movies with multiple dubbing and subtitling options, significantly expanding the reach of international programs. This commitment to linguistic accessibility has broadened the audience for both established and emerging international productions, fostering a more inclusive and diverse viewing experience. The platform's sophisticated algorithms further personalize the viewing experience by suggesting relevant content based on individual preferences, further maximizing the discovery of international programming.

The impact on local television industries is complex and multifaceted. While streaming platforms provide opportunities for smaller production companies and independent filmmakers to reach a global audience, bypassing the limitations of traditional distribution channels, it also presents challenges to established national broadcasters. The competition for viewers and advertising revenue has intensified, forcing traditional broadcasters to adapt their strategies and programming to remain competitive. This increased competition has, in many instances, spurred innovation and creativity within the broadcasting sector as well. Furthermore, many national broadcasters have also partnered with streaming platforms to distribute their content internationally, leveraging the global reach of these platforms while maintaining their local relevance and brand identity.

The rise of streaming has also fostered a greater awareness and appreciation for diverse cultures and storytelling styles. Viewers are now exposed to a wider range of perspectives and narratives than ever before. Shows like "Squid Game" (South Korea), "La Casa de Papel" (Spain), "Dark" (Germany), and "Money Heist" (Spain), to name just a few, have achieved international acclaim, breaking through language and cultural barriers to garner global viewership. These successes have highlighted the universal appeal of compelling storytelling and have demonstrated that high-quality content, regardless of its origin, can resonate with audiences around the world. This exposure has not only enriched the viewing experience but has also stimulated interest in various cultures and countries' languages, creating a more interconnected and globally aware audience.

However, the global expansion of streaming services is not without its complexities. Regulatory hurdles, differing censorship laws, and copyright issues present significant challenges. The need to adapt content to local cultural norms and sensitivities often requires extensive localization efforts. Some argue that the dominance of a few major streaming giants creates an imbalance of power within the global entertainment industry. Smaller, independent producers and distributors may struggle to compete, leading to a potential homogenization of content. Concerns have also been raised regarding the potential displacement of local content and the dominance of Western narratives, leading to calls for government interventions and support for local productions to maintain cultural diversity.

Furthermore, the business model of many streaming services relies heavily on subscription fees, creating a potential barrier to entry for viewers in developing countries with limited internet access or disposable income. This disparity raises concerns about equitable access to global television content and highlights the digital divide.

Initiatives aimed at bridging this divide, such as providing affordable internet access or offering subsidized subscriptions, are crucial for ensuring that the benefits of streaming are shared more equitably. The affordability and accessibility of high-speed internet remain significant hurdles to overcome in order for the full potential of streaming services to be realised globally.

The impact of streaming on the advertising landscape is also noteworthy. Traditional advertising models based on broadcast television are evolving to incorporate targeted digital advertising on streaming platforms. This shift creates both opportunities and challenges for advertisers. While streaming platforms offer advanced analytics and targeted advertising capabilities, it also demands a different approach to campaign design and measurement. The ongoing evolution of advertising technology and marketing strategies reflects the fundamental changes brought about by the rise of streaming.

Moreover, the evolving nature of technology itself continues to influence the global reach and accessibility of streaming services.

The development of more efficient compression techniques, improved internet infrastructure, and the proliferation of mobile devices and smart TVs are all contributing factors to the expansion of streaming's global footprint. However, ensuring compatibility across different devices and operating systems remains an ongoing challenge. The ongoing advancements in both content delivery and streaming technology will continue to shape the future of global television.

In conclusion, the role of streaming services in shaping the global television market has been profound and transformative. They have expanded the accessibility and reach of television content in ways that were unimaginable just a few decades ago. However, this global expansion is a complex process, fraught with challenges related to regulation, competition, cultural sensitivities, and equitable access. The future of global television will depend on how these challenges are addressed and how streaming services continue to adapt and innovate to meet the evolving needs and expectations of a global audience. The ongoing interplay between technology, culture, and economics will continue to define the global television landscape in the years to come.

The Future of Global Television Trends and Predictions

The preceding discussion detailed the transformative impact of streaming services on the global television landscape, highlighting both their successes and challenges. Looking forward, the future of global television promises to be even more dynamic and complex, shaped by a confluence of technological innovations, evolving viewer preferences, and ongoing geopolitical shifts. Several key trends are poised to significantly redefine how we consume and experience television in the years to come.

One of the most significant trends will be the continued proliferation of streaming services and their increasing sophistication. While the current landscape is dominated by a few major players, we can anticipate a more diverse and fragmented ecosystem emerging. Smaller, niche streaming platforms focusing on specific genres, languages, or cultural demographics will likely emerge, catering to the increasingly specialized viewing habits of global audiences. This diversification may lead to a more competitive market, potentially fostering innovation and offering viewers a broader range of choices. However, it could also lead to increased consumer fragmentation and difficulties in navigating the expanding array of options. The challenge for viewers will be to find the platforms that best suit their tastes and budgets, requiring better content discovery mechanisms and potentially leading to a need for aggregation services to help navigate the multitude of options.

Technological advancements will play a pivotal role in shaping this future. The ongoing evolution of high-definition formats, like 8K and beyond, will offer increasingly immersive and realistic viewing experiences. The integration of virtual and augmented reality (VR/AR) technologies is also poised to revolutionize the way we interact with television content, transforming passive viewing into a more active and participatory experience. Imagine experiencing a historical drama as if you were a character within the narrative, or exploring a documentary setting virtually. This is not merely science fiction; the technologies to achieve this are rapidly developing, albeit still at a nascent stage.

Artificial intelligence (AI) will continue to play an increasingly significant role in various aspects of television production and consumption. AI-powered tools are already being used for tasks such as scriptwriting assistance, editing, and content recommendation. The future may see AI taking on more prominent roles, potentially influencing the creative processes themselves and impacting the aesthetics of television productions. While the creative control of AI in these realms raises concerns for many, the potential for AI to enhance the efficiency and effectiveness of production is undeniable. The automation potential of AI can also significantly impact content localization, potentially speeding up the process of dubbing and subtitling, allowing for quicker global release of international productions.

The impact of AI on the viewer experience will be equally significant. Personalized content recommendations, powered by advanced AI algorithms, will become even more precise and sophisticated, potentially anticipating viewers' preferences before they even realize them. This personalization, while offering benefits to viewers, also raises concerns about potential biases and filter bubbles, potentially limiting exposure to diverse perspectives and creating echo chambers.

Furthermore, the convergence of television and other media platforms will continue. The lines between traditional television, streaming services, and social media will become increasingly blurred. We are already witnessing the integration of interactive elements and social features into streaming platforms, allowing viewers to engage with each other and participate in live discussions during broadcasts. This blurring of lines may lead to new forms of storytelling and audience engagement, possibly creating a more interactive and collaborative television experience. It also raises concerns about the potential for misinformation and the need for media literacy in discerning credible sources from sensationalized or manipulative content.

The future of international content creation will also be transformed. While the dominance of Western narratives remains a significant concern, the success of non-Western productions, such as

"Squid Game," has demonstrated the global appeal of compelling storytelling regardless of its origin. We can expect to see an increase in co-productions, collaborations between producers from different countries, leading to a more diverse range of narratives and perspectives. However, the challenges associated with navigating different cultural contexts and regulatory frameworks will remain a significant hurdle to overcome.

The distribution of international content will also undergo significant changes. The development of decentralized content delivery networks and the increasing availability of high-speed internet globally will contribute to improved accessibility. However, the digital divide remains a persistent problem. Addressing inequalities in internet access and affordability is crucial for ensuring that the benefits of global television are shared equitably across all regions. Governments and international organizations will have a critical role to play in bridging this digital divide.

The business models of television production and distribution are also likely to evolve. Subscription models will likely remain dominant, but we can anticipate greater experimentation with alternative revenue streams, such as ad-supported models, tiered subscription options, and microtransactions. The emergence of blockchain technology and other decentralized models may also disrupt the traditional hierarchies of power within the industry. This decentralization could empower smaller producers and give them more opportunities to participate in a wider global distribution of content.

Finally, the regulatory landscape will continue to be a major factor. Governments worldwide are grappling with the challenges of regulating streaming services, balancing the need to protect local content industries with the desire to promote innovation and competition. The complexities of copyright law, data privacy concerns, and cross-border regulation will demand sophisticated and adaptable international agreements to ensure fair and equitable practices.

In summary, the future of global television presents a landscape of immense opportunity and complex challenges. The interplay between technological innovation, evolving viewer preferences, and regulatory frameworks will shape the experience of television for decades to come. While the dominance of a few major players presents some risks, the opportunities for diversification, personalized experiences, and collaborative storytelling also hold considerable potential for a more enriching and inclusive global television landscape. Navigating these complexities, however, will require careful consideration of issues such as equitable access, cultural sensitivity, and the potential impact of artificial intelligence on the creative processes and the viewing experience. The coming years will undoubtedly be a period of significant transformation for this ever-evolving medium. The constant evolution of technology ensures a future of constant innovation and adaptation, promising an increasingly sophisticated and personalized viewing experience.

However, it will also be crucial for stakeholders to address the challenges of equitable access, cultural diversity, and responsible AI integration to fully realize the potential of global television in the years to come. The success of this transformative journey will rely heavily on international cooperation, thoughtful regulation, and the commitment to creating a truly inclusive and diverse global media ecosystem.

Televisions Role in Political Campaigns Media Coverage and Debates

The rise of television as a dominant medium in the mid-20th century profoundly altered the landscape of political campaigns. No longer were politicians solely reliant on newspapers, radio broadcasts, and public appearances to reach voters. Television offered a powerful new tool for disseminating their messages, shaping public perception, and engaging directly with the electorate. This shift fundamentally changed the strategies employed by campaigns and the way voters consumed political information. The visual immediacy of television, its ability to project charisma and personality, and its reach into millions of homes revolutionized the political process, although not without its drawbacks.

One of the most immediate impacts was the increased emphasis on visual communication. Candidates' appearances, demeanor, and even the carefully constructed sets of their televised addresses became as crucial as their policy positions. The "image" of a candidate, crafted through meticulous staging and media training, became a key element in winning over voters. This emphasis on visual appeal often overshadowed detailed policy discussions, leading to concerns about superficiality and a focus on style over substance. The Kennedy-Nixon debates of 1960 serve as a prime example. While the radio broadcasts revealed a closer contest, television viewers overwhelmingly favored Kennedy, whose youthful vigor and confident demeanor contrasted sharply with Nixon's perceived nervousness and less polished appearance. This highlighted the power of the visual medium to sway public opinion, even when the substance of the arguments might be equally compelling.

Televised political debates themselves evolved into major events, attracting huge audiences and shaping the course of campaigns. These televised confrontations allowed voters to directly compare candidates' views and personalities, providing a level of insight unavailable through other media. However, the debate format also presented opportunities for manipulation. The careful selection of topics, the strategic use of soundbites, and the exploitation of visual cues could significantly impact the viewer's perception of a candidate, regardless of the factual accuracy of their assertions. The debates between Ronald Reagan and Jimmy Carter in 1980 offer a compelling example. Reagan's confident delivery and effective use of memorable phrases, such as "Are you better off than you were four years ago?", resonated strongly with television audiences, contributing significantly to his victory.

The role of television news coverage in shaping political campaigns is equally significant. News broadcasts, both local and national, became pivotal platforms for disseminating information about candidates, their policies, and their campaigns. However, the way this information was presented could heavily influence voter perceptions. The framing of news stories, the selection of visuals, and the emphasis placed on certain aspects of a campaign could create a narrative that either favored or disadvantaged a particular candidate. The reliance on soundbites, short excerpts taken out of context, could also lead to misinterpretations and the dissemination of incomplete or inaccurate information. The intense media scrutiny accompanying presidential elections, particularly in the United States, frequently leads to a 24/7 news cycle, blurring the line between objective reporting and partisan commentary.

Furthermore, the rise of cable news and the proliferation of partisan media outlets have added another layer of complexity to television's role in politics. The 24-hour news cycle, driven by the need for constant content, has led to an environment where breaking news and sensationalism often overshadow in-depth analysis and thoughtful discussion of policy issues. The emergence of partisan news channels, which actively promote specific political agendas, further contributes to polarization and the spread of misinformation. This phenomenon has been particularly evident in recent years, with the increasing difficulty in distinguishing between factual reporting and opinion pieces, and the rise of "fake news" as a potent political weapon. The ability to target specific demographics through cable television and social media platforms, often with biased or misleading information, also creates substantial challenges to maintaining an informed electorate.

Television advertising became a crucial component of modern political campaigns, enabling candidates to reach vast audiences with targeted messages. The use of persuasive visuals, emotionally charged appeals, and catchy slogans made television advertisements particularly effective in shaping public perception. However, the high cost of television advertising created an uneven playing field, favoring candidates with substantial financial resources. Negative advertising, which attacks opponents' records or personalities, became increasingly prevalent, often employing misleading or emotionally charged imagery to sway public opinion. The impact of these negative advertisements on voter turnout and engagement remains a subject of ongoing debate, although evidence suggests it can increase cynicism and decrease voter participation.

The rise of social media and the internet has further complicated the role of television in political campaigns. While television continues to reach a broad audience, its dominance has been challenged by the increased use of online platforms for political communication. Candidates now utilize social media to bypass traditional media gatekeepers, engaging directly with voters through social media channels. However, this also opens the door to greater potential for misinformation and the spread of unsubstantiated claims. The ease of creating and disseminating videos and other digital content has led to a proliferation of propaganda, "deepfakes," and other forms of manipulated media, blurring the lines between truth and fiction and making it increasingly difficult for voters to discern accurate information.

In conclusion, television's impact on political campaigns has been profound and multifaceted. While it offers unprecedented opportunities for reaching voters and engaging in direct political discourse, it has also introduced challenges related to image over substance, the power of visual persuasion, and the potential for misinformation and manipulation. The rise of partisan media, the 24-hour news cycle, and the increased influence of social media further complicate the landscape. As we move into a future where traditional television coexists with various digital media platforms, the need for media literacy and critical thinking skills among voters has never been greater to navigate the complex, often polarized, world of televised political communication. The ability to critically evaluate information presented on television and other platforms is essential for informed political participation in a world saturated with information and competing narratives. This calls for a greater emphasis on media literacy education and the development of critical thinking skills to combat the proliferation of misleading information and ensure an informed electorate capable of making sound political choices. Only through this ongoing critical assessment can we effectively harness the power of television and other media in promoting a healthy and robust democracy.

The Influence of Television on Public Opinion Shaping Political Discourse

The pervasive influence of television extends far beyond entertainment; it profoundly shapes public opinion and, consequently, political discourse. The medium's ability to deliver information directly into homes, bypassing traditional gatekeepers like newspapers, has created a powerful tool for shaping political narratives. Televised news coverage, in particular, plays a crucial role in framing political issues and influencing public perceptions. The selection of stories, the angle from which they are presented, and the visuals accompanying the reports all contribute to a constructed reality, potentially leading to biased interpretations.

For instance, the framing of economic news can significantly impact public sentiment towards government policies. A report focusing on rising unemployment rates, accompanied by images of struggling families, might foster a sense of pessimism and dissatisfaction with the current administration. Conversely, a report emphasizing economic growth, illustrated with graphs showing positive trends and interviews with successful entrepreneurs, could create a more optimistic outlook. This selective presentation of information, even without overt bias, can subtly shape public opinion and influence voting behavior.

The strategic use of visuals is another key element in shaping political discourse on television. Images, whether they depict a candidate shaking hands with constituents or a protest turning violent, powerfully communicate emotions and perceptions. The careful selection and placement of these visuals within a news segment can manipulate viewers' emotional responses and influence their interpretation of events. A news report about a political rally might include shots of enthusiastic supporters, reinforcing a perception of popular support for the candidate, while omitting any footage of protests or dissent. Such subtle manipulations can significantly skew public perception.

Furthermore, the emphasis on soundbites – short, memorable phrases extracted from longer speeches or interviews – further simplifies and potentially distorts political discourse. While soundbites are effective in capturing attention and disseminating key messages, they often lack context and nuance. The selection of a particular soundbite can highlight a specific aspect of a politician's statement, potentially misrepresenting their overall position. For example, a politician's comment advocating for tax cuts, when taken out of context, might be interpreted as a disregard for social programs, even if the full statement included caveats and qualifiers. This manipulative use of soundbites contributes to the simplification and potential misrepresentation of complex political issues.

Political advertising on television epitomizes the deliberate manipulation of public opinion. Campaigns invest heavily in creating persuasive advertisements designed to appeal to specific demographic groups. These advertisements often employ emotional appeals, catchy slogans, and carefully chosen imagery to sway voters. Negative advertising, a particularly aggressive form of political advertising, focuses on attacking opponents, often through misleading or exaggerated claims. Such tactics can significantly damage a candidate's reputation and influence voter perceptions, even if the claims are unsubstantiated. The efficacy of negative advertising is a contentious topic, with some studies suggesting that it can demotivate voters while others suggest that it can motivate the base. However, the undeniable effect is the creation of a narrative around a candidate which can influence whether a voter will consider that candidate.

Beyond news coverage and political advertising, even entertainment programming subtly shapes political discourse. Television shows often reflect and reinforce existing societal biases, shaping viewers' perceptions of different groups and political ideologies. Sitcoms, dramas, and even reality shows can present certain political viewpoints in a positive or negative light, subtly influencing viewers' beliefs and attitudes. For example, the portrayal of specific political figures or ideologies within fictional narratives can affect viewers' perceptions of their character and stances, subtly influencing opinions.

The rise of cable news and 24-hour news cycles further exacerbates the issue of bias and influence. The constant need for new content often leads to a focus on sensationalism and breaking news, overshadowing in-depth analysis and thoughtful discussion of policy issues. The proliferation of partisan news channels, each promoting a specific political agenda, further polarizes the public and contributes to the spread of misinformation. Viewers are often exposed to a highly curated selection of information that reinforces their existing beliefs, creating echo chambers and hindering open dialogue.

The digital age and the proliferation of online platforms add another layer of complexity. The ease with which manipulated videos and false information can be disseminated online poses a significant challenge. The line between factual reporting and opinionated commentary becomes increasingly blurred, leading to confusion and distrust. The algorithms used by social media platforms further reinforce echo chambers, limiting exposure to diverse perspectives and fostering political polarization.

To mitigate the negative impacts of television's influence on public opinion, increased media literacy is crucial. Educating viewers on how to critically analyze information presented on television, identify biases, and recognize manipulative tactics is essential for fostering informed and engaged citizenry. This includes promoting critical thinking skills, encouraging the consumption of diverse news sources, and fostering a greater awareness of the inherent biases present in any form of media. Only by developing these crucial skills can we navigate the complex and often biased world of televised political communication and make informed political decisions. The constant need for critical engagement with media is a vital safeguard against misinformation and manipulation and the key to using television for positive and constructive social and political engagement.

Television and Political Power Media Control and Censorship

The inherent power of television to reach vast audiences simultaneously made it a coveted tool for those seeking to shape public opinion and exert political control. Governments worldwide quickly recognized this potential, leading to various strategies for influencing, regulating, and in some cases, directly controlling television programming. The interplay between television and political power often involved a delicate balance between freedom of expression and the need to maintain social order or advance specific political agendas. This section will explore this complex relationship, focusing on instances of media control and censorship, and the subsequent governmental regulations put in place to manage the powerful influence television holds.

One of the earliest and most significant forms of media control was the direct ownership and operation of television broadcasting by state entities. In many countries, particularly those with authoritarian regimes, television networks were wholly owned and operated by the government, making them instruments of propaganda and political indoctrination. Programming was carefully curated to promote the ruling party's ideology, suppress dissent, and shape public perceptions favorably. News broadcasts, documentaries, and even entertainment shows were often designed to reinforce the government's narrative and portray a positive image of the regime. Critical voices were silenced, oppositional viewpoints were marginalized, and alternative perspectives were effectively suppressed. This level of direct control was commonplace in several communist states throughout the 20th century, and in many cases, continues today in various forms and to varying extents. The ability to control the narrative offered a powerful tool to control the populace through shaping their beliefs and perspectives.

Beyond direct ownership, governments employed less overt but equally effective methods of influencing television content.

Licensing systems, which granted broadcasting permits to television stations, became another significant tool for control. Governments could grant or deny licenses based on the broadcaster's adherence to established guidelines and regulations, effectively influencing programming decisions. This mechanism allowed for the subtle suppression of dissenting voices, by ensuring only stations that adhered to governmental policies were granted broadcast permits.

Broadcasting was thus controlled through the indirect method of licensing, ensuring only those whose viewpoints aligned with the government's received the right to broadcast. This method remained more subtle than outright ownership, but its effectiveness in shaping the media landscape was nonetheless significant.

Censorship, often implicit rather than explicit, was another pervasive strategy. Governments might not directly ban certain topics or programs, but they could exert pressure on broadcasters to self-censor, avoiding potentially controversial subjects. This pressure could take the form of informal guidelines, threats of license revocation, or subtle warnings. Broadcasters, mindful of the potential consequences of defying the implicit or explicit directives of the government, would often opt to avoid sensitive topics, leading to a form of self-censorship that effectively limited the diversity of viewpoints presented on television. The threat of punitive action was frequently sufficient to maintain conformity with governmental expectations, ensuring that the broadcast content remained within the limits of acceptability.

The rise of globalization and the proliferation of satellite television challenged the effectiveness of these traditional forms of media control. While governments could continue to regulate domestic broadcasters, it proved significantly more difficult to control the flow of international programming through satellite channels. The increasing availability of foreign news channels and entertainment programs exposed viewers to alternative perspectives and viewpoints, weakening the grip of state-controlled media. However, governments responded by implementing new strategies to counteract this increased access to global perspectives. This included the increased use of targeted media campaigns aimed at discrediting foreign broadcasters, promoting their own news channels as authoritative sources, and using sophisticated methods of surveillance to monitor the use and consumption of alternative media channels.

Furthermore, the increasing influence of social media and digital platforms has added a new dimension to this relationship.

Governments often attempt to exert control over online content, though the challenges of effectively censoring the internet are far greater than controlling broadcast television. Governments have implemented various strategies to achieve this. These include the use of surveillance technology to track online activity, employing complex legal frameworks to regulate online speech, and directly influencing the content of online platforms. This effort, however, continues to be a battleground, as technological innovations and the spread of encryption technology continuously challenge the capability of governments to monitor and control this online landscape.

The regulation of television broadcasting also varies significantly across different countries, reflecting different political systems, cultural values, and legal frameworks. Some countries have strict regulations governing television content, aimed at protecting children, preventing the spread of hate speech, or maintaining national security. Other countries have a more laissez-faire approach, relying on market forces and self-regulation to shape the broadcast landscape. Even those countries with more relaxed regulations are confronted with evolving social and political challenges that necessitate careful attention to the effects of media on the public. In this sense, the debate over media regulation never ends; the issues involved are continuously updated and reinterpreted.

The relationship between television and political power remains a complex and dynamic one. While governments have employed various strategies to control and influence television content, the emergence of new technologies and the increasing demand for access to diverse information continue to challenge their ability to exert absolute control. The ongoing evolution of media technology and its capacity for global transmission will continue to shape the future dynamics of the interplay between governments and the television media, a relationship which has consistently evolved and changed in tandem with the technology that powers it. The coming decades will likely see this interplay continue to evolve, as governments and media providers must continue to adapt and respond to changing technologies, audience expectations, and political landscapes. The quest for balance between freedom of speech and the need to maintain social order continues to be a constant challenge.

The Impact of Social Media on Political Discourse Amplification and Polarization

The rise of social media has profoundly reshaped the landscape of political discourse, creating a complex interplay with the established influence of television. While television once held a near-monopoly on the dissemination of political information to mass audiences, social media platforms have emerged as powerful alternative channels, dramatically altering the dynamics of political communication. This shift has manifested in two key ways: the amplification of political messages and the exacerbation of political polarization.

Social media's capacity for rapid and widespread dissemination of information far surpasses that of traditional media. A single tweet, Facebook post, or viral video can reach millions within hours, bypassing the gatekeepers of traditional media—editors, producers, and network executives—who once controlled the flow of political information. This has empowered political actors, activists, and even ordinary citizens to bypass established media channels and directly engage with their target audiences. Political campaigns can now launch targeted messaging directly to specific demographics, using sophisticated data analytics to identify and reach potential voters with tailored appeals. This level of precision and direct engagement was previously unimaginable in the television era. Moreover, the immediacy of social media facilitates rapid responses to unfolding events, allowing political figures to instantly address controversies, react to news developments, and engage in real-time debates with their constituents and opponents. This direct interaction offers a level of immediacy and engagement that television, bound by production schedules and broadcast times, cannot replicate.

The decentralized nature of social media has also fostered the rise of citizen journalism and alternative news sources. Individuals can now document and share their perspectives on political events, often providing accounts that complement or even contradict the narratives presented by mainstream media outlets. This decentralized information flow empowers individuals and smaller news outlets to act as independent watchdogs, offering diverse perspectives on political events and challenging the dominant narratives propagated by traditional media or political establishments. This diversity, however, is not without its downsides. The increased volume of information—much of it unverified—makes it more challenging for citizens to discern factual accuracy and assess the credibility of sources. The ease with which misinformation can spread through social media networks exacerbates this challenge and necessitates an increased degree of media literacy from consumers.

However, the amplification effect of social media is not always positive. The rapid spread of misinformation and disinformation, commonly referred to as "fake news," poses a significant challenge to democratic discourse. The decentralized structure of social media platforms makes it difficult to regulate the flow of false information, and the algorithms that govern these platforms often prioritize engagement over accuracy, leading to the amplification of sensationalized or misleading content that can quickly spread and influence public opinion. The spread of conspiracy theories and other forms of misinformation can undermine trust in institutions and sow discord within society. This challenges the ability of traditional media outlets to effectively counter misinformation, particularly when the algorithms that dictate social media traffic favor emotionally charged and easily-shared content, regardless of its veracity.

Beyond the amplification of messages, social media has contributed to a significant increase in political polarization. Echo chambers, where individuals are primarily exposed to information that confirms their existing beliefs, are readily created and reinforced by social media algorithms. These algorithms personalize newsfeeds, suggesting content tailored to user preferences and past interactions. While this personalization can be useful for providing users with relevant content, it can also reinforce pre-existing biases and limit exposure to diverse perspectives. Consequently, individuals may become increasingly entrenched in their viewpoints, reducing their willingness to engage with alternative opinions and leading to greater division and animosity within society. This can manifest in intensified political tribalism, reduced inter-group understanding, and increased conflict.

The interaction between television and social media further complicates this issue. Television broadcasts often serve as the source of events that then become subject to extensive discussion and commentary on social media platforms. Political debates, news events, and even entertainment programming featuring political commentary all feed the online conversation, creating a dynamic feedback loop where television broadcasts shape the social media discussion and social media responses, in turn, influence television programming and reporting. This complex interplay necessitates a nuanced understanding of how these media interact to shape political discourse. The line between fact and opinion becomes increasingly blurred as information is relayed and repurposed across different media platforms, requiring viewers and users to develop heightened critical thinking skills to navigate this complex information ecosystem.

For instance, during election campaigns, television broadcasts of political debates and campaign rallies are often followed by intense discussions and analysis on social media. Candidates' appearances, verbal exchanges, and policy pronouncements are dissected, debated, and often meme-ified on various platforms. This can impact the overall perception of candidates and their platforms, influencing public opinion independently of traditional media's editorial influence. Furthermore, social media posts and commentary can then become the subject of follow-up reporting on television, creating a recursive effect where television broadcasts fuel social media discussions, which, in turn, are reflected back in subsequent television coverage. This feedback loop can amplify certain narratives while marginalizing others, making it difficult to accurately assess the overall public mood and the true influence of different political messages.

The influence of social media on political polarization is not limited to the amplification of existing divisions. It also creates new avenues for the spread of divisive rhetoric. The anonymity afforded by many social media platforms can embolden users to express extreme views or engage in aggressive personal attacks, contributing to a climate of heightened antagonism. The ease of sharing inflammatory content and engaging in online harassment contributes to the degradation of political discourse and discourages meaningful engagement between individuals with differing viewpoints. This toxic environment makes it harder for compromise and consensus-building to occur, furthering the polarization of political discourse. The spread of hateful and extremist ideologies through social media, often targeted at specific groups or individuals, is particularly troubling and requires robust countermeasures from both social media platforms and civil society organizations.

In conclusion, the impact of social media on political discourse is multifaceted and far-reaching. While it has empowered individuals and groups to bypass traditional media gatekeepers and participate directly in political debates, it has also created new challenges, including the spread of misinformation and the exacerbation of political polarization. The interplay between television and social media creates a dynamic and complex information environment that requires careful consideration and a heightened level of critical thinking to navigate. Understanding the intricate mechanisms by which these media intersect and influence public opinion is crucial for fostering informed civic engagement and promoting a healthier, more constructive political dialogue in the future. The constant evolution of both television and social media necessitates ongoing research and analysis to fully grasp the changing dynamics of this critical relationship and its impact on democratic processes. This ongoing investigation will require collaboration across multiple disciplines, from media studies and political science to computer science and social psychology, to understand the complex interplay of technology, communication, and political behavior in the digital age.

The Future of Television and Politics Adapting to a Changing Media Landscape

The convergence of television and the internet, accelerated by the proliferation of streaming services and smart TVs, has fundamentally altered the consumption of political information. Traditional broadcast television, once the dominant force in shaping public opinion, now faces a fragmented and increasingly competitive media landscape. The rise of on-demand content, personalized news feeds, and niche online communities has empowered viewers to curate their own media diets, often leading to echo chambers and reinforcing pre-existing biases. Political actors are adapting to this shift by diversifying their communication strategies, utilizing a multi-platform approach that leverages both traditional television and newer digital channels.

Political advertising, a cornerstone of television's influence on political campaigns, is undergoing a significant transformation.

While television remains a powerful tool for reaching mass audiences with broad-based messaging, the rise of targeted advertising on social media platforms allows campaigns to micro-target specific voter demographics with personalized appeals. This precision targeting, enabled by sophisticated data analytics, permits campaigns to tailor their messaging to resonate with the specific concerns and values of individual voter segments. This approach allows for more efficient resource allocation and potentially greater impact, but it also raises concerns about the potential for manipulation and the spread of misinformation. The ability to micro-target specific demographics with tailored messaging has also enabled the rise of 'dark ads'—political advertisements that are not publicly viewable and therefore lack transparency. This lack of transparency raises concerns about the accountability and potential for manipulation inherent in these covert advertising strategies.

The future of televised political debates remains uncertain. While these events still attract significant viewership, particularly among older demographics, their influence may be diluted by the parallel conversations and analyses unfolding on social media. The immediate commentary and fact-checking that accompany these events on platforms like Twitter, Facebook, and YouTube can often overshadow the impact of the broadcast itself. Viewers are increasingly likely to consult multiple sources, forming their own conclusions independent of the narrative presented by the televised debate. This necessitates a recalibration of the strategic value of participating in these events. Candidates must adapt their communication styles to engage both the live television audience and the concurrent online conversation.

The blurring lines between news and entertainment also pose challenges for the future of television and politics. The rise of infotainment programs, blending news with commentary and analysis, blurs the distinction between objective reporting and subjective opinion. This format can be particularly effective in engaging viewers, but it raises concerns about the potential for bias and misinformation. The line between hard news and soft news has become increasingly porous, making it more difficult for citizens to discern factual accuracy and assess the credibility of sources. The proliferation of opinion pieces and commentary, often presented with the same visual style and production values as traditional news broadcasts, adds to the complexity of evaluating the information presented.

Furthermore, the rise of alternative media sources presents a significant challenge to traditional television news outlets. Online news aggregators, blogs, podcasts, and social media influencers all compete for viewers' attention, diversifying the sources of political information available to the public. This democratization of information distribution has empowered individuals and groups to bypass traditional media gatekeepers, but it also creates new challenges in terms of ensuring accuracy and combating misinformation. The spread of fake news and conspiracy theories, exacerbated by algorithms that prioritize engagement over accuracy, poses a direct threat to informed civic engagement and democratic discourse. This has necessitated the development of new strategies for verifying information and educating citizens about the dangers of misinformation.

The future of television and politics will also depend on technological advancements. The integration of artificial intelligence (AI) into television broadcasting and news production holds the potential to revolutionize how political information is created, disseminated, and consumed. AI-powered tools can automate newsgathering, enhance video editing and production, and personalize news feeds based on individual viewer preferences.

However, concerns around bias in algorithms, algorithmic manipulation, and the potential for misuse of AI-powered tools in disinformation campaigns must be carefully addressed. This requires ongoing research into the ethical implications of AI and its potential impact on democratic processes.

The integration of interactive elements and augmented reality into television programming may provide opportunities for increased citizen engagement with political issues. Viewers could potentially interact directly with political events and candidates via social media feeds integrated into television broadcasts. These technological advancements, however, also pose challenges related to data privacy, security, and the potential for abuse.

The ability of political institutions and actors to adapt to these evolving media landscapes will determine the future of television's role in shaping political discourse. Those who effectively utilize a multi-platform strategy, leveraging both traditional television and new digital channels, will likely enjoy greater success in engaging with voters. However, simply transitioning to these newer platforms will not be enough; political actors must also demonstrate a commitment to accuracy, transparency, and ethical communication practices. Transparency in advertising and funding will be crucial in maintaining public trust, and combating the spread of misinformation and fake news through effective media literacy initiatives will be equally important.

The rise of streaming services and smart TVs also necessitates a re-evaluation of the role of public service broadcasting in the context of a fragmented media landscape. Public broadcasters have a crucial responsibility in providing high-quality, unbiased, and factual news and information to citizens. Maintaining public trust in these institutions will require a commitment to journalistic integrity and a proactive approach to combating misinformation. This also necessitates a thorough examination of how to make this crucial information accessible to all viewers, regardless of economic or technological barriers. Public broadcasters must leverage technological advancements to reach diverse audiences through digital platforms while continuing to provide high-quality programming on traditional broadcast channels.

In conclusion, the future of television and politics is inextricably linked to the evolution of the broader media landscape. The rise of new media technologies and platforms has fundamentally reshaped the consumption of political information, creating both opportunities and challenges for political actors, institutions, and citizens alike. Navigating this evolving environment requires a multi-faceted approach that embraces technological advancements while also addressing concerns about misinformation, bias, and the ethical implications of new communication technologies.

Maintaining a commitment to journalistic integrity, fostering media literacy, and prioritizing transparency and accountability will be critical for sustaining informed civic engagement and a robust democratic process in the age of digital media. The ongoing evolution of media technologies necessitates a continual adaptation of strategies to ensure a healthy and informed political landscape for the future.

Televisions Influence on Popular Culture Trends and Fashions

Television's pervasive influence extends far beyond the realm of politics and news. Its impact on popular culture is undeniable, shaping trends in fashion, music, language, and even social behavior in profound ways. From the brightly colored clothing of the 1960s sitcoms influencing teenage fashion to the catchphrases and slang that become embedded in everyday conversation, television's imprint on our collective consciousness is deeply ingrained. The rise of the celebrity culture, often fueled by television exposure, highlights another significant dimension of this influence. Television's ability to project idealized images of lifestyle and aspiration also plays a crucial role in defining social norms and desires.

One striking example of television's impact on fashion can be seen in the evolution of women's clothing. The stylish outfits worn by characters in iconic sitcoms like "I Love Lucy" and "The Mary Tyler Moore Show" influenced fashion trends across the country. The simple, yet elegant, attire of Lucy Ricardo, for instance, resonated with housewives across America, reflecting a shift toward practicality and comfort. Similarly, the professional yet stylish attire of Mary Richards reflected the growing independence and career aspirations of women during the 1970s, impacting workplace fashion trends for years to come. This influence extended beyond sitcoms; drama series and even reality shows also played a key role, with fashion choices of leading characters often imitated by viewers. The impact was further amplified by the creation of television-inspired clothing lines and merchandise, directly translating on-screen style into consumer products. The rise of fashion shows dedicated to showcasing outfits featured in popular shows further cemented the cyclical relationship between television and fashion trends.

The relationship between television and music is equally compelling. Television's vast reach provided a platform for emerging musical artists, transforming the way music was discovered and consumed. The advent of music-oriented television shows, from early variety programs showcasing established acts to later dedicated music video channels, played a central role in popularizing musical styles. The integration of music into television shows, both as background scores and integral plot elements, significantly influenced the tastes and preferences of viewers. Songs featured prominently in popular television shows often experienced a resurgence in popularity, reaching a much wider audience than through traditional radio or record sales. This phenomenon also led to the creation of soundtracks featuring music from popular television shows, further solidifying the interconnectedness of television and the music industry. The influence of television on music extended beyond simply promoting artists; it also played a significant role in shaping the visual style of music videos, borrowing production techniques and aesthetics from television broadcasting. The symbiotic relationship between the two media significantly shaped the cultural landscape of music.

Television's influence extends to language and communication, subtly shaping the way we speak, write, and interact. Catchphrases and slang from popular television shows often enter mainstream vocabulary, becoming ingrained in everyday conversation. Iconic lines from sitcoms, dramas, and even commercials become part of the cultural lexicon, used to express a range of emotions and opinions. This integration of television language into everyday discourse reflects the medium's deep penetration into our collective consciousness, highlighting its role in shaping linguistic trends. The use of television language is not merely a matter of adopting catchphrases; it involves the adoption of storytelling structures, comedic timing, and narrative techniques that influence the way we communicate in everyday interactions. This adoption can be seen across different communication settings, from personal conversations to professional presentations. The narrative styles and communication strategies presented on television shows become models for viewers, subtly shaping the way they articulate their thoughts and experiences.

Beyond language, television has profoundly impacted social behaviors. The portrayal of relationships, family structures, and social interactions on television can influence viewers' perceptions of what is considered "normal" or desirable. Sitcoms and dramas often present idealized versions of family life, romance, and social interactions, shaping viewers' expectations and aspirations. While these portrayals may not always reflect reality, they nonetheless play a significant role in shaping social norms and influencing viewer behavior. This influence extends beyond simple imitation; the storylines and themes presented in television programs can prompt viewers to re-examine their values, beliefs, and behavior.

The portrayal of diverse family structures, for example, can challenge societal norms and promote a greater level of acceptance and understanding. Similarly, depictions of social issues and inequalities can stimulate public discourse and encourage positive social change. The influence of television, therefore, is not merely about emulating what is shown on screen but also about engaging with the broader social narratives presented.

The rise of reality television presents another significant facet of television's influence on popular culture. These shows, often showcasing heightened drama and fabricated situations, have nevertheless played a major role in shaping social perceptions and behavior. Reality television shows often create trends by showcasing particular styles, lifestyles, and social interactions, often amplified by the constant commentary and analysis offered by various media platforms. This constant commentary and interpretation creates a feedback loop, where television influences popular culture, which in turn shapes the content and themes of future reality shows. The blurring of lines between reality and fiction inherent in these programs raises questions about authenticity and the potential for manipulation, yet their significant impact on popular culture remains undeniable. The constant exposure to these programs can influence social interactions and behaviors, often leading to the imitation of behaviors and lifestyles shown on screen.

The advent of streaming services and the rise of on-demand content have further intensified television's impact on popular culture. The ability to access an extensive library of television shows and movies at any time and from anywhere has shifted the way viewers consume content, intensifying exposure and influencing trends more rapidly than ever before. The algorithms utilized by streaming services further amplify this effect, constantly suggesting content based on viewing habits and preferences, creating highly personalized and potentially echo-chamber-like consumption patterns. The highly personalized nature of these platforms allows for extremely targeted advertising and promotional campaigns, increasing the efficiency and effectiveness of marketing strategies.

The interactive nature of many streaming platforms allows for immediate feedback and user engagement, fostering a more dynamic and responsive relationship between viewers and content providers. This dynamic interaction accelerates the dissemination of trends and fashions, reinforcing the pervasive influence of television in shaping popular culture.

In conclusion, television's influence on popular culture is a complex and multifaceted phenomenon. Its impact on fashion, music, language, and social behavior is undeniable, reflecting the medium's powerful ability to shape our perceptions, aspirations, and interactions. The ever-evolving nature of television technology, with the advent of streaming services and interactive platforms, continues to intensify this influence, demonstrating television's ongoing role in shaping the cultural landscape and our understanding of the world around us. The convergence of television with other forms of media, such as social media and online platforms, further amplifies its reach and impact, reinforcing its crucial role in shaping trends and fashions in modern society. The study of television's cultural impact requires a continuous and dynamic approach, recognizing the evolving nature of the medium and its ongoing relationship with broader societal and technological trends.

The Portrayal of Social Issues on Television Representation and Stereotypes

Television's influence extends beyond shaping trends; it profoundly impacts how we understand and perceive social issues. The small screen has served as a powerful platform, both reflecting and shaping societal attitudes towards gender, race, class, and a myriad of other social categories. However, this power comes with a significant responsibility, one that television has not always met effectively. The portrayal of social issues on television is a complex tapestry woven with threads of representation, stereotype, and the potential, albeit often unrealized, for positive social change.

One of the most pervasive areas where television's influence is felt is in its depiction of gender roles. For decades, television reinforced traditional gender stereotypes. Sitcoms of the 1950s and 60s, for example, often depicted women as homemakers primarily concerned with their families, while men were portrayed as the breadwinners and primary decision-makers. These representations, while seemingly innocuous, subtly reinforced existing power dynamics and limited the perceived aspirations of women. Even as television evolved, challenges persisted. While shows like "Mary Tyler Moore" presented independent, career-oriented women, they often faced challenges and obstacles that were largely absent from the male characters' narratives. The portrayal of female characters frequently emphasized their romantic relationships over their professional achievements, a subtle but significant imbalance that reflected and reinforced societal biases.

The evolution of female representation on television is far from uniform. The past few decades have seen a growing diversity of female characters, reflecting the changing social landscape. However, challenges remain. While there has been a notable increase in strong, independent female leads, they often adhere to specific aesthetic ideals, potentially perpetuating unrealistic beauty standards. The representation of diverse body types, sexual orientations, and ethnicities remains uneven, failing to represent fully the richness and complexity of the female experience. The presence of successful female characters shouldn't overshadow the continuing need for critical examination of how these portrayals affect audience perceptions and expectations of women in real life. The subtle ways in which female characters are portrayed – their agency, their vulnerabilities, their relationship to power – all contribute to a complex picture that requires careful scrutiny.

Similarly, the representation of racial and ethnic minorities on television has a long and often troubled history. Early television largely excluded minorities or relegated them to stereotypical roles, reinforcing negative biases and perpetuating harmful misconceptions. Black characters, for example, were often confined to roles as maids, servants, or comedic sidekicks, failing to represent the diversity and complexity of Black experiences. Latin American characters were frequently depicted as fiery or romantic, while Asian characters were often portrayed as meek and submissive. These limited and stereotypical portrayals reinforced existing prejudices and perpetuated a limited understanding of the richness of diverse cultures. The absence of positive representation fostered a lack of visibility and a diminished sense of belonging for minority communities.

The struggle for accurate and equitable representation is a continuous journey, not a destination reached. While progress has been made, with the emergence of shows that feature complex and well-rounded minority characters, the challenges remain significant.

The imbalance in representation, particularly in leading roles, continues to perpetuate a sense of exclusion. Furthermore, the way minority characters are portrayed – their interactions with majority characters, their struggles, and their triumphs – can either reinforce or challenge existing stereotypes. The mere presence of diverse characters does not automatically equate to authentic representation. In-depth analysis of the characters' experiences and their portrayal within the larger narrative structure is crucial in assessing their impact.

Class representation on television also offers a revealing perspective on societal biases. For many years, television predominantly showcased middle-class or affluent families, neglecting the experiences of the working class and the poor. When working-class families were depicted, it was often through a lens of humor or pity, reinforcing negative stereotypes and reinforcing existing social hierarchies. The lack of diverse class representation failed to reflect the social realities of a large segment of the population. This limited portrayal created a sense of disconnect between the television audience and the complex realities of socioeconomic inequalities.

The portrayal of working-class families often lacked nuance, reducing complex life experiences to simple tropes. The complexities of financial struggles, job insecurity, and the daily challenges faced by those living in poverty were often absent from the narratives. The rare instances where working-class families were portrayed often emphasized their struggles, sometimes for comedic effect, rather than exploring the resilience, strength, and cultural richness of these communities.

The depiction of social issues on television, however, is not solely about the perpetuation of stereotypes; it also holds the potential for positive social change. Shows that challenge stereotypes, explore complex social issues, and offer diverse perspectives can play a powerful role in promoting understanding, empathy, and social progress. Television's ability to reach a broad audience makes it a potentially potent instrument for initiating social dialogue and promoting positive change. Shows like "The Wire," for example, provided a nuanced portrayal of the drug trade, challenging simplistic narratives and promoting a more nuanced understanding of complex social problems.

Similarly, shows that address LGBTQ+ issues, disability rights, and other minority experiences can promote greater acceptance and understanding. The portrayal of complex relationships, interracial couples, and characters with disabilities can challenge preconceived notions and encourage greater empathy among viewers. However, the effectiveness of these portrayals depends not only on the presence of diverse characters but also on the authenticity and depth of their representation. Superficial or tokenistic portrayals can be counterproductive, potentially reinforcing stereotypes or trivializing important issues.

The effectiveness of television's role in promoting social change depends on several factors. The quality of writing, acting, and direction, the credibility of the show's portrayal of issues, and the resonance it finds with its intended audience all contribute to the ultimate impact. Furthermore, the context in which the show is received – including prevailing cultural attitudes and social norms – plays a significant role in how the messages are interpreted and adopted. Mere portrayal isn't enough; sustained engagement with the issues, leading to meaningful discussions and societal change, is crucial. The role of television in promoting social change is not automatic or guaranteed; it requires careful consideration of the narratives presented, and the potential for positive change.

In conclusion, television's portrayal of social issues is a complex and multifaceted phenomenon. While the medium has historically perpetuated stereotypes and reinforced existing inequalities, it also holds the potential for significant positive social change. The path toward responsible and effective representation requires a constant critical assessment of how social categories are portrayed, a commitment to diversity and inclusion, and a willingness to challenge prevailing biases and misconceptions. The power of television to reach millions of viewers makes its responsibility in shaping perceptions and promoting positive change paramount. The ongoing evolution of television, its formats, and its narrative structures requires a continuous reevaluation of the standards of representation, ensuring the narratives conveyed are both accurate and impactful, fostering a more inclusive and equitable society.

Televisions Impact on Family Life Changing Dynamics and Relationships

Television's arrival in homes across the globe dramatically altered the fabric of family life, reshaping dynamics, relationships, and communication patterns in profound ways. While often lauded for its entertainment value, the impact of the television screen on families is a complex tapestry woven with threads of both positive and negative consequences. Understanding this impact requires a nuanced examination of how it altered shared experiences, individual habits, and the very structure of family interactions.

One of the most immediate and noticeable changes was the shift in shared family time. Before the ubiquitous presence of television, evenings often involved shared activities – games, storytelling, reading aloud, or simply engaging in conversation. The television, with its captivating programming, offered a readily available alternative, often drawing family members away from these shared experiences. The flickering screen became a focal point, sometimes uniting the family in shared viewing, but more often fragmenting it as individuals retreated into their own private worlds of entertainment. This shift had profound implications for the development of interpersonal skills, particularly for children. The decline in face-to-face interactions could lead to reduced opportunities for developing communication skills, empathy, and social understanding. While family dinners might still occur, the presence of the television could often detract from the quality of those interactions, creating a backdrop of distraction that hindered meaningful conversation.

The rise of television also profoundly altered the dynamics between parents and children. The power of the television to influence children's attitudes, beliefs, and behaviors became a source of concern for parents. The exposure to violence, inappropriate language, and unrealistic portrayals of life raised anxieties about the impact on children's development. This led to parental efforts to control television viewing, introducing parental controls, setting viewing limits, and selecting programs deemed appropriate. These efforts, however, were often met with resistance from children who craved the entertainment and social connection offered by popular television shows. The resulting power struggle over television access became a recurring feature of family life in many households, further complicating the parent-child relationship.

The introduction of television also impacted the communication patterns within families. The shared experience of watching a program could serve as a springboard for conversation, allowing family members to connect over shared interests and experiences. However, the passive nature of television viewing often limited the opportunities for meaningful dialogue. The family might sit together in the same room, but each individual could be lost in their own separate viewing experience, effectively isolating them from each other, even in physical proximity. This phenomenon of "togetherness" without actual interaction became a defining characteristic of family life in the television age. The television itself often became a mediator, substituting for genuine interaction and creating a barrier to open and honest communication.

The impact of television also extended to the relationship between siblings. While shared viewing could sometimes foster a sense of camaraderie, it could also be a source of conflict. Disputes over program selection, viewing time, and channel control became common occurrences, often leading to sibling rivalry and strained relationships. The competition for parental attention, often fueled by the allure of television, could further exacerbate these conflicts.

The television, therefore, could become not just a source of entertainment but also a focal point of family friction, adding another layer of complexity to sibling dynamics.

The introduction of television into the family home also impacted parental roles and responsibilities. While the television offered a form of entertainment that could occupy children for extended periods, freeing up time for parents, it also brought with it new challenges. The need to monitor children's viewing habits, manage screen time, and address concerns about the influence of media added to the already substantial demands of parenting. This amplified the challenges of balancing work, household chores, and childcare. The increased availability of ready-made entertainment also raised questions about parental involvement in children's leisure activities and the role of parents in shaping their children's worldview.

The effects of television weren't limited to the immediate family unit; they also extended to the broader social network. Television viewing could impact the amount of time spent with extended family and friends. The allure of television programs could compete with other social activities, reducing the frequency and intensity of interactions with individuals outside the immediate family circle.

This could lead to feelings of isolation and a decreased sense of community, particularly for those who lacked strong social networks.

However, it is crucial to acknowledge the positive impacts television has had on family life. For many families, television provided a shared source of entertainment and connection, particularly in times of social isolation or geographical distance. Educational programs enriched the learning experience for children, while news broadcasts kept families informed about current events.

Family members could also come together to watch favorite programs, creating shared memories and bonding experiences. The potential for shared viewing facilitated family discussions and strengthened relationships when used judiciously.

The transition to cable and satellite television further diversified the available programming, catering to more specialized interests and offering opportunities for families to explore diverse cultures and perspectives. The rise of streaming services further enhanced this accessibility, providing a wealth of on-demand content that catered to the preferences of individual family members. This greater diversity of programming allowed families to tailor their viewing habits to their specific needs and interests, facilitating a more personalized experience.

The impact of television on family life is an ongoing process of adaptation and change. As television technology continues to evolve, so too does its influence on family dynamics. The advent of mobile devices and the internet has created new forms of media consumption, challenging the traditional dominance of the television screen and further fragmenting family time. Families are constantly negotiating the balance between shared activities and individual screen time, continually seeking to integrate technology into their lives in a way that supports healthy relationships and meaningful interactions.

The challenge for families today is not to eliminate television entirely but to navigate its use responsibly. Setting clear limits on screen time, engaging in shared viewing experiences, and promoting open communication about television content are crucial steps in mitigating the potential negative impacts and maximizing the positive ones. Parents need to actively participate in their children's viewing habits, guiding them towards age-appropriate programming and using television as a tool for education and conversation. Families need to find a balance between the convenience and entertainment that television offers and the importance of face-to-face interaction, shared activities, and meaningful communication. Only then can families leverage the positive aspects of television while minimizing its potentially disruptive influence on their dynamics and relationships. The ongoing evolution of the media landscape requires a continuous adaptation of family strategies to maintain strong, healthy, and meaningful connections within the family unit.

Television and Education Informative and Educational Programming

The democratizing power of television extended beyond entertainment; it also held significant potential as an educational tool. From its earliest days, visionaries recognized the medium's capacity to reach vast audiences simultaneously, offering unprecedented access to information and learning opportunities previously confined to classrooms or expensive printed materials.

The post-World War II era witnessed a burgeoning interest in utilizing this powerful medium to address educational needs, fostering literacy, and promoting civic engagement. This led to the development of dedicated educational programming, aiming to bridge geographical and socioeconomic divides in access to quality instruction.

Early examples of informative programming often took the form of documentaries, which capitalized on television's ability to visually convey complex information. Series like "The March of Time," initially a newsreel series, adapted to the television format, offering viewers engaging glimpses into historical events, scientific discoveries, and social issues. The intimate nature of the television screen allowed viewers to experience events in a more personal way than was previously possible through other media. These documentaries often utilized compelling narratives, dramatic reconstructions, and expert interviews to make complex topics accessible to a broad audience, fostering a sense of shared understanding and stimulating further inquiry.

The emergence of public broadcasting in many countries significantly expanded the reach and impact of educational programming. In the United States, the Public Broadcasting Service (PBS) emerged as a crucial platform for educational television. Programs like "Sesame Street" and "Mister Rogers' Neighborhood" demonstrated the effectiveness of television in reaching young children, employing catchy songs, engaging characters, and age-appropriate content to teach basic literacy, numeracy, and social skills. These shows cleverly blended entertainment and education, proving that learning could be enjoyable and accessible to even the youngest viewers. Their success underscored the medium's power to capture children's attention and instill valuable life lessons, impacting early childhood development in profound ways.

Beyond early childhood education, television also found its place in secondary and higher education. Programs offering instruction in diverse subjects, from science and history to literature and the arts, began to appear on public and commercial channels. While the quality and depth of these programs varied considerably, they demonstrated the potential of television to supplement traditional classroom instruction, offering a flexible and accessible learning resource. The ability to visually depict scientific processes, historical events, or artistic techniques provided a dynamic complement to textbooks and lectures, making abstract concepts more concrete and engaging for learners.

The introduction of educational channels specifically dedicated to broadcast teaching further solidified television's role in the educational landscape. These channels offered structured curricula, often aligned with national educational standards, providing comprehensive instruction in various subjects. The use of interactive elements, quizzes, and assignments aimed to enhance engagement and monitor student progress. These channels often collaborated with educational institutions and expert educators to ensure the accuracy and relevance of the content, bridging the gap between formal schooling and the accessible world of television.

However, the integration of television into education wasn't without its challenges and limitations. Critics raised concerns about the passive nature of television viewing and its potential to detract from active learning and critical thinking. The lack of direct interaction with educators and the absence of immediate feedback posed limitations in comparison to the more dynamic classroom environment. Furthermore, the quality of educational programming varied widely, with some programs being more effective and engaging than others. The reliance on visual stimuli could also overshadow the importance of textual literacy and critical analysis, potentially hindering the development of essential learning skills.

The potential for bias and the propagation of inaccurate

information also presented significant challenges. The influence of commercial interests on programming content raised concerns about objectivity and the potential for manipulative or misleading representations of facts. The selection and presentation of information became a critical aspect of educational television, requiring rigorous vetting and adherence to pedagogical principles. The need to maintain balance and present multiple perspectives was essential to ensure that viewers received a comprehensive and unbiased understanding of the subject matter.

The technological advancements of the late 20th and early 21st centuries further revolutionized the potential of television in education. The rise of cable and satellite television brought greater diversity and specialization to educational programming, offering a wider range of subject matter and catering to diverse learning styles. The advent of interactive television, incorporating features that allowed viewers to participate in quizzes, provide feedback, and access additional resources, enhanced the learning experience, moving beyond passive viewing.

The digital revolution profoundly impacted the role of television in education. The emergence of online platforms, streaming services, and educational apps broadened access to educational content beyond the constraints of broadcast schedules. Educational videos became readily available on demand, offering learners flexibility and control over their learning experience. This shift extended the reach of educational television significantly, making it available to individuals in geographically remote areas, or those with unconventional learning schedules. The ability to access educational content at any time and from virtually anywhere transformed the way people learned and consumed knowledge.

However, the digital landscape also presented its own challenges. The sheer volume of available content, coupled with the lack of quality control in some online platforms, created a need for discerning curation and critical evaluation. The potential for misinformation and the spread of unreliable educational materials underscored the need for caution and responsible online learning practices. The digital divide, the unequal access to technology and internet connectivity, created another barrier, preventing certain populations from fully benefiting from the potential of online educational resources.

The future of television and education appears intertwined with the ongoing evolution of technology and media consumption.

Interactive learning platforms, virtual reality applications, and personalized learning experiences are likely to become increasingly prevalent in educational television programming. The integration of artificial intelligence could potentially personalize the learning experience even further, tailoring content to individual student needs and learning styles. This ongoing evolution of the media landscape necessitates a continual reassessment of the role of television in education, ensuring that this powerful medium is used effectively to advance learning and knowledge acquisition for all.

The enduring legacy of television in education lies not solely in its ability to disseminate information but also in its potential to inspire curiosity, foster critical thinking, and promote lifelong learning. As technology continues to reshape the media landscape, the challenge remains to leverage the unique strengths of television – its accessibility, engaging visuals, and storytelling potential – while addressing its limitations and ensuring that it serves as a powerful tool for empowering individuals through education. The journey of television as an educational tool is a continuous evolution, reflecting the dynamic interaction between technology, pedagogy, and the evolving needs of learners. The future holds immense potential for using this powerful medium to bridge learning gaps and unlock the learning potential within us all.

The Future of Televisions Cultural Impact Shaping Values and Beliefs

The democratizing influence of television, as explored in the preceding section, extends far beyond its role in education. Its profound impact on the formation and dissemination of cultural values, beliefs, and social norms is a subject worthy of significant attention. As television continues to evolve, so too will its capacity to shape societal perspectives, and understanding these potential shifts is crucial for navigating the future.

One critical area of concern is the potential for the reinforcement of existing biases and stereotypes. While television has historically served as a platform for challenging social norms and promoting inclusivity, it has also been criticized for perpetuating harmful stereotypes through its portrayal of different groups. The algorithms driving personalized content recommendations on streaming services present a particular challenge, as they may inadvertently limit viewers' exposure to diverse perspectives, reinforcing existing biases through an echo chamber effect. This risk is amplified by the increasing sophistication of AI-driven content creation and recommendation systems. Without careful oversight and ethical considerations implemented in these systems, the future of television risks becoming a fragmented landscape, where individuals are exposed only to content that confirms their existing worldview, hindering productive dialogue and social cohesion.

The rise of reality television presents another significant challenge. While reality shows offer ostensibly unscripted glimpses into the lives of ordinary individuals, their constructed nature and the often manipulative editing techniques employed raise serious concerns about their impact on viewers' perceptions of reality and social norms. The emphasis on conflict, competition, and sensationalism in many reality formats can foster a culture of superficiality and a distorted understanding of human relationships and social interactions. Moreover, the normalization of aggressive behavior, unrealistic expectations of success, and idealized lifestyles in reality television can contribute to feelings of inadequacy and social comparison among viewers. The long-term consequences of prolonged exposure to such programming remain a significant area of research and concern.

The increasing influence of social media and its integration with television further complicates the issue. The blurred lines between traditional television programming and user-generated content, interactive platforms, and live-streaming features have created a dynamic and interconnected media landscape. This interconnectivity offers opportunities for participation, engagement, and the creation of diverse voices, but it also carries the potential for the rapid spread of misinformation, polarization, and the erosion of trust in traditional media outlets. The challenges of moderating online interactions and preventing the spread of harmful content become exponentially more difficult within this dynamic and rapidly evolving media ecosystem.

However, the future of television's cultural impact is not solely characterized by negative trends. The evolution of television technology also offers unprecedented opportunities for promoting positive social change and fostering intercultural understanding. High-quality documentaries, meticulously researched and ethically produced, can continue to educate viewers about critical social issues, promoting empathy, understanding, and informed engagement in public discourse. Interactive programming formats allow for greater audience participation and can encourage thoughtful reflection on complex topics, fostering a culture of critical thinking and informed decision-making. The potential of virtual reality and augmented reality technologies to immerse viewers in diverse cultural contexts and perspectives presents further opportunities for fostering intercultural understanding and empathy.

The development of sophisticated AI-driven tools capable of translating languages in real-time has the potential to break down communication barriers and facilitate the sharing of diverse cultural narratives across national borders. The potential for international collaborations in television production could lead to more nuanced and comprehensive portrayals of different cultures, challenging stereotypes and promoting cross-cultural understanding. The integration of these technologies into television production and distribution could lead to a more inclusive and representative media landscape, reflecting the diverse experiences and perspectives of global communities.

However, realizing the positive potential of these technologies requires conscious and proactive efforts from policymakers, media producers, and technology developers. Establishing clear ethical guidelines for the development and implementation of AI-driven content creation and recommendation systems is crucial to prevent the unintended perpetuation of biases and the erosion of trust in media. Investing in media literacy education is essential to equip viewers with the skills and critical thinking abilities needed to navigate the complexities of the modern media landscape and engage thoughtfully with diverse perspectives.

Furthermore, the development of effective mechanisms for moderating online interactions and countering the spread of misinformation is paramount. International cooperation and collaboration between governments, technology companies, and media organizations are essential to address the challenges posed by the global dissemination of harmful content and the spread of disinformation campaigns. The future of television's cultural impact rests on the active engagement of all stakeholders in creating a more equitable, inclusive, and informative media landscape.

The role of television in shaping political discourse also requires careful consideration. The proliferation of partisan news channels and the rise of "infotainment" have blurred the lines between news reporting and opinion, creating an environment ripe for the spread of misinformation and the polarization of political viewpoints. The potential for AI-powered deepfakes and sophisticated disinformation campaigns poses a significant threat to the integrity of political discourse, challenging the ability of viewers to distinguish fact from fiction. The development and implementation of effective strategies for detecting and countering disinformation, including media literacy education and fact-checking initiatives, is essential for preserving the integrity of the democratic process.

The economic aspects of the television industry also play a vital role in shaping its cultural impact. The concentration of ownership in the hands of a few powerful media conglomerates can limit diversity of content and perspectives, leading to a homogenization of cultural narratives. The influence of advertising revenue on programming decisions can also lead to the prioritization of entertainment value over educational or socially responsible content. Addressing the issue of media concentration and promoting greater diversity in media ownership is essential for ensuring a vibrant and representative television landscape.

Looking ahead, the future of television's cultural impact is likely to be characterized by increasing personalization, interactivity, and the integration of various media platforms. The rise of virtual reality and augmented reality technologies offers the potential for immersive and engaging storytelling, but also raises concerns about the potential for escapism and the erosion of social interaction. The development of AI-driven content creation tools offers opportunities for greater efficiency and the production of personalized content, but also raises concerns about the potential for biases and the displacement of human creativity.

Navigating this complex landscape requires a multi-faceted approach, involving collaboration between policymakers, media producers, technology developers, educators, and viewers themselves. The future of television's cultural impact depends on our ability to harness the power of this powerful medium for positive social change while mitigating its potential risks. This requires a continuous dialogue and a commitment to ethical principles, responsible innovation, and media literacy education.

Only through such proactive engagement can we ensure that television continues to evolve in a way that reflects and enriches the diverse cultures and values of global communities. The challenges and opportunities are immense, demanding a concerted effort to shape a future where television fosters understanding, promotes inclusivity, and serves as a powerful tool for positive social transformation.

Technological Advancements Predictions and Innovations

The trajectory of television technology beyond its current state promises a captivating array of advancements, each with the potential to redefine our viewing experience and reshape the very fabric of the medium. Higher resolutions, already making inroads with 4K and 8K displays, are poised to become the norm, ushering in an era of unparalleled visual fidelity. Imagine watching your favorite films and television shows with such clarity that every detail, every subtle nuance of expression, is rendered with breathtaking accuracy. This increased resolution will demand corresponding advancements in content creation, pushing the boundaries of visual storytelling and special effects. The production pipeline will need to adapt, requiring investments in new cameras, editing software, and post-production techniques capable of handling the exponentially larger data files associated with these higher resolutions. The implications extend beyond mere aesthetic improvement; the increased realism will enhance the immersive quality of the viewing experience, blurring the lines between the on-screen world and the viewer's reality.

Beyond mere resolution, the pursuit of immersive viewing experiences is gaining momentum. Three-dimensional television, while having experienced its share of technological hurdles and market challenges, continues to evolve, offering a more engaging and captivating viewing experience. However, true immersion transcends 3D; the advent of virtual reality (VR) and augmented reality (AR) technologies promises to revolutionize television viewing. Imagine stepping into your favorite fictional world, exploring its environments, and interacting with its characters—a level of engagement previously confined to the realm of science fiction. VR headsets, already finding applications in gaming and other entertainment sectors, will inevitably integrate more seamlessly with television content, offering viewers a completely new way to experience narratives and explore virtual worlds. This technology, however, presents its own set of challenges. The cost and accessibility of VR headsets remain barriers to widespread adoption, and the potential for motion sickness and other physical discomforts needs to be addressed. Furthermore, the creation of compelling VR television content requires significant investment in specialized equipment and expertise.

The personalization of the television viewing experience is another key area of innovation. Streaming services have already begun to personalize content recommendations, using algorithms to suggest shows and movies based on individual viewing habits and preferences. However, this is just the beginning. Future television systems will likely employ increasingly sophisticated AI-powered algorithms to curate not only content but also the very viewing experience itself. This may involve adjusting aspects such as picture settings, audio levels, and even the pacing of the narrative to match the individual viewer's preferences. Personalized advertisements and interactive elements could be seamlessly integrated into the viewing experience, creating a dynamic and tailored entertainment ecosystem. The ethical implications of this hyper-personalization warrant careful consideration. Concerns regarding data privacy, the potential for algorithmic bias, and the creation of echo chambers that limit exposure to diverse perspectives will need to be addressed proactively. Transparency in data collection and usage, along with robust mechanisms to mitigate bias, are crucial to ensuring that personalized television remains a positive and enriching experience.

Artificial intelligence is destined to play an increasingly pivotal role in the future of television. Beyond personalized content recommendations, AI is poised to transform content creation itself.

AI-powered tools are already being used for tasks such as scriptwriting, editing, and special effects, and their capabilities will undoubtedly expand in the coming years. Imagine AI assisting in the creation of realistic virtual characters, generating dynamic and interactive storylines, and even composing original music scores. This integration of AI, however, raises concerns about the potential displacement of human creativity and the need to maintain artistic integrity. The question of authorship and copyright in AI-generated content will require careful legal and ethical consideration.

Moreover, the risk of bias in AI-driven content creation needs to be addressed proactively to prevent the perpetuation of harmful stereotypes and viewpoints. Ensuring that AI enhances human creativity rather than replacing it will be a crucial challenge for the future of television.

The evolution of television extends beyond the screen itself. The integration of television with other smart home devices and platforms promises to create a seamlessly interconnected entertainment ecosystem. Voice control, already a common feature in many modern televisions, will become even more sophisticated, allowing for effortless control of all aspects of the viewing experience. Smart homes will integrate television viewing with other activities, allowing viewers to seamlessly transition between watching a show, controlling their home's lighting and temperature, and interacting with other smart devices. This integration will blur the boundaries between television and other aspects of daily life, creating a more personalized and immersive home entertainment experience. However, ensuring seamless interoperability between various devices and platforms will require significant standardization efforts. Furthermore, security concerns regarding data privacy and the potential for hacking and malicious intrusion into smart home systems must be addressed proactively.

Predicting the exact form television will take in the decades to come is inherently challenging. Nevertheless, the trends discussed above point toward a future where television will be defined not just by its technology but also by its capacity to personalize, immerse, and connect viewers in unprecedented ways. The pursuit of higher resolutions, immersive viewing experiences, personalized content, and the increasingly sophisticated integration of artificial intelligence are just a few of the factors driving the ongoing transformation of television. This evolution will require a collaborative effort involving technologists, content creators, policymakers, and viewers themselves. Ethical considerations, data privacy concerns, and the preservation of human creativity will need to be at the forefront of this ongoing evolution to ensure that the future of television is both technologically advanced and socially responsible. The interplay between technological innovation and societal impact will shape not only the form but also the very function of television, making the continuing study of this medium a vital and compelling endeavor. The journey towards a truly personalized, immersive, and intelligently driven television ecosystem is sure to be filled with both challenges and extraordinary opportunities. The evolution of television is an ongoing story, one that unfolds with each technological leap and societal shift. It is a story that deserves our close attention, as it profoundly impacts not only our entertainment but also our understanding of the world around us.

Changing Viewing Habits Adapting to New Technologies and Platforms

The rise of on-demand streaming has fundamentally altered how we consume television. No longer tethered to rigid broadcast schedules, viewers now dictate when and what they watch. This shift has empowered audiences, fostering a more personalized and individualized viewing experience. The linear model, once the cornerstone of television viewing, is rapidly fading into the background, replaced by a fragmented yet vibrant landscape of streaming services, each vying for audience attention with tailored content and unique features. This transformation has profound implications for both content creators and viewers alike. The traditional broadcast model, with its reliance on large, homogenous audiences, is giving way to a more niche-focused approach, where content is tailored to specific demographics and viewing preferences.

This move towards personalized content extends beyond simple genre categorization. Streaming services leverage sophisticated algorithms to analyze viewer data, tracking viewing history, preferences, and even social media activity to generate highly targeted recommendations. This level of personalization has led to both benefits and drawbacks. On the positive side, it allows viewers to discover content they might otherwise miss, creating serendipitous viewing experiences and fostering a sense of connection with platforms that seemingly understand their tastes. However, this hyper-personalization also raises concerns about filter bubbles and echo chambers. The algorithms, while effective in recommending similar content, might inadvertently limit exposure to diverse viewpoints and perspectives, potentially contributing to societal polarization. The challenge lies in balancing personalization with exposure to a broader range of content, ensuring a rich and diverse viewing experience.

The fragmentation of the television landscape has also led to a proliferation of platforms, each with its unique content library and user interface. Navigating this increasingly complex ecosystem can be overwhelming for viewers. The sheer number of options, from established players like Netflix and Hulu to newer entrants vying for market share, creates a sense of choice overload, making it difficult for viewers to discern the value proposition of each platform. This abundance of choice, while seemingly beneficial, can paradoxically lead to viewer fatigue and indecision, creating a "paradox of choice" where the sheer number of options hinders rather than helps the selection process. This challenge underscores the need for innovative solutions, such as improved content discovery tools and more intuitive user interfaces, to help viewers navigate this fragmented landscape and locate content that aligns with their preferences.

Furthermore, the shift towards on-demand streaming has impacted the very nature of television viewing. The traditional "appointment viewing," where families gathered around the television at a specific time to watch a particular program, is less prevalent. Viewers now engage with television content on their own schedules, often consuming multiple episodes of a show in a single sitting or watching short-form videos in between other tasks. This change in viewing habits has necessitated adaptations in content production, with series increasingly designed for binge-watching and short-form video content gaining significant traction. The episodic structure of television shows has undergone a transformation, with seasons becoming shorter and more focused, mirroring the demands of a fragmented and on-demand viewing audience.

The technological advancements driving these changes are not limited to streaming services. The integration of television with other smart home devices and platforms is blurring the lines between different forms of media consumption. Voice assistants, smart speakers, and other connected devices now facilitate seamless navigation through various entertainment options, making it easier for viewers to switch between television shows, music playlists, and other digital content. This interconnectedness offers a new level of convenience and personalization but also presents challenges related to data privacy and security. The vast amount of data collected by these devices raises concerns about potential misuse of personal information and the vulnerability of these systems to cyberattacks. The challenge for technology companies is to develop systems that are both user-friendly and secure, protecting viewer privacy while offering a seamless and immersive entertainment experience.

The emergence of new screen sizes and viewing technologies also profoundly influences viewing habits. The proliferation of smartphones and tablets has introduced a mobile viewing experience, allowing viewers to consume television content on the go, regardless of their location. The rise of large-screen smart TVs has enhanced the home viewing experience, providing a more immersive and cinematic quality. These developments have created a fragmented yet interconnected ecosystem of screens, each offering a unique viewing experience tailored to specific contexts and situations. The challenge for content creators is to adapt to this multi-screen environment, producing content that is engaging and enjoyable across different screen sizes and viewing contexts.

The evolution of interactive television technologies also holds implications for future viewing habits. Interactive features, such as interactive games, polls, and quizzes integrated within television programs, are becoming increasingly common. These features foster a more engaging and participatory viewing experience, blurring the lines between passive consumption and active participation. This level of interactivity can foster a sense of community among viewers, allowing them to interact with each other and with the content in real-time. However, the development and implementation of such features require a significant investment in technology and expertise, presenting a barrier to widespread adoption.

The future of television will be shaped by the interplay between technological innovation and evolving viewing habits. As new technologies emerge, viewers will adapt their consumption patterns, creating a dynamic feedback loop that continually reshapes the television landscape. Predicting the exact form television will take in the future is a complex undertaking, but it's clear that personalization, interactivity, and cross-platform integration will play pivotal roles. The challenge lies in harnessing the potential of these advancements while addressing the ethical and practical challenges associated with data privacy, security, and algorithmic bias. The ongoing evolution of television is a testament to its adaptability and enduring appeal. The medium's future will depend on how effectively it navigates the challenges and opportunities presented by these rapidly advancing technologies and the evolving preferences of its audience. The story of television is far from over; it is an ongoing narrative shaped by technological innovation and the ever-changing relationship between the screen and the viewer.

The Role of Artificial Intelligence Personalized Content and Enhanced Experiences

The integration of artificial intelligence (AI) is poised to revolutionize the television landscape, ushering in an era of unprecedented personalization and enhanced viewer experiences. AI's role extends far beyond simple content recommendations; it's fundamentally reshaping how television programs are created, distributed, and consumed. The sophisticated algorithms powering AI-driven platforms analyze vast amounts of viewer data, including viewing history, preferred genres, demographic information, and even social media interactions, to curate highly tailored content suggestions. This level of personalization goes beyond simply suggesting similar shows; it anticipates viewer preferences, proactively offering content that aligns with evolving tastes and interests.

For example, a viewer who consistently watches crime dramas and documentaries about historical events might receive recommendations for similarly themed content, perhaps including lesser-known independent films or international series that match their specific niche interests. The algorithms can even adjust recommendations based on time of day or viewing context –perhaps suggesting lighter fare in the evening after a long day of work, or recommending more intellectually stimulating content during weekend downtime. This dynamic adjustment ensures a constantly evolving and personalized viewing experience, catering to the individual's unique tastes and evolving preferences.

However, the hyper-personalization facilitated by AI raises crucial ethical considerations. The risk of creating "filter bubbles" and "echo chambers" is substantial. While algorithms excel at identifying patterns and predicting preferences, they can inadvertently limit exposure to diverse viewpoints and perspectives, potentially reinforcing pre-existing biases and hindering intellectual growth. A viewer constantly receiving recommendations within a narrow ideological or thematic spectrum might become increasingly isolated from opposing viewpoints, creating an echo chamber where their perspectives are consistently reinforced without exposure to challenging or contrasting ideas. This effect can have broader societal implications, contributing to societal polarization and limiting opportunities for critical thinking and intellectual debate. Consequently, responsible development and deployment of AI in content curation is crucial to mitigate these risks. Transparency in algorithmic processes, along with mechanisms allowing users to easily broaden their recommendations, are critical considerations for platform designers.

Beyond personalized recommendations, AI is also playing a significant role in content creation itself. AI-powered tools are being utilized to automate various aspects of production, from scriptwriting and editing to post-production processes. AI algorithms can analyze existing scripts, identify recurring themes, and even generate new plotlines or dialogue, potentially accelerating the writing process and assisting screenwriters in overcoming creative blocks. Similarly, AI can automate tasks like color grading, sound mixing, and special effects, streamlining the post-production workflow and enabling more efficient content creation. This increased efficiency translates to lower production costs and potentially a wider range of content available to viewers.

Moreover, AI is transforming interactive television experiences. AI-powered chatbots are being integrated into television programs, allowing viewers to interact with characters or participate in plot development through real-time dialogue. AI can personalize these interactions, adapting the chatbot's responses to individual viewer preferences and behaviors. Furthermore, AI algorithms can facilitate interactive games and quizzes integrated within television shows, encouraging viewer engagement and fostering a sense of community among viewers. This participatory approach enhances the viewing experience, transforming passive consumption into an active and social activity.

The integration of AI also significantly impacts television advertising. AI algorithms can analyze viewer data to target advertising more effectively, delivering ads that are more relevant to individual viewers' interests and preferences. This increased relevance can lead to higher engagement rates and improved advertising ROI for businesses. However, the potential for invasive data collection and targeted manipulation raises serious ethical and privacy concerns. The fine line between personalized advertising and intrusive surveillance must be carefully navigated to ensure viewers' privacy is protected. This requires transparency regarding data collection practices and mechanisms for users to control their data sharing preferences.

The application of AI in content accessibility is another area of growing significance. AI-powered tools can automatically generate subtitles and closed captions, improving accessibility for viewers with hearing impairments. Similarly, AI can create audio descriptions for visually impaired viewers, bringing the richness of visual storytelling to a wider audience. This inclusive approach expands the accessibility of television content, ensuring that everyone can participate in the viewing experience regardless of their abilities.

Despite the significant potential benefits, the widespread adoption of AI in television also presents challenges. The algorithmic bias inherent in AI systems can perpetuate and amplify existing societal inequalities. If the data used to train AI algorithms is biased, the resulting recommendations and content will likely reflect and reinforce those biases, leading to unfair or discriminatory outcomes. Addressing algorithmic bias requires careful data curation, ongoing algorithm monitoring, and the development of mechanisms to identify and mitigate bias in AI systems.

Furthermore, the reliance on AI raises concerns about job displacement in the television industry. As AI automates various production tasks, there is a risk that human workers in areas like scriptwriting, editing, and post-production could be replaced by AI-powered systems. The need to adapt to these changes necessitates a proactive approach to workforce retraining and the development of new skill sets relevant to the AI-driven media landscape.

Ultimately, the future of television hinges on the responsible development and deployment of AI. While the potential benefits – increased personalization, improved content creation, enhanced interactivity, and greater accessibility – are substantial, the ethical and practical challenges surrounding algorithmic bias, data privacy, and job displacement cannot be overlooked. Striking a balance between leveraging the transformative potential of AI while mitigating its risks is crucial to ensuring a future where television remains a valuable and enriching form of entertainment for everyone. This requires a collaborative effort among technology developers, content creators, policymakers, and viewers to create a sustainable and ethically sound media ecosystem. The continued evolution of this dynamic medium will be shaped by the ongoing dialogue between technological innovation and the evolving needs and expectations of its audience. The narrative of television continues, constantly adapting and responding to the ever-changing relationship between technology and the viewer.

The Convergence of Media Televisions Place in a MultiPlatform World

The television of the future isn't just a standalone device; it's a nexus, a central point in a complex web of interconnected media experiences. The convergence of television with streaming services, social media platforms, and immersive technologies like virtual reality (VR) and augmented reality (AR) is reshaping how we consume content and interact with the television medium itself. This convergence presents both unprecedented opportunities and significant challenges for the industry and viewers alike.

Streaming services have fundamentally altered the television landscape. Initially envisioned as supplementary to traditional broadcast television, streaming platforms like Netflix, Hulu, Amazon Prime Video, and Disney+ have become dominant forces, offering vast libraries of on-demand content and original programming that rivals, and in some cases surpasses, the quality and reach of traditional networks. This shift has empowered consumers, providing them with unprecedented choice and control over their viewing habits. The traditional reliance on scheduled broadcasts has largely been replaced by a more flexible, personalized approach to content consumption, with viewers able to watch what they want, when they want, and on whatever device they choose.

This shift also impacts the economics of television production and distribution. Streaming services have disrupted traditional advertising models, offering subscription-based access to content rather than relying heavily on commercial interruptions. This has forced traditional broadcasters to adapt, exploring new revenue streams and adopting hybrid models that incorporate both advertising and subscription fees. The competition for viewers and content creators is fierce, leading to a surge in high-quality programming and innovative storytelling formats. However, the rise of streaming has also raised concerns about the sustainability of smaller production companies and independent filmmakers, who may struggle to compete with the deep pockets of major streaming giants.

The integration of social media into the television experience is another significant aspect of media convergence. Viewers now routinely engage with television programs through platforms like Twitter, Facebook, and Instagram, sharing opinions, reactions, and predictions in real-time. This fosters a sense of community and shared viewing experience that transcends geographical boundaries.

Television programs are increasingly designed with social media integration in mind, incorporating interactive elements, hashtags, and online contests that encourage viewer participation and engagement. This two-way communication between viewers and broadcasters has transformed television from a passive, one-way medium into a dynamic, interactive space where audiences actively participate in the conversation surrounding their favorite shows.

This convergence, however, presents challenges. The proliferation of platforms and content can lead to viewer fatigue and an overwhelming sense of choice. Finding what to watch can become a daunting task, even with sophisticated recommendation algorithms.

Moreover, the constant barrage of information and notifications across multiple platforms can be distracting and detract from the immersive viewing experience. The challenge for content creators and platform providers lies in curating a streamlined and engaging experience that balances choice with ease of navigation and avoids overwhelming the viewer.

Virtual reality and augmented reality technologies are poised to further revolutionize the television experience, offering new ways to engage with content and interact with the virtual world. VR headsets can transport viewers into the heart of their favorite television shows, allowing them to explore virtual sets, interact with characters, and experience narratives in a deeply immersive way. AR overlays, on the other hand, can enhance the viewing experience by adding interactive elements to the real world, allowing viewers to access additional information, participate in virtual games, or interact with characters beyond the screen.

The potential of VR and AR in television is immense. Imagine watching a documentary about ancient Rome and being able to virtually explore the ruins of the Colosseum, or experiencing the thrill of a sporting event as if you were sitting in the stadium. These technologies could revolutionize news broadcasts, allowing viewers to witness events unfold as if they were on the scene, or even participate in virtual news discussions. However, the widespread adoption of VR and AR technologies in television faces significant hurdles, including the cost of headsets, the development of high-quality VR and AR content, and the challenge of creating seamless and intuitive user interfaces.

The convergence of media is also reshaping the nature of television advertising. Traditional television commercials are becoming less effective as viewers increasingly utilize ad-blocking technology and skip commercials on streaming services. Consequently, there is a shift towards more personalized and interactive forms of advertising, such as sponsored content, product placement, and targeted online advertisements. This requires advertisers to adapt their strategies, focusing on creating engaging and relevant content that aligns with viewers' interests and preferences rather than simply relying on interrupting the viewing experience.

The ethical implications of media convergence are equally profound. The increasing collection and use of viewer data by streaming services and social media platforms raises concerns about privacy and data security. Algorithms used to personalize content recommendations and target advertising can create filter bubbles and echo chambers, limiting exposure to diverse viewpoints and reinforcing pre-existing biases. The challenge lies in finding a balance between personalized experiences and protecting individual privacy and promoting intellectual freedom. Transparency in data collection practices and user control over data sharing are crucial to maintaining trust and ensuring ethical data usage.

In conclusion, the future of television lies in its ability to adapt and integrate with other forms of media. The convergence of streaming services, social media, and immersive technologies is fundamentally reshaping how we consume and interact with television content.

This convergence presents both exciting opportunities and significant challenges. The success of the television industry in the years to come will depend on its ability to embrace innovation, address ethical concerns, and create engaging experiences that cater to the evolving needs and expectations of its audience. The interplay between technological advancements, creative storytelling, and ethical considerations will shape the evolving narrative of television, ensuring that this enduring medium continues to connect with and engage future generations. The future of television is not about a single device or platform, but about a fluid, interconnected ecosystem of media experiences.

The Enduring Power of Television Adapting and Thriving in a Digital Age

Despite the rise of streaming services and the proliferation of digital media, television retains a remarkable resilience. Its enduring power stems not from technological dominance alone, but from its unique ability to adapt and evolve while retaining its core function: to bring people together through shared experiences and compelling narratives. The very fabric of television has been woven into the social and cultural tapestry of numerous generations, creating a legacy that extends far beyond the technical specifications of its devices. This deep-seated cultural embedding is a crucial factor in its continued success.

One key element of television's enduring appeal is its capacity to foster a sense of shared cultural experience. While streaming allows for individualized viewing choices, broadcast television—and even the scheduled programming of many streaming services—still provides a common ground for water-cooler conversations, sparking discussions and bonding experiences around nationally televised events, sporting matches, or popular prime-time shows. The collective viewing of live events, from award ceremonies to presidential addresses, creates a shared moment in time, fostering a sense of national community and shared identity. This shared cultural experience is difficult to replicate within the fragmented landscape of on-demand streaming.

The evolution of television content also contributes to its ongoing relevance. While early television relied heavily on live broadcasts and limited programming options, the modern television landscape offers a dizzying array of genres, styles, and formats. From meticulously crafted dramas to reality TV's unscripted narratives, from cutting-edge documentaries to animated series that appeal to audiences across generations, television constantly adapts to changing tastes and preferences. The creative ingenuity of producers and writers continues to push boundaries, experimenting with innovative storytelling techniques, and creating compelling characters and narratives that resonate with audiences.

Furthermore, the integration of new technologies into the television experience has not diminished its appeal, but rather enhanced it. High-definition screens, surround sound systems, and sophisticated remote controls have significantly improved the viewing experience, offering a level of visual and auditory immersion that was unimaginable in the early days of television. The advent of smart TVs, which offer access to a multitude of streaming services and interactive applications, has transformed television sets into interactive entertainment hubs, further solidifying their position at the heart of the home entertainment ecosystem.

The rise of 4K and 8K resolution technologies represents another significant leap forward in image quality, offering unparalleled levels of detail and clarity. These improvements go beyond mere aesthetic enhancements; they can significantly impact the viewer's experience of the content. The richer visuals allow for greater immersion in the narrative, particularly beneficial for genres such as documentaries and nature programs, where a realistic and detailed image can transport viewers to another place or time. The potential for even higher resolutions in the future promises an even more immersive and engaging viewing experience.

However, the evolution of television hasn't been without its challenges. The rise of streaming platforms and the decline of traditional cable subscriptions have significantly impacted the television industry's business model. The shift from advertising-supported television to subscription-based streaming models has forced broadcasters and networks to adapt their revenue strategies.

This transformation has led to some consolidation within the industry, with larger media companies acquiring smaller networks and streaming services to expand their reach and content libraries.

Despite these challenges, the television industry has shown a remarkable capacity for innovation and adaptation. The emergence of new business models, such as hybrid models that combine advertising and subscriptions, and the ongoing development of new content formats, demonstrate the industry's willingness to evolve and meet the changing needs of its viewers. Moreover, the ability of television to adapt and thrive in a digital environment extends beyond its business model. Its ability to deliver compelling narratives and provide a platform for cultural commentary remains a cornerstone of its enduring appeal.

The integration of interactive elements and social media into the television viewing experience has significantly enhanced audience engagement. Viewers can now participate in real-time conversations surrounding their favorite shows, sharing their opinions, reactions, and predictions online. This fosters a sense of community and shared experience, and it often leads to more passionate and involved audiences. Television producers and broadcasters are increasingly incorporating interactive elements into their programs, encouraging viewers to participate and influence the narrative.

Looking ahead, the future of television will likely be defined by its ongoing integration with other technologies and media platforms. Virtual reality (VR) and augmented reality (AR) technologies hold immense potential to revolutionize the television experience by creating immersive and interactive environments for viewers.

Imagine experiencing a historical documentary as if you were physically present at the events being depicted, or watching a sporting event from the perspective of a player on the field. VR and AR technologies have the potential to blur the lines between the virtual and real worlds, offering entirely new ways to engage with television content.

However, the widespread adoption of VR and AR technologies in television faces significant hurdles. The cost of VR and AR headsets, the development of high-quality content tailored to these platforms, and the need for user-friendly interfaces are all significant challenges that must be addressed before these technologies become mainstream. Nevertheless, the potential rewards are substantial, and as the technology continues to develop and become more affordable, we can expect to see a greater integration of VR and AR into the television experience.

The interplay between technology and content remains crucial for the future of television. While technological advancements will continue to enhance the viewing experience, it's the creative vision of producers, writers, and directors that will ultimately determine the success of television programs. The future of television will be shaped by the ability of the industry to create high-quality, engaging content that appeals to a diverse range of audiences. This requires a commitment to innovation, a willingness to experiment with new formats and storytelling techniques, and a deep understanding of the evolving needs and preferences of viewers.

The ethical considerations surrounding television's evolution also deserve attention. The increasing collection and use of viewer data by streaming platforms and social media companies raise concerns about privacy and data security. The use of algorithms to personalize content recommendations and target advertising can lead to filter bubbles and echo chambers, limiting viewers' exposure to diverse viewpoints and potentially reinforcing pre-existing biases.

Transparency in data collection practices, user control over data sharing, and responsible algorithm design are crucial to mitigate these risks.

In conclusion, television's continued success is not merely a matter of technological prowess. It's a reflection of its ability to adapt to changing technological landscapes, its capacity to foster shared cultural experiences, and its capacity to tell compelling and engaging stories. The evolution of television is a testament to its resilience, its adaptability, and its enduring power to connect with audiences across generations. The future of television will be shaped by a dynamic interplay between technological innovation, creative storytelling, and ethical considerations, ensuring that this medium remains a central part of our cultural and entertainment landscape for many years to come. Its ability to evolve and connect will ensure its continued relevance in a world of ever-changing media consumption habits.

Glossary

Analog Television: A television system using continuously variable signals to transmit images and sound.

Cathode Ray Tube (CRT): The vacuum tube used in older television sets to display images.

Digital Television: A television system using digital signals to transmit images and sound, offering improved clarity and other features.

High-Definition Television (HDTV): A digital television standard offering significantly improved resolution compared to standard definition.

NTSC: National Television System Committee, the analog television standard used in North America.

PAL: Phase Alternating Line, an analog television standard used in many parts of the world.

SECAM: Sequential Couleur à Mémoire, an analog television standard used primarily in France and Eastern Europe.

Smart TV: A television set with internet connectivity and access to various applications and streaming services.

Streaming: The delivery of digital media content over the internet in real time.

Ultra High Definition (UHD) Television (4K/8K): Television systems with significantly higher resolution than HDTV.

www.ingramcontent.com/pod-product-compliance
Lightning Source LLC
LaVergne TN
LVHW051224050326
832903LV00028B/2246